Women and New Hollywood

Women and New Hollywood

Gender, Creative Labor, and
1970s American Cinema

EDITED BY AARON HUNTER
AND MARTHA SHEARER

Rutgers University Press

New Brunswick, Camden, and Newark, New Jersey

London and Oxford

Rutgers University Press is a department of Rutgers, The State University of New Jersey,
one of the leading public research universities in the nation. By publishing worldwide, it furthers
the University's mission of dedication to excellence in teaching, scholarship, research, and
clinical care.

Library of Congress Cataloging-in-Publication Data

Names: Hunter, Aaron, editor. | Shearer, Martha, editor.
Title: Women and new Hollywood : gender, creative labor, and 1970s American cinema /
    edited by Aaron Hunter and Martha Shearer.
Description: New Brunswick : Rutgers University Press, 2023. | Includes bibliographical
    references and index.
Identifiers: LCCN 2022036897 | ISBN 9781978821798 (paperback) | ISBN
    9781978821804 (cloth) | ISBN 9781978821811 (epub) | ISBN 9781978821835 (pdf)
Subjects: LCSH: Women in the motion picture industry—United States—History—
    20th century
Classification: LCC PN1995.9.W6 W64 2023 | DDC 791.43/082—dc23
LC record available at https://lccn.loc.gov/2022036897

A British Cataloging-in-Publication record for this book is available from the British Library.

References to internet websites (URLs) were accurate at the time of writing. Neither the author
nor Rutgers University Press is responsible for URLs that may have expired or changed since the
manuscript was prepared.

rutgersuniversitypress.org

Contents

Part II   Text

Part III   Theory and Criticism

Women and New Hollywood

Introduction

AARON HUNTER AND
MARTHA SHEARER

Gwen Verdon is watching the Oscars ceremony on television. Her estranged husband, Bob Fosse, has won the Best Director award for *Cabaret* (1972). During his speech, after thanking the film's stars, studio head, and songwriters, he thanks "a dear friend of mind by the name of Gwen Verdon." As Fosse moves on to the film's producer, their daughter, Nicole, asks her mother, "Why didn't he thank me?" to which Gwen replies, "Because you didn't help direct his movie, darling." This scene takes place in the fourth episode of *Fosse/Verdon* (FX, 2019) and encapsulates both the show's concern with Fosse's neglect of his family and its project to position Verdon not simply as Fosse's romantic partner and "muse" but also as his collaborator, as someone who, among other things, helped direct his movies. Verdon was one of many women whose crucial work on New Hollywood films has been marginalized and obscured, in both academic and popular contexts. Now, particularly in the wake of #MeToo, we are in the midst of a cultural reckoning with the legacy of the 1970s and its film culture, ranging from the (re)emergence of sexual harassment, abuse, and misconduct allegations against major

1

New Hollywood figures, including Dustin Hoffman, Jon Peters, and Roman Polanski; to the season of Karina Longworth's podcast *You Must Remember This* on production designer, screenwriter, and producer Polly Platt; and a series of historical television shows reassessing the 1970s and their legacy, including not only *Fosse/Verdon* but also *The Get Down* (Netflix, 2016–2017), *The Deuce* (HBO, 2017–2019), *Mrs. America* (FX, 2020), and *The Offer* (Paramount+, 2022). Such reckonings are important and necessary, but those focused on cinema also risk inadvertently maintaining the central position of men in the New Hollywood narrative, even perpetuating the decade's reputation as an era of so-called mavericks.[1] This collection focuses on women's authorship and creative labor in the New Hollywood era. We contend that women like Verdon, Platt, and *Cabaret*'s screenwriter, Jay Presson Allen (not named in Fosse's acceptance speech either in the show or in reality), were integral to the growth and creative development that American cinema underwent in the 1970s—inside and outside of Hollywood—even as they remained underrepresented in all fields and faced substantial sexism, harassment, and institutional barriers.

The standard account of the New Hollywood is a familiar tale of creative transformation and financial recovery. On the brink of collapse in the late 1960s, Hollywood studios underwent massive corporate and financial realignment as many of the old guard producers and studio heads retired or died, while a new wave of filmmakers—educated in film schools, in the cheaper, quick-turnaround world of television, or under the tutelage of Roger Corman and his "you can do anything, if you do it cheap" approach to moviemaking—produced an innovative, auteur-driven cinema that thrived until the reassertion of studio control with the turn to the blockbuster model later in the decade. The New Hollywood has a privileged place in U.S. film culture, regularly celebrated as an era of unparalleled artistic achievements. In scholarship too, the New Hollywood has maintained a consistent presence in academic publication since the early 1980s.[2] The dominant account of New Hollywood was cemented in the popular imagination by Peter Biskind's *Easy Riders, Raging Bulls: How the Sex-Drugs-and-Rock 'n' Roll Generation Saved Hollywood* (1998), where he describes the period as "the last time it was really exciting to make movies in Hollywood."[3] But that characterization can also be found in scholarly accounts of the New Hollywood; Geoff King, for example, describes it as "an era when Hollywood produced a relatively high number of innovative films."[4] As these characterizations suggest, central to the standard New Hollywood narrative is the auteur.

It is difficult to overestimate the influence that auteurism—albeit a particularly American, popular auteurism—has had on the construction of the

New Hollywood narrative. By the mid-1970s, auteurism's broad influence was such that one could speak of several different, overlapping auteurisms. For some critics and scholars, auteurism could remain an analytical approach, an effort to discern more about a film's meaning through comparison with other films by the same director. There was also, however, the alignment of the auteur figure with a sense of genius, tied to the notion that auteur directors were the singular artists of their films. There was further the use of the auteur figure as a marketing device, particularly as the notion that individual studios had house styles or genres was waning, and in many ways cemented by the growing use of possessory credits on films and in marketing throughout the decade.[5] Some critics and scholars have resisted these constructions almost since their origins: Pauline Kael famously argued against Andrew Sarris and the *Movie* critics, most notably in her 1963 article "Circles and Squares" in *Film Quarterly*.[6] Kael was joined in the era by writers such as journalist Richard Corliss and scholar Graham Petrie in their resistance to the constructs that were developing around the figure of the auteur.[7] But even so, and even as the notion of the author as the source of a text's meaning was being questioned across the academic humanities, overlapping concepts of auteurism were percolating throughout film journalism, education, production, and marketing.

Since the 1970s, New Hollywood auteurism has become a prized object of nostalgia. Jeffrey Sconce characterizes that critical nostalgia as an elitist reaction against the blockbuster-driven Hollywood that followed and for a period when "critics felt they still had some impact on shaping the future of cinematic practice, and the East Coast was still the bastion of taste that kept the philistines of Hollywood in check."[8] A tension between art and commerce is foundational to the Romantic idea of the artist as individual creative genius that underpins auteurism. Terry Eagleton notes that the "birth of aesthetics as an intellectual discourse coincides with the period when cultural production is beginning to suffer the miseries and indignities of commodification. The peculiarity of the aesthetic is in part spiritual compensation for this degradation: it is just when the artist is becoming debased to a petty commodity producer that he or she will lay claim to transcendent genius."[9] A critical nostalgia for the 1970s as an auteurist pinnacle of American cinema, then, needs to be understood in the context of what followed, where, according to Timothy Corrigan, in the "so-called international art cinema of the sixties and seventies, the auteur has been absorbed as a phantom presence within a text," while in the 1980s, the auteur "rematerialized" as "a commercial performance of *the business of being an auteur*."[10] The New Hollywood is, among other things, the origin point of the "visionary director" discourse of contemporary movie marketing.

In the era itself, the labor of women of the New Hollywood was often obscured and marginalized, even on some of the period's most canonical films. When *Bonnie and Clyde* was released in 1967—often considered the birth of New Hollywood—the film's nontraditional approach to editing was often commented on, but its editor, Dede Allen, was rarely mentioned. Anti-auteurist Kael, in a hint at how powerful the auteur paradigm already was, does mention Allen once in her influential review of the film, while also undermining her input: "The editing of this movie is, however, the best edit-ing in an American movie in a long time, and one may assume that Penn deserves credit for it along with the editor, Dede Allen."[11] Likewise, reviews of *The Last Picture Show* (1971) discuss its windswept realism but rarely men-tion designer Polly Platt. Roger Ebert describes Bobby Dupea (Jack Nich-olson), the protagonist of *Five Easy Pieces* (1970), as "one of the most unforgettable characters in American movies" but does not name his creator, screenwriter Carol Eastman.[12] There are exceptions to such slights, of course, but in the main, most of the women who shaped the successes of New Hol-lywood films were decidedly overlooked.

In scholarship, too, the foundational inquiries focused overwhelmingly on white male directors.[13] And that foundation has proved durable. Even though turns toward areas such as genre and industry studies were often framed in direct opposition to auteurism—such as Thomas Schatz's characterization of it as "effectively stalling film history and criticism in a prolonged stage of ado-lescent romanticism"—the New Hollywood's auteurist identity has gone rela-tively unchallenged.[14] Revisiting the era in the edited collection *The Last Great American Picture Show* (2004), Thomas Elsaesser professes awareness that "it (almost) goes without saying that these auteur-directors . . . are male" but then attempts to preempt criticisms of this formulation because "the male values on display are, however, suitably multiple and ambivalent."[15] As recently as 2020, the collection *The Other Hollywood Renaissance* offers "a revisionist account of this creative resurgence by discussing and memorializing twenty-four direc-tors of note who have not yet been given a proper place in the larger history of the period." While the collection includes welcome chapters on Elaine May and Joan Micklin Silver, it also deems filmmakers such as Hal Ashby, Peter Bogdanovich, Michael Cimino, Brian De Palma, and William Friedkin as not having "been given a proper place" and in need of "memorializing."[16]

Until recently, feminist scholarship has also neglected the New Holly-wood. In feminist film theory of the 1970s, the primary object was instead the studio era.[17] In feminist criticism of the 1970s and 1980s, meanwhile, some of the most vociferous criticism was reserved for the handful of women who gained some degree of prominence or creative control, such as Elaine May and Ellen Burstyn.[18] Molly Haskell's influential declensionist narrative, meanwhile, constructed the studio era as a lost golden age of women's on-screen representation, especially in comparison to the 1970s.[19] Scholarly discussions of women and 1970s Hollywood cinema at the time tended to focus on questions of representation and narrative, often privileging films directed by men.[20] Auteurism has long had a vexed relationship to feminism. As Shelley Cobb notes, auteur "is a term that, because of its masculine connotations, has neither been readily available for women filmmakers nor wholly accepted by feminist film theorists."[21] Work on women's cinema, however, has also often focused on directors. That work includes a small, and growing, cluster of work on Barbara Loden and Claudia Weill, but women who did not direct have received little attention.[22]

It is well established that the New Hollywood is a critical construct; Noel King, for example, argues that since "different critical accounts" make "different claims for what is significant" about the period, "'New Hollywood' does not remain the same object across its different critical descriptions," and in particular there are "a series of competing accounts of 'the new' in relation to 'New Hollywood.'"[23] We contend that focusing on women in this era highlights the fact that it is a critical construct built around white masculinity, whether Biskind's rebel auteurs or Thomas Elsaesser's unmotivated heroes.[24] Film scholarship has too often accepted New Hollywood's auteurist definitions of itself, perpetuating the disingenuous notion that the great creative outbursts and industrial challenges of 1970s U.S. cinema were all performed by men and reinforcing a cultural identification of creativity with masculinity. As in Geneviève Sellier's account of the French New Wave—not coincidentally another cinematic reference point closely tied to a notion of "the film's auteur as he who masters the whole of the creative process"—the New Hollywood remains a "cinema in the masculine singular."[25] Rebecca Sheehan contends that the "masculinist cult of auteur theory likely helped to bolster beliefs about male creative superiority into the 1970s."[26] An academic cult of the auteurist New Hollywood only replicates and reinforces the industry's own exclusions.

In this book we contend that the auteur paradigm has been both historically and politically unhelpful, serving to confine women to the historical margins. And yet, Judith Mayne argues that despite the risk that privileging female authorship appropriates "an extremely patriarchal notion of cinematic creation," female authorship is not only a "useful political strategy" but also "crucial to the reinvention of the cinema that has been undertaken by women filmmakers and feminist spectators."[27] Indeed, Seán Burke contends, "It would scarcely be an exaggeration to say that the struggles of feminism have been primarily a struggle for authorship—understood in the widest sense as the arena in which culture attempts to define itself."[28] To do justice to women's creative labor, then, we need to take authorship seriously, if not necessarily the auteur.

Women *and* New Hollywood

There are other ways to tell the story of 1970s American cinema. A wave of new scholarship has reframed the period by situating auteurism as a cynical marketing ploy and simply a reconfiguration of existing hierarchical Hollywood structures, by stressing continuities with the corporate blockbuster era that followed rather than presenting the New Hollywood as an auteurist break, by shifting attention to the era's "hacks," and by arguing for a multiple authorship model.[29] In recent years, there has been growing scholarly interest in cinema and the feminist 1970s, most notably Maya Montañez Smukler's *Liberating Hollywood: Women Directors and the Feminist Reform of 1970s American Cinema* (2018).[30] Montañez Smukler explains how from the 1960s, in part due to the achievements of second-wave feminism, women "were in a position to gain access, for the first time in generations, to creative and economic power in the motion picture business."[31] Montañez Smukler is specifically describing the situation of female directors, but much the same could be said for women working as screenwriters, editors, costume and production designers, and, in some cases, producers. Montañez Smukler, along with Sheehan and Philis Barragán Goetz, discusses key texts, filmmakers, and efforts at institutional reform and training, such as the American Film Institute (AFI) Directing Workshop for Women.[32] This work has emerged alongside efforts to both analyze and memorialize 1970s feminist film theory and criticism.[33] Beyond the academy, there have also been modest cults formed around certain 1970s women filmmakers—notably Barbara Loden, Elaine May, and Polly Platt—that have produced dedicated festivals, screening series, podcasts, and even T-shirts.

We do not want to overstate either the creative or the industrial power that women held in the 1970s. For one thing, those women who did achieve positions where they could create significant work were overwhelmingly white. We are alert, too, to what Jane Gaines has identified as the risks of both under- and overestimation in feminist film history. Writing of the "amount of evidence of women's work in the early US industry," she notes that "the

numerical differential evidenced in increased numbers even worldwide, unde-
niable as the numbers may be, is not as significant as the conclusions that have
rushed in, sometimes in advance of the numbers, at every juncture of interest
in the topic of women filmmakers in an industry considered hostile to women."[34]
The number of women in either above-the-line or below-the-line positions
in the New Hollywood was never especially large. Even the oft-vaunted cadre
of 1970s female editors includes only a handful of women like Marcia Lucas,
Dede Allen, and Verna Fields. No feature film of the 1970s was shot by a female
cinematographer. Sheehan cites numerous examples of male executives and
crew unwilling to tolerate the possibility of their female colleagues' basic com-
petence.[35] The experience of women in 1970s Hollywood was characterized by
persistent, ingrained misogyny and racism as least as much as it was by under-
examined creative breakthroughs.

We argue that when shifting our focus to women, we therefore need to
contest, expand, and even explode the New Hollywood's boundaries. While
Annette Kuhn has argued that New Hollywood's characteristic openness
and ambiguity are especially evident in the "new women's cinema" of the
1970s—films including *Julia* (1977), *Girlfriends* (1978), and *An Unmarried
Woman* (1978)—New Hollywood scholarship has regularly defined the category, implicitly or otherwise, to exclude other Hollywoods of the time, not
only much new women's cinema but also often Blaxploitation.[36] Furthermore,
women's filmmaking in the 1970s took place in the context of intense creative and feminist activity that shaped and defined women's relationship to
Hollywood. For some of the women discussed in this book, there was a clear
rejection of the mainstream industry for political and/or artistic reasons; for
others, pathways were blocked or unthinkable. In this project we therefore
bring New Hollywood into dialogue and tension with other American cinemas of the 1970s, including New York independent filmmaking, exploitation film, Blaxploitation, and the L.A. Rebellion. Exploitation film, for
example, was a route into Hollywood for male filmmakers (Peter Bogdanovich, Francis Ford Coppola, Martin Scorsese) but not for women who also
wished to follow that trajectory (Stephanie Rothman, as discussed by Alicia
Kozma in this volume). Those non-Hollywood filmmaking cultures were
always to some degree, even if outright rejection, in dialogue with Hollywood.
This book, then, both is and is not about "New Hollywood" specifically. It is
a book about woman *and* New Hollywood, but not necessarily women *in*
New Hollywood.

The book is structured in three parts: history, text, and theory and criticism. This allows us to place more traditional text-based analysis alongside

work from a media industries perspective and to situate both alongside the decade's rich and important theoretical and critical interventions. Paula Rabinowitz situates New Hollywood as one of several film practices of the "long 1968," alongside documentary and the Underground, all of which is paralleled by feminist film practice. She suggests that in contrast to the 1968 of "the white male New Left," the long 1968 "for the integration of feminism and film in the United States stretches between 1965 and 1972, from Gunvor Nelson's and Dorothy Wiley's *Schmeerguntz* to the founding of Women Make Movies." By 1975—in a shift Rabinowitz argues was signaled by Laura Mulvey's "Visual Pleasure and Narrative Cinema"—"feminist film practice ... was firmly institutionalized, unleashing an extraordinarily rich field that has been instrumental in refashioning the humanities."[37] We take Rabinowitz's vision of feminist film culture—one that cuts across distinctions between theory, criticism, and practice, and between wildly different modes of filmmaking—as a model for reconceptualizing 1970s filmmaking. We see 1970s American cinema as both a constellation of cinemas that need to be understood in relation to each other and as part of a broader film culture that encompasses not only production but also film theory and criticism.

The chapters in part I focus on histories of 1970s women filmmakers—some in Hollywood, some outside, and others who straddled the line between mainstream and independent filmmaking—and also historiography, exploring how women have, and have not, been situated in New Hollywood and in film history. Alicia Kozma's critique of the "Rothman Renaissance"—the resurgence of interest in Stephanie Rothman since 2015, after forty years of neglect—highlights the problems with ahistorical recoveries of women filmmakers. In contrast to accounts that frame Rothman as an "exceptional woman" or as "subversive," Kozma argues for the necessity of grounding women filmmakers in their historical context and working conditions and for paying attention to the cultural and institutional barriers that produce their obscurity. Nicholas Forster draws on extensive archival research to paint a detailed and nuanced picture of Jessie Maple's early years. Maple would become the first Black woman admitted to the New York camera operators union, and a director of documentary and feature films. Recounting Maple's early careers in journalism, television, and elsewhere, Forster constructs a convincing depiction of the role that community connections often play in the development of women's filmmaking careers. In his chapter on Jay Presson Allen, Oliver Gruner illustrates how the screenwriter was forced to negotiate a Hollywood writing terrain still heavily dominated by men, who often demanded extensive compromise. Drawing on script notes, drafts, and interviews, Gruner demonstrates how within this milieu, Allen deftly crafted a body of work with consistent themes featuring complex female protagonists who resisted simple description. In his chapter on Barbra Streisand in the 1970s, Nicholas Godfrey notes that Streisand's trajectory is typically framed in parallel to, but never intersecting with, the New Hollywood. He explores the ways in which, as a singularly powerful figure but not yet a director, Streisand frustrated both distinctions between Old and New Hollywood and conventional ideas of authorship in 1970s Hollywood. In the part's final chapter, Maya Montañez Smukler traces Maya Angelou's extensive filmmaking career and the ways that Hollywood exploited her name recognition while also denying her the opportunity to direct films. Angelou was an accomplished, revered writer, the first Black woman to script a feature film, and the only Black woman member of the AFI's inaugural Directing Workshop for Women, but her efforts to make films on her own terms were blocked. Montañez Smukler articulates how Angelou's ambitions were thwarted by the sexism and racism of Hollywood's hierarchical system.

Part II comprises chapters that perform close textual analysis, some focusing on a singular work, some a selection of work by one practitioner, and still others the films of a group of practitioners working in close proximity. These chapters share an approach that foregrounds the creative labor of female filmmakers in ways that have historically been reserved for the work of male auteurs. The part begins with Karen Pearlman's close examination of the work of three key New Hollywood editors—Dede Allen, Marcia Lucas, and Verna Fields—on New Hollywood texts. Pearlman shows how vital each film's editing is to its narrative and thematic success and demonstrates how these editors imbued their films with elements of character, narrative, and theme that were never scripted, but rather were results of the editors' own creative, imaginative interpretations of the film. James Morrison explores awkwardness in Elaine May's films of the 1970s, especially the awkward women in central roles in *A New Leaf* (1971) and *The Heartbreak Kid* (1972). Morrison argues that May's films "revel in a certain dislocated quality" and use awkwardness "as a route to bare little-seen realities." Abigail Cheever's chapter builds on work that has connected the New Hollywood to the rise of the professional-managerial class by examining how Claudia Weill's *Girlfriends* (1978), in its depiction of the development of a photographer, imagines a "feminist professionalization" by attempting to reconcile professionalism's emphasis on impersonal, formalized knowledge with the demands of second-wave feminism, where, by contrast, the personal is political. Cheever argues that the film does this by drawing on both a modernist aesthetics of form and the era's auteurism. She further points out the political limitations of doing so in a system where the creative autonomy granted to male filmmakers remained inaccessible to women. Further afield from Hollywood during the 1970s were the members of the L.A. Rebellion, young Black filmmakers who were defiant in the face of Hollywood's whitewashing and racism. Virginia Bonner's chapter performs a close formal analysis of the work of two female members of the movement, Alile Sharon Larkin and Barbara McCullough. Bonner argues that the films' formal composition and style establish a filmic vocabulary that counters the hegemonic whiteness of Hollywood, creating and exploring a space of female Blackness that had not been seen on-screen, thereby modeling the possibilities for a transgressive, nuanced countercinema in U.S. filmmaking. Finally, Anna Backman Rogers explores *Wanda*'s (1970) aesthetics of failure and radically negative anti-capitalist politics of refusal, an aesthetics and a politics that radically diverged from the masculine "pathos of failure" that Elsaesser identifies with the New Hollywood and rendered the film illegible within the frameworks of 1970s feminism (a point picked up later in the volume by Amelie Hastie).

The 1970s saw the rise of feminist film theory as well as several prominent female film critics. Both cohorts had complex relationships with contemporary women practitioners, and the book's final part explores those tensions and the broader legacies of the decade's feminist film theory and criticism. Focusing on both women's filmmaking and popular and academic feminist film criticism, Amelie Hastie discusses three films that originated with women "trying to make feature films in an era on the cusp of liberation": *Wanda, A New Leaf,* and *Alice Doesn't Live Here Anymore* (1974), films that she argues evaded the era's classification systems. Hastie argues instead for a feminist historiographical approach that enables the construction of histories that expand "not through straight lines or even superficial likenesses but through multiple directions, associations, differences, and interconnections at once." Perhaps the most influential film critic of the New Hollywood era, Pauline Kael had a tremendous impact on the reception of female performance and direction. At the same time, her relationship with the era's feminism and female performers and filmmakers was ambiguous and often rife with tension. Adrian Garvey develops extensive analysis of Kael's writing on filmmaking, feminism, and women in the industry, teasing out the often-contradictory nature of Kael's reception of New Hollywood's women, in front of and behind the camera. Maria Pramaggiore focuses on the legacies and afterlives of Laura Mulvey's "Visual Pleasure and Narrative Cinema," situating the essay in relation to its "sibling theoretical construct": auteurism. She tracks the ways in which the essay's reception has constructed Mulvey herself as an academic auteur, closing off its potential for generating more radical and expansive conceptions of film authorship. Finally, she suggests that ideas of multiple authorship, including posthuman collaborations, provide models for alternative academic authoring practices that reject the anti-feminist, auteurist limitations of the academic star system.

Our collection emerges from and is in dialogue with contemporary work in feminist film history that has sought not simply to fill in gaps in conventional film history but also to transform it, in Shelley Stamp's words, to "take women—and our own scholarship—out of the little grey boxes relegated to the sidelines of film history," to "disrupt conventional narratives with new avenues and new possibilities," to "trace the shapes defined by women's absence."[38] In contrast to what Charlotte Bunch has famously called the "add women and stir" approach to change, what these chapters demand is a fundamental rethinking of both authorship and 1970s American cinema.[39] As Christine Gledhill and Julia Knight have argued, "The questions that asking about women pose to traditional ways of doing film history demand new ways of thinking cinema itself. Insofar as these challenge the dominance of the director, recognize co-creation and collaboration, refuse dominant conceptions of cinematic essence, and reorganize notions of aesthetic value, it is not only women who stand to gain. Asking about women promises new perspectives on film history itself and the many cinemas it generates, both past and future."[40] The chapters in this collection construct and engage these "new ways of thinking cinema" and in so doing challenge the dominant New Hollywood construction that has persisted since the era's earliest days.

Notes

1 Indeed, as Steven Cohan and Dara Milovanovic have pointed out, *Fosse/Verdon* neglects Fosse's other female collaborators and focuses on the peak of Fosse's career as opposed to the earlier peak of Verdon's. Steven Cohan, "*Fosse/Verdon* and the #MeToo Moment," in *American Television During a Television Presidency*, ed. Karen McNally (Detroit: Wayne State University Press, 2022), 203–220; Dara Milovanovic, "*Fosse/Verdon* and All That Jazz: Who Is the Real Star Here?" (paper presented at the London Metropolitan University/virtual conference "Behind the Screen and Off the Stage: Film and Television Representations of American Entertainment," November 11–13, 2021).

2 For recent examples, see Peter Krämer and Yannis Tzioumakis, eds., *The Hollywood Renaissance: Revisiting American Cinema's Most Celebrated Era* (London: Bloomsbury, 2018); Jonathan Kirshner and Jon Lewis, eds., *When the Movies Mattered: The*

New Hollywood Revisited (Ithaca, NY: Cornell University Press, 2019); Dominic Lennard, R. Barton Palmer, and Murray Pomerance, eds., *The Other Hollywood Renaissance* (Edinburgh: Edinburgh University Press, 2020); Gregory Frame and Nathan Abrams, eds., *New Wave, New Hollywood: Reassessment, Recovery, and Legacy* (New York: Bloomsbury, 2021).

3 Peter Biskind, *Easy Riders, Raging Bulls: How the Sex-Drugs-and-Rock 'N' Roll Generation Saved Hollywood* (New York: Simon & Schuster, 1998), 17.

4 Geoff King, *New Hollywood Cinema: An Introduction* (London: I. B. Tauris, 2002), 13.

5 After years of dispute between the Directors Guild of America, the Writers Guild of America, and the Alliance of Motion Picture and Television Producers, an agreement reached in April 1968 allowed individual directors to negotiate for a possessory credit on a film-by-film basis. See Directors Guild, "Possessory Credit Timeline," *DGA Quarterly*, February 2004, https://www.dga.org/Craft/DGAQ /All-Articles/0402-Feb-2004/Possessory-Credit-Timeline.aspx.

6 Pauline Kael, "Circles and Squares," *Film Quarterly* 16, no. 3 (Spring 1963): 12–26.

7 See, for example, Richard Corliss, *Talking Pictures: Screenwriters in the American Cinema* (New York: Overlook, 1974); Graham Petrie, "Alternatives to Auteurs," *Film Quarterly* 26, no. 3 (Spring 1973): 27–35.

8 Jeffrey Sconce, "Movies: A Century of Failure," in *Sleaze Artists: Cinema at the Margins of Taste, Style, and Politics*, ed. Jeffrey Sconce (Durham, NC: Duke University Press, 2007), 275.

9 Terry Eagleton, *The Ideology of the Aesthetic* (Oxford: Blackwell, 1990), 64–65.

10 Timothy Corrigan, "The Commerce of Auteurism: A Voice without Authority," *New German Critique* 49 (Winter 1990): 47.

11 Pauline Kael, "Bonnie and Clyde," *New Yorker*, October 13, 1967, https://www .newyorker.com/magazine/1967/10/21/bonnie-and-clyde.

12 Roger Ebert, "Five Easy Pieces," *Chicago Sun-Times*, January 1, 1970, https://www .rogerebert.com/reviews/five-easy-pieces-1970.

13 In addition to Elsaesser, see also Diane Jacobs, *Hollywood Renaissance: The New Generation of Filmmakers and Their Works* (New York: Delta, 1980); Robert Phillip Kolker, *A Cinema of Loneliness: Penn, Kubrick, Coppola, Scorsese, Altman* (Oxford: Oxford University Press, 1980).

14 Thomas Schatz, *The Genius of the System: Hollywood Filmmaking in the Studio Era* (New York: Metropolitan Books, 1988), 5.

15 Thomas Elsaesser, "American Auteur Cinema: The Last—or First—Great Picture Show," in *The Last Great American Picture Show: New Hollywood Cinema in the 1970s*, ed. Thomas Elsaesser, Alexander Horwath, and Noel King (Amsterdam: Amsterdam University Press, 2004), 37–70.

16 Lennard, Palmer, and Pomerance, *The Other Hollywood Renaissance*.

17 Jane Gaines, *Pink-Slipped: What Happened to Women in the Silent Film Industries?* (Urbana: University of Illinois Press, 2018).

18 Karyn Kay and Gerald Peary, "*Alice Doesn't Live Here Anymore*: Waitressing for Warner's," *Jump Cut*, no. 7 (1975): 5–7; Molly Haskell, *From Reverence to Rape: The Treatment of Women in the Movies*, 2nd ed. (Chicago: University of Chicago Press, 1987), 376.

19 Haskell, *From Reverence to Rape*.

20 See, for example, Joan Mellen, "The Return of Women to Seventies Film," *Quarterly Review of Film and Video* 3, no. 4 (1978): 525–543; Charlotte Brunsdon, "A Subject for the Seventies," *Screen* 23, no. 3–4 (October 1982): 20–29.

21 Shelley Cobb, *Adaptation, Authorship, and Contemporary Women Filmmakers* (Basingstoke: Palgrave Macmillan, 2015), 1. See also Angela Martin, "Refocusing Authorship in Women's Filmmaking," in *Auteurs and Authorship, A Film Reader*, ed. Barry K. Grant (Malden, MA: Blackwell, 2008).

22 Annette Kuhn, *Women's Pictures: Feminism and Cinema*, 2nd ed (London: Verso, 1994), 130–136; Sue Thornham, *What If I Had Been the Hero? Investigating Women's Cinema* (London: BFI, 2012), 65–75; Elena Gorfinkel, "Wanda's Slowness: Enduring Insignificance," in *On Women's Films: Across Worlds and Generations*, ed. Ivone Margulies and Jeremi Szaniawski (London: Bloomsbury Academic, 2019), 27–48.

23 Noel King, "'The Last Good Time We Ever Had': Remembering the New Hollywood Cinema," in *The Last Great American Picture Show: New Hollywood Cinema in the 1970s*, ed. Thomas Elsaesser, Alexander Horwath, and Noel King (Amsterdam: Amsterdam University Press, 2004), 20. "New Hollywood" remains a contested term. While we are aware of both competing terms to describe the 1970s and competing definitions of "New Hollywood," we have chosen this term for the collection because it best represents both the promise of the era and the irony that, in terms of gender, much about the 1970s was decidedly *not* new. For the purposes of this collection, we consider New Hollywood to span roughly 1967 to 1980, although these dates are also subject to debate.

24 Thomas Elsaesser, "The Pathos of Failure: American Films of the 1970s: Notes on the Unmotivated Hero" (1975), in *The Last Great American Picture Show: New Hollywood Cinema in the 1970s*, ed. Thomas Elsaesser, Alexander Horwath, and Noel King (Amsterdam: Amsterdam University Press, 2004), 279–292.

25 Geneviève Sellier, *Masculine Singular: French New Wave Cinema* (Durham, NC: Duke University Press, 2008), 221.

26 Rebecca J. Sheehan, "'One Woman's Failure Affects Every Woman's Chances': Stereotyping Impossible Women Directors in 1970s Hollywood," *Women's History Review* 30, no. 3 (2021): 489.

27 Judith Mayne, *The Woman at the Keyhole: Feminism and Women's Cinema* (Bloomington: Indiana University Press, 1990), 97.

28 Seán Burke, ed., *Authorship: From Plato to the Postmodern, A Reader* (Edinburgh: Edinburgh University Press, 1995), 145.

29 Derek Nystrom, "Hard Hats and Movie Brats: Auteurism and the Class Politics of New Hollywood," *Cinema Journal* 43, no. 3 (Spring 2004): 18–41; King, *New Hollywood Cinema*, 114; Thomas Elsaesser, "Auteur Cinema and the New Economy Hollywood," in *The Persistence of Hollywood* (New York: Routledge, 2012), 237–255; J. D. Connor, *The Studios after the Studios: Neoclassical Hollywood (1970–2010)* (Stanford, CA: Stanford University Press, 2015); Julie A. Turnock, *Plastic Reality: Special Effects, Technology, and the Emergence of 1970s Blockbuster Aesthetics* (New York: Columbia University Press, 2015); Aaron Hunter, *Authoring Hal Ashby: The Myth of the New Hollywood Auteur* (New York: Bloomsbury Academic, 2016); Peter Labuza, "Putting Penn to Paper: Warner Bros.' Contract Governance and the Transition to New Hollywood," *Velvet Light Trap*, no. 80 (Fall 2017): 4–17; Jeff Menne, *Post-Fordist Cinema: Hollywood Auteurs and the Corporate Counterculture* (New York: Columbia University Press, 2019); Ben Rogerson, "'Nobody Knows Anything': Professionalism and Publics in *The Great Waldo Pepper*," *JCMS: Journal of Cinema and Media Studies* 58, no. 2 (Winter 2019): 91–114.

30 Maya Montañez Smukler, *Liberating Hollywood: Women Directors and the Feminist Reform of 1970s American Cinema* (New Brunswick, NJ: Rutgers University Press,

2018). See also Miranda Banks, *The Writers: A History of American Screenwriters and Their Guild* (New Brunswick, NJ: Rutgers University Press, 2015); Shilyh Warren, *Subject to Reality: Women and Documentary Film* (Urbana: University of Illinois Press, 2019); Anna Backman Rogers, *Still Life: Notes on Barbara Loden's "Wanda" (1970)* (Santa Barbara, CA: Punctum Books, 2021); Sheehan, "'One Woman's Failure Affects Every Woman's Chances.'" See also forthcoming work on *Wanda* (1970), from Elena Gorfinkel; on Elaine May, from both Elizabeth Alsop and Carrie Courogen; and on Jane Fonda's work on *Klute* (1971), from Amelie Hastie.

31 Montañez Smukler, *Liberating Hollywood*, 41–42.

32 Philis M. Barragán Goetz, "Breaking Away from Reverence and Rape: The AFI Directing Workshop for Women, Feminism, and the Politics of the Accidental Archive," *Moving Image* 15, no. 2 (Fall 2015): 50–71; Montañez Smukler, *Liberating Hollywood*; Sheehan, "'One Woman's Failure Affects Every Woman's Chances.'" On parallel efforts in the 1970s television industry, see Miranda J. Banks, "Unequal Opportunities: Gender Inequities and Precarious Diversity in the 1970s US Television Industry," *Feminist Media Histories* 4, no. 4 (2018): 109–129.

33 See, for example, B. Ruby Rich, *Chick Flicks: Theories and Memories of the Feminist Film Movement* (Durham, NC: Duke University Press, 1998); Patrice Petro, *Aftershocks of the New: Feminism and Film History* (New Brunswick, NJ: Rutgers University Press, 2002), 157–173; Amelie Hastie, "The 'Whatness' of *Ms.* Magazine and 1970s Feminist Film Criticism," *Feminist Media Histories* 1, no. 3 (2015): 4–37; Laura Mulvey, "Introduction: 1970s Feminist Film Theory and the Obsolescent Object," in *Feminisms: Diversity, Difference and Multiplicity in Contemporary Film Cultures*, ed. Laura Mulvey and Anna Backman Rogers (Amsterdam: Amsterdam University Press, 2015), 17–26; Amelie Hastie, Lynne Joyrich, Patricia White, and Sharon Willis, "(Re)Inventing Camera Obscura," in *Feminisms: Diversity, Difference and Multiplicity in Contemporary Film Cultures*, ed. Laura Mulvey and Anna Backman Rogers (Amsterdam: Amsterdam University Press, 2015), 169–183; Clarissa K. Jacob, "Women & Film: The First Feminist Film Magazine," *Feminist Media Histories* 1, no. 1 (2015): 153–162.

34 Gaines, *Pink-Slipped*, 18–19.

35 Sheehan, "'One Woman's Failure Affects Every Woman's Chances,'" 483–505.

36 Kuhn, *Women's Pictures*, 135.

37 Paula Rabinowitz, "Medium Uncool: Women Shoot Back; Feminism, Film and 1968—A Curious Documentary," *Science and Society* 65, no. 1 (Spring 2001): 74–75.

38 Shelley Stamp, "Feminist Media Historiography and the Work Ahead," *Screening the Past*, 2015, http://www.screeningthepast.com/2015/08/feminist-media-historiography-and-the-work-ahead/.

39 Charlotte Bunch, *Passionate Politics: Feminist Theory in Action, Essays, 1968–1986* (New York: St. Martin's Press, 1987), 140, 302–303.

40 Christine Gledhill and Julia Knight, "Introduction," in *Doing Women's Film History: Reframing Cinemas, Past and Future*, ed. Christine Gledhill and Julia Knight (Urbana: University of Illinois Press, 2015), 11.

Part 1

History

The Rothman Renaissance, or the Politics of Archival (Re)Discovery

ALICIA KOZMA

Archives have long frustrated feminist scholars, as institutions popular, academic, and museological consistently overlook or marginalize women's historical traces. Critically, the embrace of postmodernism in the 1990s radically transformed how archival collections were understood, as scholars eschewed ideas of unbiased and equitable preservation, and embraced archives as the end result of complex subjective processes. The contemporary archival landscape takes for granted the idiosyncrasy of archival collections and their curators; any notion of a single-origin history and its objective preservation is passé. This has been particularly beneficial for cinema scholars, as film history has been retired in favor of histories, and the concession of archival subjectivisms has broadened the breadth and depth of the discipline's historiography. Yet for many feminist film scholars this conceptual opening is not enough because it does not explicitly call for the type of reparative work necessary to uncover and appraise women's myriad past and present contributions to the global evolution of cinema. Feminist interventions into film histories and their associated archives, then, are continually necessary and yet unsparingly fraught. As Vicki Callahan explains in her introduction to the critical women-in-film archives collection *Reclaiming the Archive*: "Much of the feminist work in the arena of film history functions as a double-edged sword: on one level reviewing received notions of what and who counts in film history ... and on a second level rethinking the ongoing tension in feminist film studies between cinema as a machine of pleasure and cinema as a machine of oppression."[1] Grappling with this paradox is as indicative of the work of feminist archival reappraisals as are the newly proffered histories of women film laborers, as scholars like Judith Mayne, Kaja Silverman, Erin Hill, Jane Gaines, and Vivian Sobchack all interrogate the desire for, their positionality to, and the process of feminist archival interventions into cinema histories.[2] Undeniably, a critical component of this process is avoiding what Helen Buss calls "reading from above," wherein the privileges afforded to academics are used to appropriate rather than elucidate.[3] This self-reflexive work forces academics to reconcile with several indefatigable conditions: their intersectional privilege and role as "discoverer;" enduring capitalist filmic systems; and the interconnection between women film laborers, the films their labor helped produce, and various mechanisms of erasure said women and films have been subjected to.

Or not. There have been numerous reparatives of women's filmic labor in and outside of the academy that have ignored the thornier, and necessary, questions addressed by the scholars mentioned here. Despite my glibness, this is a questionable interventional method; any ahistorical reconsideration of women's filmic labor must be scrutinized for the ways in which reappraisal can, itself, eradicate the very subjects it claims to foreground. In this chapter, I consider the reverberations of ahistorical recovery and appraisal through director Stephanie Rothman and her return to public consideration forty-plus years after she retired from filmmaking. Indeed, when I consider the recent renaissance of her work, I do so with great skepticism. Not because the recognition is not warranted—it certainly is—but because of the implications of revitalizing a career out of context and the elisions of women's labor, archival presence, and cultural contributions that type of recovery can facilitate. I am interested in teasing out the ways that rediscoveries of women filmmakers can mask the archival lack of women directors and the persistent disparity in gendered labor in the entertainment industries, holding up "rediscovered" women as emblematic of the mythic meritocracy of Hollywood. I begin this process with a short recounting of Rothman's career and her recent renaissance, moving then to the problematics of the rhetoric of subversion attached to her rediscovery and closing with the intertwined issues of archives, labor, and memory.

The Death and Life of Rothman's Oeuvre

Born in 1936 in New Jersey and raised in Los Angeles, filmmaker Stephanie Rothman was one of the most productive women filmmakers of New Hollywood. Yet, until recently, she was a minor footnote in film histories, in part because Rothman made exploitation films. Exploitation films have a long history as a shadow industry in Hollywood, their classical period running from 1919 to 1959 and their second wave from 1960 to 1980.[4] The two discrete cycles are differentiated by their style and content but linked by their production, distribution, and reputation. Second-wave exploitation films were a critical training ground for many of the writers, directors, and producers who made up New Hollywood, including Francis Ford Coppola, Peter Fonda, Jack Nicholson, John Sayles, Peter Bogdanovich, Martin Scorsese, and Jonathan Demme. Yet for those exploitation filmmakers who were unable to migrate to mainstream filmmaking, second-wave exploitation films and their filmmakers are often lost to cinema history.

A graduate of the University of Southern California film school and the first woman to win the Directors Guild of America student filmmaking fellowship, Stephanie Rothman made seven feature films between 1966 and 1974 and was vice president at the production and distribution outfit Dimension Pictures. Although independent, Rothman's films were screened all over the United States and were economically successful. Her filmmaking career began at Roger Corman's Filmgroup, where she made her first two features, *Blood Bath/Track of the Vampire* (1966) and *It's a Bikini World* (1967). Rothman was not particularly interested in working in second-wave exploitation, and she left Corman in 1966 with hopes of transitioning to mainstream film work. Rothman faced a double bind: breaking into Hollywood as a woman was exceedingly difficult made more so by her exploitation experience. Rothman returned to Corman's employ in 1969 as a production executive on the film *Gas-s-s-s* (Roger Corman, 1970). In 1970, she joined Corman at his new production and distribution company, New World. Continually discontented with the salacious content demands of second-wave exploitation, Rothman developed a set of informal but consistent filmmaking rules to balance content requirements with her own ethics. These included equitable male and female nudity; avoiding filmic rape and, when forced to include rape scenes, filming them as nonvoyeuristic; avoiding nudity as a form of vengeance; forsaking violence whenever possible, and when it is represented it is shown as harsh, noneroticized, and with significant consequences; and, finally, choices made by female characters should be done outside of their relationship with male characters.[5] She directed two films at New World under these guidelines—*The Student Nurses* (1970) and *The Velvet Vampire* (1971)—and would continue to employ them throughout her career.

In 1972, New World was preparing to film a new picture with a larger than normal budget and a more seasoned cast than was typical for the company's slate. As a proven director and sound investment under Corman's employ, Rothman felt her spirit buoyed. She recalled: "I was hoping that if anything came along, Roger would give me more resources. He was always very laudatory and has always said good things about me, both to me and to other people in my presence. I had hoped that if he was going to finance a film that would allow for more time and better actors, all those things that I hadn't had before when making films for him, he would choose me to direct."[6] In spite of her reasoned anticipation, the film—*Boxcar Bertha* (1972)—was given to neophyte director Martin Scorsese.[7] Hyperaware of her limitations under Corman, Rothman left New World to help cofound Dimension Pictures. She served as Dimension's vice president, responsible for development of new film ideas, viewing preproduced films for possible acquisition, and advising on recutting/shaping acquired films. Her primary responsibilities, however, remained writing, directing, and overseeing preproduction on her own films. Rothman made three films at the company: *Group Marriage* (1972), *Terminal Island* (1973), and *The Working Girls* (1974). They were her last. Pushed out of Dimension in 1974 in a bid for economic control over the company, she would spend the next ten years trying to work in mainstream Hollywood. During this time, she sold several scripts but was continuously locked out of directing. Rothman quit the industry in 1984 and never returned. The legacy of her oeuvre is one that foregrounds progressive politics and the lived experiences of contemporary women from a humanist perspective.

What I term the "Rothman Renaissance" began in earnest in 2015.[8] While there are scattered moments of recognition before 2015, I trace her resurgence to this origin point of recurrent, sustained activity. To wit, the following chronology. In 2015, the Academy Film Archives struck a new print of *The Student Nurses* from a negative donated to the Academy of Motion Pictures Arts and Sciences by Corman,[9] and financial support from Cinema Conservancy and the New York Women in Film & Television Cinema Preservation Fund. The film screened at New York City's Museum of Modern Art (MoMA) in February of that year.[10] Also in 2015, Rothman was solicited by the Academy of Motion Picture Arts and Sciences to participate in a video oral history for the "Women in Film" section of its new museum. Rothman was skeptical. She said, "I told them I found it rather ironic that an organization that would never have me as a member wanted to have my history in its archive. But I changed my mind when I saw the list of other people they had interviewed. We had all been chosen not for our fame or celebrity but for our historical significance."[11] Finally, that year an entry about Rothman appeared in the Routledge book *Fifty Hollywood Directors*.[12]

A partnership between Rothman and MoMA was extended in 2016, and the museum embarked on a campaign to secure the necessary monies to strike new prints of *Group Marriage*, *Terminal Island*, and *The Working Girls*. Distributor Vinegar Syndrome owns a positive print of *Terminal Island* it has agreed to share with MoMA for the project, but there are no positive prints of *Group Marriage* or *The Working Girls* to be found.[13] Rothman, who does not own the rights to her movies, agreed to provide the museum with copies she has of two films for the project.[14] Both need significant, and expensive, color correction.[15] In March 2016, *Interview Magazine* featured Rothman ahead of *The Student Nurses* playing at New York City's luminary art house theater Metrograph.[16] The theater brought Rothman to speak alongside the film. *The Student Nurses* and *Group Marriage* also screened at Film Forum as part of its "Genre Is a Woman" Festival.[17] In 2017, she was featured on the cover of *Camera Obscura* and as part of the "In Focus" section of the journal.[18] That year, Roger Corman presented her with the Inspiration Award at the Etheria Film Festival.[19] In 2018, Rothman appeared on Blumhouse and Fangoria's *Shock Waves* podcast;[20] there, cohost Rebekah McKendry, in conjunction with the Etheria Film Festival, announced the Stephanie Rothman Fellowship for Women Student Filmmakers.[21] In March 2018, Rothman received the Vanguard Award from the Nevada Women's Film Festival.[22] Most recently, *The Student Nurses* screened at the tenth TCM Classic Film Festival; Rothman was on hand to discuss the film.[23]

Reconciling the Renaissance

The renewed and sustained interest in Rothman's work over the past five years has been incredibly valuable in exposing her body of work to newer and broader audiences. This is undeniably good. Less equivocal, however, is the impact of a ahistorical revival that denies the cultural and institutional factors that led to forty years of near obscurity. Rothman exists marginally in cinematic and popular histories. Much of the limited information that can be found about her is superficial, contradictory, or simply incorrect: she has been labeled a pornographic director; the star—not director—of one of her films, Corman was given directorial credit for another; and three of her films referenced her husband as director.[24] Misinformation about Rothman is rampant, so much so she has demanded some corrections. For example, a 1981 interview with Rothman in the *Journal of Popular Film and Television* was so misrepresentative that she wrote a letter of correction to the journal; it was published, and the journal amended part of their policies around interviews.[25] Rothman's misrepresentation in the press left a lasting impression. As she told me, "I do want to author my own story, but only because I don't want it distorted. I had some early press interviews that were so inaccurate and sloppy that I learned my lesson and I have never forgotten it."[26]

Interestingly, historical and contemporary rhetorical refrains around Rothman and her films pull at the same thread. Writing extemporaneous to her career often focused on her so-called outsider status in second-wave exploitation, emphasizing the novelty of a woman working in a stereotypically masculinized cinematic style.[27] This incongruity was often rationalized through her liberal politics and ideologically progressive films: Rothman as an undercover rebel. Yet Rothman did not see herself as an outsider. Indeed, her strident goal was a career in mainstream Hollywood. In the Rothman Renaissance, "outsider" transformed into "subversive."[28] Instances include: "Rothman's low-budget movies have been recognized in the proceeding decades for their subversive content;"[29] "Stephanie Rothman's subversive sensibility;"[30] and "a double feature of her films, the provocative and subversive movie."[31] The application of subversion is not uncommon in evaluations of second-wave exploitation films or of women filmmakers. The idea of women's directorial labor as a subversive, a label applied to a broad range of women from Lois Weber to Roberta Findlay, constitutes what Jane Gaines call an "unimaginabilities."[32] Historiographical unimaginabilities—those realities that seem impossible to have existed in the past but which regularly confront historians with their subsistence—require us to "imagine what we can't imagine . . . because the historical past is by definition full of unimaginabilities or surprises,"[33] like an influential producer and director of the early silent era (Weber) or an infamous adult film director and cinematographer in the 1970s and 1980s (Findlay). The sobriquet of subversion is more indicative of the historian's narrow imagination than it is of the past lives and careers of the women the title is applied to.

Even so, subversion has a particular staying power in public discourse, and it is used both as a marker of "hidden" value and as a justification for considering the traditionally derided films worthy of study.[34] Critically, however, it obscures directorial and industrial context. For example, an *Interview Magazine* profile from 2016 describes Rothman as "packaging subversive content into movies that marketed themselves solely on the promise of nudity and violence." Putting aside the impossibility of claiming second-wave exploitation films marketed themselves solely on anything, in statements like this Rothman is "subverting" her industrial home. This causes three interrelated problems. First, it values the films' impacts as exploitation artifacts solely. By this I mean that Rothman's films are antidotes to *all* commercial filmmaking in the 1960s and 1970s—mainstream and independent. Claiming Rothman's films as subversive only to second-wave exploitation ignores the fact that nuanced, political, progressive stories about women's lives and experiences are anathema to most filmmaking. Second, it compresses second-wave exploitation into a monolith that universally demanded subversion. While all film industries have practices to ensure standardization toward production efficiency and return on investment, second-wave exploitation is stereotypically regarded as hyperformulaic filmmaking whose repetitive output bred insurgency. Rothman may have undermined the stereotypical idea of exploitation, but the stereotype is certainly not representative of what was an extremely productive and varied industry.

Third, and here I return to archival considerations, is that a blanket application of subversion ignores the history of Rothman's career. Indeed, her limited archival presence should trouble any simplistic label, as knowing and evaluating Rothman's career presents particular problems. For example, *The Student Nurses* is often described as subversive, adding fodder to Rothman's reputation as such. However, it was not until Rothman saw a review of the film in *Variety* calling it exploitation that she realized she was directing exploitation films.[35] Claims of subversion ignore the lived experiences of her career; reconsiderations of women filmmakers cannot be divorced from their historical contexts. Rothman's career was not defined by subversion but rather by persistence and resilience. She first met Corman because USC sent her to his office for to interview to be his secretary; she convinced him that she could do more. After Corman saw the first cut of *The Student Nurses*, he thought it was too political and wanted Rothman to change it; she refused.[36] When a studio executive called her in to ask for insight on how to make a

"Stephanie Rothman" movie, she offered her employment; the executive equivocated, and Rothman left.[37] Rothman fought her entire career to simply have a career. Labeling it subversion upholds historical unimaginabilities and is too reductive; rediscovery cannot come without context.

Rothman's archival representation, or lack thereof, is not uncommon for many women filmmakers. The same archival neglect that surrounds Rothman holds true for her industrial contemporaries like Marilyn Tenser, Doris Wishman, and Barbara Peeters, among others. This both narrows the history of women working behind the camera while also troubling the mythologized relationship between New Hollywood and second-wave exploitation. Doubtlessly, part of New Hollywood lore involves the beginnings of many key figures in second-wave exploitation, generally, and Roger Corman, specifically. The colloquially named "Corman school" has become as legendary as many of its graduates mentioned in this chapter, as "the exploitation generation stormed the gates of Hollywood's citadel and paved the way for filmmakers with backgrounds in media that didn't even exist in the 1970s."[38] Yet while the industry that trained these men for radical reinventions of cinema did the same for competent and successful women filmmakers, the door to mainstream Hollywood was closed to them. The masculinization of New Hollywood, combined with the persistent "great men" narrative of auteurism, sidelines women's filmic labor and reinforces their historiographical lack. Additionally, acontextual rediscovery sidesteps the minefield that is women's labor in Hollywood and its parallel industries. This is compounded when textual or filmic analysis overwhelms the circumstances of production and labor. Focusing solely on the filmic output of a career exempted from the working conditions that impacted them downplays the disparity in gendered labor in the industry and the hostile working conditions that develop from them. An ahistorical or acontextual rediscovery of any woman director that does not specifically understand filmic contributions in the context of her everyday working conditions upholds Hollywood's mythic, and toxic, meritocracy.

In "Vision and Visibility," Yvonne Tasker suggests that the public visibility of women filmmakers is one rejoinder to their continued industrial precarity and marginalization.[39] This is particularly salient in the post-#MeToo Hollywood reckoning. Pre-2017, before the onslaught of public exposure around Hollywood's culture of rampant sexual assault and harassment, the conversation around gender in Hollywood was primarily focused on hiring and pay equity.[40] While mainstream and trade news outlets reported on gender parity in hiring, there was little conversation about what happens *after* a woman has been hired, reifying a singular focus on one aspect of compounded issues. Women in the industry at all levels shared stories of consistent and persistent working atmospheres filled with sexual harassment, abuse, institutional misogyny, and open hostility. The professional structures that condone these behaviors, naturally, offer little to no recourse for their victims. These stories force us to make the connection between misogynistic hiring practices, hostile and volatile work environments, rampant sexual abuse and harassment, and the way we as scholars narrate the historical and present life of women film workers. The forces of institutional sexism and misogyny that nurture sexual harassment and abuse also structured the careers of women like Stephanie Rothman. They are the same networks that foster the current lack of women film workers in key creative positions in the industry and the miserable, abusive working environments for those working within it. Sexual harassment and abuse, the labor conditions of Hollywood past, present, and future, and ahistorical recoveries of women film laborers cannot be untangled from one another.

Intimately related is how rediscovery feeds into what I refer to as cinema histories' paradigm of exceptional women. The paradigm of exceptional women encapsulates the idea that women filmmakers are routinely positioned as exceptions to the rule of male dominance in directing, thereby conveying aspirational-only status for current and future women directors while simultaneously denormalizing the very concept of women directors. Indeed, "the emergence and success or failure of women filmmakers is also a question of women who visibly, publicly appropriate titles perceived as male."[41] This is grounded in the particular industrial assumption that women filmmakers are exceptions to the rule of the accepted, routinized maleness of directors. To be clear, the term "exceptional" in no way refers to the talent or skill of women directors, or to the success of their films. Any woman who has overcome the misogynistic hurdles of most filmmaking industries to direct a film is exceptional in the most extraordinary sense. The exceptionalism I posit is that of tokenism masquerading as parity. Exceptional women directors are limited symbols of a long and unexamined history of women as film workers. Constructing the exceptional woman director is key to maintaining patriarchal control in Hollywood employment and labor environments. The exceptional woman "provides men with an excuse to blame women for their own pain and struggles while simultaneously assuring women that sexism only needs to be outwitted to be overcome. She tells us that the system is survivable for women—you simply have to be the right kind of woman."[42]

I have previously argued that the paradigm of exceptional woman is created through academic and popular canons, publishing, and restrictive film archives and histories. Here I add contemporarily fraught rediscovery to that list. Acontextual and ahistorical extant rediscovery of women filmmakers reinforces the exceptional woman paradigm by holding up a small group of women filmmakers as an example of the potentialities of a meritocratic labor and employment landscape while obscuring the systemic, institutionalized prejudice and oppression facing all women film workers. Screening Rothman's films at MoMA or adding her to the academy's museum does nothing to acknowledge an industrial system that beat her down until she left. It does nothing to acknowledge that the same working conditions for women in Hollywood in the 1960s and 1970s that have been replicated throughout decades constitute today's prevailing professional landscapes. It does nothing to broaden or equalize filmic archives and histories. It is imperative to remember that the exceptional women paradigm is not an isolated phenomenon divorced from cinematic history. It is a circular process of erasure. The dearth of accessible archival information becomes a substantial hurdle in the process of constructing a history of women in film. This encourages ahistorical and acontextual rediscoveries. The failure of cinematic archives to include women like Stephanie Rothman and others stresses the limits of the exceptional women paradigm in film history as one that constructs women directors as aberrations in directorial labor, resulting in their continued disintegration into film production and dehumanizing, exploitative, professional conditions.

There are solutions to these pernicious problems. Feminist archival interventions like those mentioned previously are spaces that connect author, text, and labor. Adjacent and complementary work in queer and affect studies provides templates for politicized and alternative archive creation. A small set of varied examples include Kathleen Stewart's anthropological investigation into the everyday; Michael Shetina's examination of citation, affect, and queer pleasure in reality television; Allison Page on the imbrication of cute animal video and labor; and Paul Michael Leonardo Atienza's ethnography of gay dating apps in Manilla.[43] Such scholarship provides templates for moving, and perhaps erasing, archival borders, bringing to light what Antoinette Burton calls small stories: "fragments of lives and dramas that we have only glimpses of but that serve as testimony to the fugitive work of gender and equally fleeting presence of women as subject across a vast landscape of the past."[44] New historiographical methods turn those small stories into broader narratives, moving them from historical fragment into holistic construction, rebalancing power differentials endemic to normative historical memory and ahistorical remembrances.

Without a doubt, historiographical research can move beyond institutions and traditional archives and unfold the complicated and brilliant careers of women film laborers. The archive can be a variant site of knowledge formation and is a crucial node in linking labor patterns across the past, present, and future, opening up spaces for understanding and progressive intervention. Combining a focus on filmic analysis *alongside* the conditions of labor and employment may, at first glance, seem small, but these approaches come with a cumulative power. They are practical, and frankly achievable, interventions that build more robust and comprehensive archives, filmic histories, and public understanding for women film workers. These efforts are critical in normalizing women's participation in cinema creation and memory. Transforming the traditional role of archives and histories as repositories of the past into active sites of investigation and interventions aids in explicating contemporary issues of women's labor in the film industry and in cultural memory. For, as Stephanie Rothman herself says, "It is very important for everyone to recognize that women can make films. It is important for social justice, for the sense of identity of all women and for the art of filmmaking."[45]

The Rothman Renaissance continues to reinforce this message, albeit in the complicated ways that always accompany the valuation of women's filmic labor. In October 2020, *The Student Nurses* and *The Velvet Vampire* were featured on The Criterion Channel, a subscription-based streaming service from the cinephilic Criterion Collection. But, in line with the involute memorialization of women's filmmaking labor, they were but two films featured in a programming block called the Women Filmmakers of New World Pictures. Also featured were films from Barbara Peeters, Amy Holden Jones, and Penelope Spheeris. The introductory text for the titles describes these filmmakers as "a handful of trailblazing women" who exist as "fascinating examples of how the transgressive pleasures of exploitation cinema can be wedded to a subversive approach to gender and genre,"[46] driving home the enduring obfuscatory power of exceptionalism, subversion, and tokenism and fortifying the necessity of archival and historiographical disruption as critical upending forces.

Notes

1   Vicki Callahan, "Introduction: Reclaiming the Archive," in *Reclaiming the Archive: Feminism and Film History*, ed. Vicki Callahan (Detroit: Wayne State University Press, 2010), 3.

2   See Jane Gaines, *Pink-Slipped: What Happened to Women in the Silent Film Industries?* (Urbana: University of Illinois Press, 2018); Erin Hill, *Never Done: A History of Women's Work in Media Production* (New Brunswick, NJ: Rutgers University Press, 2016); Judith Mayne, *The Woman at the Keyhole: Feminism and Women's Cinema* (Bloomington: Indiana University Press, 1990); Kaja Silverman, "The Female Authorial Voice," in *Film and Authorship*, ed. Virginia Wright Wexman (New Brunswick, NJ: Rutgers University Press, 2003), 59; Vivian Sobchack, "'Presentifying' Film and Media Feminism," *Camera Obscura* 21, no. 1.61 (2006): 65–68.

3   Helen Buss, "Constructing Female Subjects in the Archive," in *Working in Women's Archives: Researching Women's Private Literature and Archival Documents*, ed. Marlene Kadar (Ontario: Wilfrid Laurier University Press, 2001), 34.

4   For a definitive history of classic exploitation film, see Eric Schaefer, *Bold! Daring! Shocking! True: A History of Exploitation Films, 1919–1959* (Durham, NC: Duke University Press, 1999).

5   Alicia Kozma, "Stephanie Rothman," in *Fifty Hollywood Directors*, ed. Yvonne Tasker and Suzanne Leonard (London: Routledge, 2014), 377–383.

6   Rothman quoted in Alicia Kozma, "Stephanie Rothman Does Not Exist: Narrating a Lost History of Women in Film," *Camera Obscura* 32, no. 1.94 (2017): 183.

7   Kozma, "Stephanie Rothman Does Not Exist."

8   My own role, however small, in the Rothman Renaissance requires a note of contextualization. While I cannot claim a hand in her reemergence into the cinematic zeitgeist, I can draw direct lines between presentations of my research and the Rothman pieces in *Fifty Hollywood Directors*, *Camera Obscura*, and this volume. I wrote them all, and each one came about as a result of academic conference presentations I gave on Rothman. I have been friends with Rebekah McKendry—the cohost of Blumhouse and Fangoria's *Shock Waves Podcast*—for more than a decade, but I had no more knowledge of, or influence over, the show's honoring of Rothman than any other loyal listener. This is a long-winded way of saying that while I can claim some influence in increased academic attention to Rothman, I truly believe her renaissance is the result of increased access to her films.

9   Stephanie Rothman, email to author, February 18, 2015.

10 "What's On," The Museum of Modern Art, accessed June 2, 2020, https://www.moma.org/calendar/events/818.

11 Stephanie Rothman, email to author, February 18, 2015.

12 Kozma, "Stephanie Rothman."

13 Dave Kehr, curator in the Museum of Modern Art Department of Film, conversation with author, July 7, 2020.

14 Stephanie Rothman, email to author, May 30, 2016.

15 Dave Kehr, conversation with author, July 7, 2020.

16 Colleen Kelsey, "The Cult of Stephanie Rothman," *Interview Magazine*, last modified March 7, 2016, https://www.interviewmagazine.com/film/stephanie-rothman.

17 "GENRE IS A WOMAN" Festival, Film Forum, accessed July 2, 2020, https://filmforum.org/series/genre-is-a-woman-series.

18 Kozma, "Stephanie Rothman Does Not Exist."

19 Chris Alexander, "Etheria 2017: Roger Corman to Present Stephanie Rothman with Award," *ComingSoon.net*, last modified June 1, 2017, https://www.comingsoon.net/horror/news/854113-etheria-2017-roger-corman-to-present-stephanie-rothman-with-award.

20 "Episode 90: Stephanie Rothman!," *Shock Waves*, last updated March 30, 2028, https://www.stitcher.com/podcast/mrw-productions-llc/shock-waves/e/53914000.

21 "The Stephanie Rothman Fellowship for Women Student Filmmakers," *Film Freeway*, accessed July 2, 2020, https://filmfreeway.com/TheStephanieRothmanSch olarshipForWomenStudentFilmmakers.

22 "Featured Guest Filmmaker: Stephanie Rothman," Nevada Women's Film Festival, accessed July 2, 2020, https://www.nwffest.com/featured-guest-filmmaker -stephanie-rothman.

23 "Films," 10th TCM Classic Film Festival, accessed July 8, 2020, http://2019 .filmfestival.tcm.com/programs/.

24 Jean Callahan, "Women and Pornography," *American Film*, March 1982, 62–63; Valerie J. Nelson, "Charles Swartz, 67; Took Film to the Digital Age," *Los Angeles Times*, February 14, 2007, http://articles.latimes.com/print/2007/feb/14/local/me -swartz14; Alicia Kozma, "Stephanie Rothman and Vampiric Film Histories," in *Women Make Horror*, ed. Alison Peirse (New Brunswick, NJ: Rutgers University Press, 2020), 24–32.

25 See Stephanie Rothman, "A Letter of Correct from Stephanie Rothman," *Journal of Popular Film and Television* 10, no. 3 (Fall 1982): 137.

26 Stephanie Rothman, email to author, April 13, 2013.

27 For example, see Linda Gross, "A Woman's Place Is in. . . . Exploitation Films? A Trendsetter in the Youth Market," *Los Angeles Times*, February 12, 1978, 35.

28 Kelsey, "The Cult of Stephanie Rothman."

29 "The Equal Opportunity Exploitation of Stephanie Rothman," University of Wisconsin–Madison Cinematheque, accessed July 9, 2020, https://cinema.wisc.edu /series/2017/fall/stephanie-rothman.

30 "The Student Nurses," Brooklyn Academy of Music, accessed July 9, 2020, https:// www.bam.org/events/production_cinema/2018/the-student-nurses.aspx.

31 "Legendary Director Stephanie Rothman Is Back! And She's at the Ritz This Wednesday," Alamo Drafthouse Cinema, last modified April 12, 2010, https:// drafthouse.com/news/legendary-director-stephanie-rothman-is-back-and-shes-at -the-ritz-this-wedn.

32 Gaines, *Pink-Slipped*, 197.

33 Gaines, 197.

34 Horror films offer an interesting corollary, particularly those seen as "elevated horror." For example, see the films of Ari Aster, Jordan Peele, and Jennifer Kent's *The Babadook* (2014). My thanks to Michael Shetina for first pointing out this idea.

35 Stephanie Rothman, interview by Alicia Kozma, February 4, 2014, transcript.

36 Stephanie Rothman, interview by Alicia Kozma.

37 Ben Sher. "Q&A with Stephanie Rothman. *CSW Update Newsletter*, UCLA Center for the Study of Women, last modified April 1, 2008, http://escholarship.org /uc/item/4jx713vz.

38 Maitland McDonagh, "The Exploitation Generation or: How Marginal Movies Came in from the Cold," in *The Last Great American Picture Show: New Hollywood Cinema in the 1970s*, ed. Thomas Elsaesser, Alexander Horwath, and Noel King (Amsterdam: Amsterdam University Press, 2004), 109.

39 Yvonne Tasker, "Vision and Visibility," in *Reclaiming the Archive: Feminism and Film History*, ed. Vicki Callahan (Detroit: Wayne State University Press, 2010), 213–230.

40 It seems our news outlets and entertainment systems cannot hold two thoughts about women in their metaphoric heads at the same time.

41 Tasker, "Vision," 214.

42 Sady Doyle. "The Problem with Exceptional Women." *Elle*, last modified December 15, 2016. http://www.elle.com/culture/career-politics/a41444/ivanka-trump -distraction/.

43 See Kathleen Stewart, *Ordinary Affects* (Durham, NC: Duke University Press, 2007); Michael Shetina, "Snatching an Archive: Gay Citation, Queer Belonging and the Production of Pleasure in *RuPaul's Drag Race*," *Queer Studies in Media & Popular Culture* 3, no. 2 (2018): 143–158; Allison Page, "'This Baby Sloth Will Inspire You to Keep Going': Capital, Labor, and the Affective Power of Cute Animal Video," in *The Aesthetics and Affect of Cuteness*, ed. Joshua Paul Dale, Joyce Goggin, Julia Ledya, Anthony P. McIntyre, and Diane Negra (New York: Routledge), 75–94; Paul Michael Leonardo Atienza, "Censoring the Sexual Self: Reflections from an Ethnographic Study of Gay Filipinos on Mobile Dating Apps in Manila," *The Asia Pacific Journal of Anthropology* 19, no. 3 (2018): 231–244.

44 Antoinette Burton, "Forward: 'Small Stories' and the Promise of New Narratives," in *Contesting Archives: Finding Women in the Sources*, ed. Nupur Chaudhuri, Sherry J. Katz, and Mary Elizabeth Perry (Urbana: University of Illinois Press, 2010): i.

45 Rothman quoted in Alicia Kozma, "Stephanie Rothman Does Not Exist: Narrating a Lost History of Women in Film," *Camera Obscura* 32, no. 1.94 (2017): 183.

46 "Women Filmmakers of New World Pictures," The Criterion Channel, accessed December 12, 2020, https://www.criterionchannel.com/women-filmmakers-of-new -world-pictures.

2

Watering the Grapevine

Jessie Maple, Self-Narration, and the Trajectory of a Career in Community

NICHOLAS FORSTER

Jessie Maple sent a telegram and, perhaps, she waited. It was the mid-1970s, and the aspiring filmmaker had reached out to Redd Foxx. Foxx had become a celebrity, known for his role as the curmudgeonly Fred Sanford in *Sanford and Son*, NBC's most popular show between 1972 and 1976. At the time, Maple was breaking into the television industry: in 1973 she became the first Black woman in the cameraperson's union, IATSE Local 644. The note, a Western Union telegram, was brief. Maple asked Foxx if he would consider her "to work as a second camera person on [the] film *Norman ... Is That*

You."[1] Produced by MGM and adapted from a popular stage play, *Norman* was to be Foxx's breakthrough as a lead film actor. His rising star status carried with it some power and possible leverage for the crew behind the scenes. The film was to begin shooting in April 1976. Maple reached out to make a connection.[2]

Connections mattered. Though there is no response from Foxx in Maple's papers at Indiana University's Black Film Center/Archive, the telegram reflects what Maple describes as her "method," of shrewdly making the best of every situation and finding inroads where she could.[3] "It's not what you know, it's who you know" was a truism with which Maple was intimately familiar. She had faced lies and deceit trying to break into the union. Technicians had sabotaged her application and attempted to disqualify her, proclaiming that she was too weak to carry heavy camera equipment. Nevertheless, Maple made it, all the while knowing that the union's apprenticeship system often operated on prejudicial favoritism that she could not take advantage of. Between 1975 and 1976, determined to create, with or without the assistance of an industry that rejected Black creativity, she finished her documentary on the systemic failure of New York's drug rehabilitation programs: *Methadone: Wonder Drug or Evil Spirit*. Featuring interviews with recovering addicts, doctors, and administrators, *Methadone* is a critique of state and federal programs that failed to address local communities, since, in the words of the Reverend Oberia Dempsey, the world "doesn't really want to cure drug addicts because there is a lot of profit." The documentary is just one work that demonstrated how the networks of care in Harlem were the arteries in the system of support Maple worked in and around.

Over the last thirty years, scholars have pointed to Maple's entry into the union as a landmark in the history of race, labor, and cinema. Her journey was hard-fought in legal battles, in discussions in corporate offices, and in the everyday challenges of her professional life. This essay looks backward and outlines the roots of Maple's career to better understand the routes she took and her place within a cohort of Black creatives based in New York. Maple was a member of what Michele Prettyman and I have called the "New York Scene." Where members of the L.A. Rebellion frequently shared a decolonial politics and an anti-Hollywood position, and were foundationally shaped by a university, the New York Scene was, even while predicated on spatial proximity, more diffuse and "characterized by independent, often experimental, narrative and documentary film production . . . and the convergence of poetic and political discourse."[4] Maple was a part of this scene as a mentor, writer, curator, and filmmaker. I draw out the significance of her early career, prior to entering the union, to illuminate how Maple was dedicated to widely sharing her insider knowledge. Reflecting on her life, Maple claimed that filmmaking allowed her to "be near the people."[5] This mantra is key to understanding Maple's place within an emerging class of Black artists entering the nation's culture industries.

Rather than narrate the production history of any single film, I offer a production history of Maple's career as a filmmaker. To do this, I focus on three things: Maple's journalistic work at the *Manhattan Tribune* and the *New York Courier*, two autobiographical books (*How to Become a Union Camerawoman* and *The Maple Crew*), and her experiences in apprentice programs housed by Third World Cinema (TWC) and New York's public television station WNET. I argue that Maple repeatedly provided a map to audiences that was both a product and a reflection of the importance of creative networks and connections. Where her documentaries and feature films offered ways of making sense of systemic issues through individual stories, Maple's writings created a schematic for aspiring artists to follow. Examining Maple's early work clarifies how her career was threaded together by a conscious attempt to open space for Black artists who were otherwise excluded.

My investment in Maple's writings is guided, in part, by a desire to move away from long-standing fixations on "firsts" in histories of Black creativity. Just as sociological renderings of Black film have inadvertently suppressed discussions of aesthetic form and blunted the sharp contradictions of art into a frictionless mirror of representation, a preoccupation with firsts too often reifies an artist as an isolated genius. Recognition is necessary, accolades are critical, and the marking of a "first" can offer an easy shorthand to complex histories. However, Maple's status as one of the first Black women to make a feature film and as *the* first Black woman to enter the cameraperson's union too often obfuscates the networks of support and collaboration so integral to her work. Critical to understanding this is Maple's own narration, which reveals the multifarious trajectories available for Black entertainers as well as the worlds that shut them out. Time and again, she reflected on jobs she held prior to becoming a filmmaker. In a 2005 interview, when asked, "How did you break through?" Maple did not begin with her time in the film and television industry. Instead, she replied, "Well . . . I was a bacteriologist."[6] This surprising response is an invitation to think about the significance of Maple's labor prior to her breakthrough as a "first" in the union and how that work shaped her creative approach and ethics. As a freelance cameraperson on news crews, she "would shoot . . . in a way where they couldn't cut the black person out of the story."[7] This shrewd artistic-political dedication to providing a space for Black people to appear, not as symbols but as complicated and contradictory individuals, was the project of extending the grapevine. And that work began even before Maple picked up a camera.

Recognition, Location, and the Black Press: Maple Meets a Broad Public

To have one's name in print was to be introduced to a broader public. It signaled that an individual was part of a community that people should know. In 1964 Maple's name appeared in Toki Schalk's famous *Pittsburgh Courier* column, "Toki's Types." In the Black press, society editors, like Schalk, held power and influence; they noted who was dining with whom and what events were necessary to attend if one was hip. Perhaps most significantly, they orchestrated and publicized the lives and aspirations of a developing Black middle class. As *Ebony* noted years earlier: "No one in America is closer to the pulse of colored life . . . [society editors] do more to interpret the social patterns of the community than the sociologist or psychologist."[8] Within this small world, Schalk was a legend. In the pages of the *Pittsburgh Courier*, she let readers know that Maple, "a versatile young lady, [who] has had courses in modeling and merchandising," was a business owner who had just opened a restaurant.[9] The café, Peggy's, named after Maple's sister, was a zone for Black customers to learn from one another. Materially, the restaurant supplied financial support so that Maple could pursue other passions. Peggy's also provided a source of employment for friends and family and was ultimately, in Maple's words, a place where she "could go serve the community and be treated wonderfully."[10] In the era of civil rights legislation and (un)officially segregated lunch counters, places to eat and gather functioned as vibrant sites of sociality, respite, and relief.[11]

It was Maple's time working at Peggy's that inspired her to make the short film *Methadone*. In her 2019 memoir, *The Maple Crew*, she explains that her interest in the documentary started since "one of our coffee shops [which] was next to a methadone clinic . . . people would come into our diner and have coffee before or after their treatments. I heard their stories and said, 'I'm going to do a film about you all.'"[12] During New York's frigid winters, Peggy's became a shelter of warmth for those waiting outside the clinic; Maple took interest in their lives, asking, "Are you being treated properly?"[13] As people came and went, regulars developed. Over time, a sense of community formed the lineaments for creative endeavors. Like nightclubs, cafés could "mitigate the effects of social and spatial isolation," incubate networks of support, and "help to sustain and enhance social capital among groups."[14] Serving, cooking, and working behind the counter, Maple would listen and learn as people gossiped and shared parts of their lives.

While running the coffee shop, Maple also worked in a bacteriology lab in the Hospital for Joint Diseases and the Medical Center on Madison Avenue. In both *The Maple Crew* and *How to Become a Union Camerawoman*, she details her time in the lab and juxtaposes the medical apprenticeship model with the structure of creative unions like IATSE. Doctors are named, dates are given, and processes are explained, lending readers a method to survive and navigate hostile spaces, which are analogized with the film industry. For example, lab supervisors pushed Maple to work in hematology (considered less skilled) rather than bacteriology, a practice she describes as rooted in "the privilege of bacteriology of whites."[15] This division proves informative, as Maple compares the split between bacteriology and hematology to the gendered division of labor in film and television, where industry professionals tried to "steer women into editing."[16] Having worked in bacteriology for seven years, Maple narrativizes her experience, suggesting that her time in the lab was a kind of training ground. It prepared her for the film and television world and illuminated the specific ways Black women are classified and refused entry into scientific and innovative work. After nearly a decade in the lab, and to the surprise of family and friends, Maple resigned. A steady paycheck only meant so much, and Maple wanted to "help other people."[17] Writing was the next place to turn.

Planting the Seeds and Authoring the Profile: Building the Newspaper Network

Labs and coffee shops offered the chance to connect to people, but they were not the place to tell stories. Now it was time to become a writer, and it was through the grapevine that Maple's friend, Alice Hille Jackson, first informed her about a local newspaper and its apprenticeship program. Though only in her twenties, Hille Jackson was also one of Toki's Types; she had quickly risen through the ranks in the television industry and, by 1968, was an associate producer on the groundbreaking arts and culture program *Soul!*[18] Hille Jackson told Maple of the *Manhattan Tribune*, a new periodical that offered a training program for aspiring Black and Latino journalists.[19] One could have goals in solitude, but it was among friends that those dreams often took shape.

The *Manhattan Tribune* was one of New York's many short-lived alternative weeklies. Founded in the summer of 1968 by William Haddad and Roy Innis and funded, in part, by the Ford Foundation, the *Tribune* saw its mission as reflecting a larger movement to reform media in New York and "increase nonwhite editorial representation."[20] In Haddad's words, the paper sought "to bridge the gap between the frustrated, angry black community and the frightened white community," which was literalized in dueling editorial pages by Innis and Haddad.[21] For Haddad, the consummate integrationist with liberal bona fides, and Innis, a conservative Black nationalist and the director of the Congress on Racial Equality, the *Tribune* was a space to beat back the stream of misinformation from the dominant press and forge sympathy between Upper West Side whites and Black Harlemites. The paper's ambition was clear in the cost (weekly issues sold for ten cents) and content, which featured articles written in English and Spanish. It was at the *Tribune* that Maple began a career in media and began to sculpt her skills as a storyteller of Black life.

Whether the product of a disorganized editorial staff or a funding fallout, the *Manhattan Tribune* training program collapsed almost as soon as it started. Maple's time at the paper was short, but she built contacts that allowed her to move to the *New York Courier*, a weekly Black newspaper. Critically, Maple was not alone at the *Courier*—her editor was Pat Patterson, who she worked with at the *Tribune*. It was her preexisting relationship with Patterson that gave Maple the autonomy to write profiles of Black artists in a column called "Jessie's Grapevine."[22]

At the *Courier*, Maple struck up relationships with emerging artists and successful talent. The job granted access to film premieres, theater openings, and record companies. Read cumulatively, "Jessie's Grapevine" represents a concerted effort to reveal the various material pathways to becoming an artist. The conversational style, which was shaped by the focus on pop music and media as well as the voices of Maple's subjects, rather than the prominent use of vernacular, created an intimacy with each subject. The essays were punctuated with the particulars of the everyday and affection typically evident in deep friendships. Maple covered everything from an artist's astrological sign and culinary loves to family life. Neither a reprint of publicity material nor an unearthing of the scandalous, each profile featured an insightful and exciting story of an artist's life. There was a sense of warmth in each piece. Decades later, Maple explained that "everything I wrote was positive; I didn't write anything negative about anybody. I just did profiles."[23] Rather than wrangle complicated lives within a rhetoric of uplift, Maple coated each story with idiosyncrasies that could inspire.

These details were wrapped in a kind of care for both the reader and the person profiled. Where Hollywood publicity turned on a claim that *stars are just like us!*, Maple rejected false relatability and instead laid out how creative expression was always created in community and alongside difference. Artists were not to be divided from the people; they were made up of the people. Maple's refusal to deify also took shape in the column's polyphonic address. While each profile provided exposure for a working artist, the articles also contained lessons for readers looking to pursue their own creative passions. Firsthand accounts of singers like Esther Morrow being "discovered" while singing in the Garment District revealed the labyrinthine but not impossible routes into the entertainment landscape.[24] Even when covering world-renowned artists Maple kept it familiar. A profile of Gordon Parks considers his career with the same sincerity as it lists the photographer's sleeping habits (he did not get up until 11:00 a.m.) and his suggestion that aspiring filmmakers "stay close to the theatre."[25] These details—yoked as they were to advice—offered a set of orientating references for aspiring actors and filmmakers.

The specifics of each profile untethered the mythology of celebrity and emphasized how small the world of Black New York art was. Maple's column was structured by and expanded artistic social networks in the city. For example, on February 12, 1970, Melba Moore, who had not yet released her debut album, appeared on *Soul!* Less than two weeks later, Moore was featured in one of the first entries of "Jessie's Grapevine." Maple describes Moore's relationship to acting and singing and the complications of performing in nude scenes; she informs readers "who are fighting for the mini[skirt] . . . that even though [Moore] likes to look sort of out of fashion on occasion, she nonetheless still 'digs' the mini."[26] Five months later, Maple profiled Clifton Davis, who wanted to let the world know that, unbeknownst to many, he and Moore had just gotten engaged.[27] This effectively turned the profile into a kind of marriage announcement. By including this note, Maple extended the world of Black performance to her readers. The personal, the professional, and the artistic were fastened together.

In other profiles, cultural laborers working below the line came to the forefront. In a February 27, 1971, piece on Anna Marie Horsford, Maple outlines the curves of Horsford's career, highlighting how behind-the-scenes work was tied to artists in front of the camera. Horsford had worked as an actress, but she secured her job as an associate producer on *Soul!* when Alice Hille Jackson (Maple's friend who had pointed her to the *Manhattan Tribune*) asked her to read for a small part, giving her entry into the show. Maple describes Horsford's education and the professional challenges she faced alongside the specifics of Horsford's presence as she "fuss[es] over a glass of orange juice" and explains that "her only quibble about living alone is that she doesn't know how to cook."[28] These moments of quotidian perception solidified the relationship between the column and its readers, all while clarifying that there were, quite simply, Black people working behind the camera. Social lives shifted professional careers, and the entertainment world was sculpted not only by those with their names on marquees but also by people who traveled through juke joints, bars, and underground sites of creative expression, like Peggy's.

Maple's consistent interest in lesser-known artists associated with *Soul!* was part of an unstated commitment to clarifying the different pathways to a public presence in the entertainment world. Where "Jessie's Grapevine" laid out the arc of a subject's career, there was also a cartography of allusions that framed certain places as hubs for Black talent. Over the course of eighteen months, Maple profiled at least six figures who worked on Ossie Davis's play *Purlie*; five involved with the musical *Hair*; three artists associated with Davis's debut film, *Cotton Comes to Harlem*; and four people who worked on *Shaft*. For readers who opened the *Courier* each week, there was a shared language and set of references and, subsequently, a listing of job opportunities. Nestled alongside profiles were ads for films like *Shaft*. The spatial proximity of these ads to "Jessie's Grapevine" created a kind of synchronicity that seemed to reach to the reader and say, "If you want to be in a film like this, well here are some things to know!"

There was also the name of Maple's column, which suggested that her profiles carried important information otherwise absent from dominant media. For decades the metaphor of the grapevine had served as shorthand for the dispersal of information through informal conversations, rumors, and Black gossip networks. The phrase was itself an abbreviated version of what was previously called the "grapevine telegraph," a term that dates to the mid-nineteenth century, often as a descriptor for unreliable information that traveled far and wide.[29] In Black life, the grapevine was a tool of survival. Booker T. Washington, in his autobiography, describes how the "grapevine telegraph" connected plantations: "I heard my mother and the other slaves on the plantation ... they kept themselves informed of events by what was termed the 'grape-vine' telegraph.... The news and mutterings of great events were swiftly carried from one plantation to another."[30] Maple's invocation of the colloquial expression resonates with the historical significance of alternative forms of Black communication, while also alluding to Marvin Gaye's smash rendition of "I Heard It through the Grapevine" (1968). Ronald Jacobs argues that the Black press has historically "provide[d] a forum for debate and self-improvement . . . monitor[ed] the mainstream press . . . [and] increase[d] black visibility in white civil society."[31] Even as specific newspapers came and went, the Black press "served to solidify in the black person's mind concepts of race and racial struggle."[32] The name "Jessie's Grapevine" called on that history, all the while clarifying how communities engaged in a cultural struggle during the Black Power era. With its title, Maple marked her column as both a lifeline for (artistic) safety and the product of communitarian sharing during the era, when publications were still asking, "Is the Black press needed?"[33]

Maple had developed her skills as a writer, and by 1971 it was clear that it was time to turn to television. Connections greased the friction of another career change. At the *Courier* she met Charles Hobson and Carol Morton. Hobson was a prolific producer working on Black current events programs like *Inside Bedford Stuyvesant* and *Black Journal*. Maple began studying with Hobson, taking notes during the shooting of the program *Like It Is*. At the same time, Morton, a producer at WNET's *Black Journal*, informed Maple of a new training program housed by the station. Just as Hille Jackson connected Maple to the *Tribune*, Morton brought Maple into WNET.

Radiating Outward: Apprenticing in a Network

The *Manhattan Tribune* and the *Courier* were laboratories where Maple had autonomy to develop her talents as a storyteller and write about what she wanted. The film and television industry, with its production costs and hierarchy of labor, presented new challenges. In 1969, the *Los Angeles Times* reported that less than 5 percent of employees in Hollywood were Black, and there were few institutions that addressed this disparity.[34] Two of the most significant programs to address this disparity were Third World Cinema and WNET's Television Training School.

The capacious and dimly lit history of Black independent cinema is made up not merely of individuals who became trailblazers but also the institutions they built and the people they trained. Often the names of those artists remain in the dark. For Maple, though, it was the founder of WNET's training program, Peggy Pinn, who "unraveled the puzzle of filmmaking."[35] Pinn was, as the *New York Times* described, a "black woman with a mission" who, after becoming the first Black secretary at New York's City College, developed WNET's training program before moving on to direct film and TV production at Howard University.[36] WNET's program first took shape as the volunteer-run Black Journal Workshop, which included twenty-two students and ran three nights a week from July through August 1968.[37] With the aid of several grants, Pinn expanded the workshop in 1970 into WNET's Television Training School. The school included a thirty-six-week-long program that trained hundreds of technicians who, in William Greaves's words, "radiated into the industry."[38]

It did not take long for word about the revolutionary workshop to travel across the country. The activist and filmmaker Michelle Parkerson, then living in Philadelphia, learned of Pinn's initiative and was so excited that she "almost left Temple University [to go to New York] . . . because I thought that was a more expeditious way to get at what I wanted to do, and I was overjoyed that the instructors were black."[39] At WNET, staff recognized that the program was "one of the few places where students literally came off of the city streets to learn film."[40] This was one of Pinn's most remarkable achievements, and it distinguished WNET from university-led initiatives. Further, the program's ethos reflected Maple's own investments in her community. As Pinn explained in the program's brochure, WNET's successful workshop eradicated the myth that "broadcasting belongs to the white and semi-white world . . . [by] fill[ing] the industry with beautiful, talented, creative and knowledgeable Brothers and Sisters."[41] In a business where opportunities were so often limited by nepotism, sexism, and racism, the school provided students with the certification necessary to discredit the oft-touted claim there were not any "qualified" Black technicians. Further, because of its affiliation with a television station, the program created a circuit of apprenticeship and work. Alongside luminaries like Kathleen Collins and Ronald Gray, Maple became one of those trainees when she graduated from WNET's program in 1972, having completed a "372-hour course covering still photography, film editing, sound recording and cinematography."[42]

Eager to learn about every aspect of filmmaking, Maple also enrolled in a training program offered by Third World Cinema. Third World Cinema had grown out of the Community Film Workshop Council (CFWC), which connected aspiring filmmakers of color to film productions like *The Landlord*, *A New Leaf*, and *Cotton Comes to Harlem*.[43] The Community Film Workshop Council was a success: the Ford Foundation reported that the council placed "68 people on 110 jobs" over two years.[44] In 1971, the activist Cliff Frazier drew on his experience with CFWC to found TWC with a collective of artists that spanned the artistic and literary worlds. These included filmmakers like Ossie Davis; journalists like Hannah Weinstein; actors, singers, and dancers, including Brock Peters, James Earl Jones, Rita Moreno, and Diana Sands; and writers such as Piri Thomas and John Oliver Killens. Managing politics and funding streams was necessarily complicated, but, as Eithne Quinn notes, TWC and CFWC "moved beyond the mainstream/independent and reformist/radical dichotomies, modeling ways of organizing and financing film production that were at once alternative, entrepreneurial, community oriented and state funded."[45] Where Pinn fomented a sense of comradery among a close-knit group of creative voices working in television, TWC set its sights on something bigger but less communal. Striking an agreement with 20th Century Fox, where members would write and produce work, TWC looked to connect artists to film production and distribution.[46]

At TWC, Maple studied under Harry "Moe" Howard, who, alongside Hugh Robertson and John Carter, was one of the first Black editors working in Hollywood. Under Howard, Maple worked on a couple of films directed by Gordon Parks. Little time had passed since Parks was profiled in "Jessie's Grapevine," where Maple described the director as a pathfinder, writing that "it wasn't long ago that the thought of a black man directing a major film . . . would have been considered an impossible dream."[47] Two years later, she and Parks were making that dream a different reality. Their meeting again was less a fortuitous twist in history than an actualization of Maple using her position to chart entryways into the industry. Social networks among Black artists in the industry were deep; Maple helped them become wider.

Maple's training at TWC was the product of her ties to Black artists throughout New York. Still, her apprenticeship was fraught. In *How to Become a Union Camerawoman*, she explains that her training at TWC was less fruitful than her time at WNET due, in large part, to the dictates of the union, which forced her "to stand around and see what I could pick up by watching."[48] If craft unions offered protections to some, they also acted as gatekeepers. That Maple gives less space in her memoirs to TWC than she does to her time at the *New York Courier* is telling. At WNET she could follow her "method" and "tak[e] advantage of lunch hours" to learn about various facets of the job, whether operating a camera or setting up lighting.[49] Maple's portrayal of WNET and TWC maps the limits and possibilities of educational projects while also providing a set of critical details that readers could consider before enrolling in any similar programs. Her journey is framed as historic, but it was critical that her own narrative pointed out certain failures, since Maple saw her trajectory as part of a communal endeavor. In her words, she was, "tell[ing] these stories to others, so they can keep moving forward . . . [and] begin again."[50]

Finding the Work and Creating Her Own

Most accounts of Maple's life and work begin after her time at TWC and WNET, focusing on her entry into the union. There remains so much more to be amplified and historicized, but concentration on her status as a first in the union has also obscured an understanding of the significance of community to Maple's career. Self-published in 1977, *How to Become a Union Camerawoman* reproduces several primary sources that address the anti-Black structures of various arms of the industry and American society. Notably, in the book, Maple reprints primary documents of her appeals to the Human Rights Commission and the discrimination lawsuits she filed against major television networks alongside specific accounts of the costs and tactics of those legal trials. In other words, Maple turns *How to Become a Union Camerawoman* into a guidebook for those interested in navigating the various material challenges of filmmaking. Accompanying letters, contracts, and photos are critical miscellany, like a reading list for aspiring filmmakers, as well as a section titled "Where the Work Is (for all categories)." This encyclopedic litany serves as a reference text that catalogs "mixing houses" and "recording studios" and includes the contact information for equipment and unions, organized by state. Maple also details the number and different types of technicians that would be needed for various crews, whether readers were interested in working on documentaries, feature films, or television news programs. Though *How to Become a Union Camerawoman* is less than one hundred pages long, Maple's multilayered text extended the grapevine to Black readers who might otherwise be disoriented in a deeply segregated marketplace.

I have argued that Maple's career and writings constitute a road map that reveals the significance of social connections across New York's landscape for Black artists. Her first fiction feature, *Will* (1981), actualizes and allegorizes that ethics of care in its depiction of Will Hastings, a recovering addict. The film begins with Hastings in his bedroom as he feels the pain of withdrawal. The past inserts itself with flashbacks of Will playing basketball, collapsing his earlier possibility with painful moments of the present. He writhes on the bed. A needle is shown. As his arms flail, Will smacks the radio and turns it on. An early draft of the script, known as *Higher Ground*, reads: "He bends over and clutches his stomach, the pain subsides, he turns on the radio and switches the dial around, he stops when he hears a man's voice giving a lecture, he becomes interested and listens."[51] Will hears the calls of a preacher who proclaims, "All you have to do, people, is take a look around you, and you'd know that just about anything is possible . . . we're all somebody very special to this universe . . . the beautiful riverside hall church at 81st and 2nd avenue." The radio brings Will into the world; media connects him to others, and that bond proves to be lifesaving.

Maple uses a deft touch in the filmed version of this scene. There is no naive suggestion that the church heals all. We see Hastings run to the bathroom to vomit before eventually telling his significant other, Jean, that he will recover "his [own] way," before asserting, "I'll help myself just give me some money." Of course, he cannot do it alone—his "way" goes only so far.

Will concludes in a church, the site of fellowship acknowledged in the opening scene. There Will tells a young child, bored by the sermon on "confidence," that he just needs to trust himself. In that trust, shared by a community, but held by one, is the possibility of life. The film's power is in its depiction of small, intimate collectives within rarely filmed Harlem landmarks such as Marcus Garvey Park, the Joseph P. Kennedy Community Center, and Sydenham Hospital (which was closed shortly after shooting, even as activists locked themselves in to protest Mayor Ed Koch's decision to shut it down). From its story to its location shooting, *Will* represents what was at the basis of Maple's career. Whether on the page, in a lab, or in film, Maple was devoted to projects where she could "be near the people." In that work was an insistence that without a community of care, all is lost.[52] Long before she entered the union, Maple made sure that such a community would survive and grow.

Notes

1   Jessie Maple to Redd Foxx, box 1, folder 7, Jessie Maple Collection, 1971–1992, Black Film Center/Archive, Indiana University, Bloomington, IN.
2   "Pictures: New York Sound Track," *Variety*, February 11, 1976, 30, 34.
3   Jessie Maple, *How to Become a Union Camerawoman: Film-Videotape* (New York: L. J. Film Productions, 1977), 11.
4   Nicholas Forster and Michele Prettyman, "Introduction: A Scene of New Worlds," *Black Camera* 10, no. 2 (Spring 2019): 53.

5 Jessie Maple with E. Danielle Butler, *The Maple Crew* (Atlanta: EvyDani Books, 2019), 32.

6 Jessie Maple transcript of interview with Audrey T. McCluskey, September 20, 2005, Black Film Center/Archive. Indiana University, Bloomington, IN.

7 Jessie Maple in Alexis Krasilovksy, Harriet Margolis, and Julia Stein, *Shooting Women: Behind the Camera, Around the World* (Chicago: Intellect, 2015), 244.

8 "Society Editors: They Work Hard to Chronicle Gay Doings of Cadillac Set," *Ebony*, March 1950, 52.

9 Toki Schalk Johnson, "Toki Types," *New Pittsburgh Courier*, July 4, 1964, 6.

10 Maple with Butler, *The Maple Crew*, 36.

11 See Chin Jou, "Neither Welcomed, nor Refused: Race and Restaurants in Postwar New York City," *Journal of Urban History* 40, no. 2 (2014): 232–251.

12 Maple with Butler, *The Maple Crew*, 64.

13 E. Danielle Butler, telephone interview with author, October 14, 2020.

14 Marcus Anthony Hunter, "The Nightly Round: Space, Social Capital, and Urban Black Nightlife," *City and Community* 9, no. 2 (June 2010): 166.

15 It is hard to read this and not see the distinction as racialized, since hematologists frequently work with sickle cell anemia, a disease that disproportionately affects Black Americans.

16 Maple with Butler, *The Maple Crew*, 13.

17 Maple and Butler, 7.

18 Toki Schalk Johnson, "A New Generation: Secretary in TV Office Is Just 22," *New Pittsburgh Courier*, April 10, 1965, 6.

19 Maple, *How to Become a Union Camerawoman*, 7.

20 "Media Jobs Urged for Minorities" *New York Times*, April 8, 1969, 29.

21 See "Paper Splits Endorsement," *New York Times*, November 1, 1969, 20.

22 Maple, *How to Become a Union Camerawoman*, 9.

23 Maple with Butler, *The Maple Crew*, 30.

24 Jessie Maple, "Jessie's Grapevine," *New York Courier*, July 4, 1970, 18.

25 Before *Shaft* became a smash hit for MGM, Maple noted, in a column on the actor Leon Frederick, that "if you are black and interested in a movie career MGM seems to be the place to cash in on the new black awareness," "Jessie's Grapevine," *New York Courier*, November 28, 1970, 24.

26 Jessie Maple, "Jessie's Grapevine," *New York Courier* February 21, 1970, 18

27 Jessie Maple, "Jessie's Grapevine," *New York Courier*, June 6, 1970, 17.

28 Jessie Maple, "Jessie's Grapevine," *New York Courier*, February 27, 1971, 21.

29 The term seems to have been popularized in the middle of the nineteenth century and circulated in reference to oral claims that moved between camps, prisons, plantations, or Civil War military regiments.

30 Booker T. Washington, *Up from Slavery: An Autobiography* (New York: Doubleday, 1901), 8.

31 Ronald Jacobs, *Race, Media, and the Crisis of Civil Society: From Watts to Rodney King* (New York: Cambridge University Press, 2000), 21.

32 Charlotte G. O'Kelly, "Black Newspapers and the Black Protest Movement: Their Historical Relationship, 1827–1945," *Phylon* 43, no. 1 (1982): 5.

33 James Williams "Is the Black Press Needed?," *Civil Rights Digest* 3, no. 1 (Winter 1970): 8–15.

34 See Dan Knapp, "An Assessment of the Status of Hollywood Blacks," *Los Angeles Times*, September 28, 1969, Q1, Q17–Q18.

35   Maple, *How to Become a Union Camerawoman,* 11.

36   Beatrice Berg, "Pinning Their Hopes on Peggy," *New York Times,* July 4, 1971, D15.

37   Frances E. Ruffin, "Peggy Pinn's Television Training School," box 1, folder 6, Jessie Maple Collection, 1971–1992, Black Film Center/Archive, Indiana University, Bloomington, IN.

38   William Greaves, interview with Pearl Bowser, January 9, 1988, Special Collections, Black Film Center/Archive, Indiana University, Bloomington, IN.

39   Michelle Parkerson, "Interviews with Filmmakers: Michelle Parkerson," in *Struggles for Representation: African American Documentary Film and Video,* ed. Phyllis R. Klotman and Janet K. Cutler (Bloomington: Indiana University Press, 1999), 374.

40   Lenora Clodfelter Stephens, "Telecommunications and the Urban Black Community" (PhD diss., Emory University, 1976), 127.

41   NET Television Training School Brochure, box 1, folder 6, Jessie Maple Collection, 1971–1992, Black Film Center/Archive, Indiana University, Bloomington, IN.

42   NET Television Training School Graduate Certificate, box 1, folder 2, Jessie Maple Collection, 1971–1992, Black Film Center/Archive, Indiana University, Bloomington, IN.

43   Aron Noelle Griffis, "Filmmaking to Save the City in Crisis: New York on Location, 1966–1975" (PhD diss., Indiana University, 2018), 70.

44   Griffis, 99.

45   Eithne Quinn, *A Piece of the Action: Race and Labor in Post–Civil Rights Hollywood* (New York: Columbia University Press, 2020), 135.

46   The plan was not successful. Though TWC and Fox were to work on *Lady Sings the Blues,* this arrangement fell through following a deal cut between Paramount and Berry Gordy's Motown Records.

47   Jessie Maple, "Jessie's Grapevine," *New York Courier,* November 21, 1970, 24.

48   Maple, *How to Become a Union Camerawoman,* 11.

49   Maple, 11.

50   Maple with Butler, *The Maple Crew,* 88.

51   Higher Ground, box 1, folder 14, Jessie Maple Collection, 1971–1992, Black Film Center/Archive, Indiana University, Bloomington, IN.

52   Maple with Butler, *The Maple Crew,* 32.

3

"It Was a Little Late in the Day for All That Prissy Business"

The New Hollywood Career of Jay Presson Allen

OLIVER GRUNER

Speaking to the *Los Angeles Times* in October 1982, Jay Presson Allen offered a blunt assessment of her screenwriting career thus far: "When I hear people talk about their *careers*, I think it's a joke," she observed. "What is a career? Who plans one? I have no idea at all."[1] Such nonchalance was hardly unusual for a woman renowned for her wit, caustic put-downs and mischievous ability to slice through any artistic pretensions leveled at her or her Hollywood peers. "I've really written for the money" was a favorite mantra.[2]

Another: "'I'm the only child of a widowed mother and even she wouldn't claim I'm a prose stylist.'"[3] Or, when asked in 1975 why she had specialized in film adaptations as opposed to original screenplays, Presson Allen replied that she had "a normal streak of greed . . . the big money comes from the secondary sale of a book or a play to pictures."[4] In one fell swoop she appeared to explain away her stage play-turned-film *The Prime of Miss Jean Brodie* (1966, 1969) and novel-turned-film *Just Tell Me What You Want* (1975, 1980) as crafty attempts to squeeze the moguls for all they were worth.

Comments such as these only skim the surface of the playful, contradictory persona Presson Allen cultivated throughout her professional life ("blunt, but slippery," as one interviewer put it) and, perhaps more important, are liable to underplay her creative achievements.[5] Between 1969 and 1980 she garnered six feature film screenplay credits: *The Prime of Miss Jean Brodie*, *Cabaret* (1972), *Travels with My Aunt* (1972), *Forty Carats* (1973), *Funny Lady* (1975), and *Just Tell Me What You Want*. She was nominated for an Academy Award (*Cabaret*) and also began work on *Prince of the City* (released in 1981), which brought her second Oscar nomination. In between these projects, she created a successful television series (*Family*, 1976–1980) and wrote a novel (*Just Tell Me What You Want*). Indeed, whether or not a "career" was intended, Jay Presson Allen has a strong claim to being New Hollywood's most successful female screenwriter.[6] Film historian Lizzie Francke describes her as "the one [woman] writer to sustain her career through the 60s and 70s."[7] By the early 1980s she was being touted as one of the highest-paid scribes in the industry.[8]

This chapter discusses the New Hollywood career of Jay Presson Allen. Popular and scholarly approaches to late 1960s and 1970s cinema have overwhelmingly privileged the director as primary creative force. And while in recent years scholars have begun to rethink the status of the screenwriter and screenplay, at this time, the role of individual writers—and especially female writers—remains underresearched.[9] I begin by situating Presson Allen's career within broader debates on screenwriting, gender, and 1960s and 1970s Hollywood. In different ways, her screenplays and public persona resonated with political, cultural, and industrial issues bedeviling Hollywood and American society throughout the period. The chapter's second half focuses in particular on *The Prime of Miss Jean Brodie*, *Cabaret*, and *Just Tell Me What You Want* as case studies of her creative and collaborative efforts. Through her screenplays—and through a carefully cultivated public persona—Presson Allen negotiated the competing demands of a male-dominated movie business, a burgeoning women's movement with its own set of expectations, and an industrial production system that frequently undervalued writers' contributions. In doing so, she enjoyed status rarely afforded women screenwriters in the 1970s and played a key role in numerous psychologically complex, thematically daring, formally interesting—decidedly "New Hollywood"—feature films.

Women Screenwriters and New Hollywood

Presson Allen informed the film critic Mary McCreadie that she "hit the movies at the right time," when Hollywood was "run by moviemakers" as opposed to businesspeople, and always worked with "top talent."[10] Her most prolific string of screenplay credits coincided with the New Hollywood era renowned for its artistic innovation and taboo-breaking content.[11] However, as film scholars such as Miranda J. Banks and Maya Montañez Smukler have discussed, although Hollywood might have been pushing certain boundaries on-screen, gender politics remained a contentious issue. On the one hand, feminist campaigns and a small but growing group of female creatives drew attention to women's roles within the industry. On the other hand, the 1970s was an epoch dogged by discrimination and unfair hiring practices.[12] Countless surveys of the early 1970s revealed the stark inequalities in terms of employment opportunities.[13] In line with broader struggles for equality being waged by feminists throughout the late 1960s and 1970s, the era witnessed an explosion of activism from film and television unions the Writers Guild of America (WGA), Screen Actors Guild (SAG), and, later on, the Directors Guild of America (DGA).

Female screenwriters such as Carole Eastman (*The Shooting,* 1966; *Five Easy Pieces,* 1970), Joan Tewkesbury (*Thieves Like Us,* 1974; *Nashville,* 1975), and Elaine May (*A New Leaf,* 1971; *Heaven Can Wait,* 1978) did enjoy a modicum of success, with Tewkesbury and May also managing to secure directing jobs with the studios. But by the late 1970s, "a sense of fatigue settled in," with industry feminists frustrated by years of Hollywood elites paying lip service to the equal rights agenda and "good will" policies leading to very little substantive change.[14] Historians of 1970s cinema also note the lack of diversity in terms of acting roles available to women, limited opportunities in above-the-line professions (writers, producers, directors), a preponderance of male-centered narratives, and an emphasis—in the era's biggest hits—on subject matter and themes intended to appeal to male audiences.[15]

In later years, Jay Presson Allen would be celebrated as a rare female creative to maintain a presence in the industry through the late 1960s and 1970s. She was a recipient of the 1982 Crystal Award for "Women in Film," honored for her "excellence, endurance and expansion of the role of women within the entertainment industry."[16] And Presson Allen has, in many ways, become a go-to voice for commentators on women screenwriters of the time. "A woman writer is a doubly lowly thing," she told film historian Patrick McGilligan in a much-cited interview, "perceived as so unthreatening they [male film-makers] can say anything to you."[17] Comments such as these—along with her much-touted status as "lone" woman in a Hollywood boys club—indicate the pressures under which her career was shaped. As Shelley Cobb argues, the celebration of "exceptional" women filmmakers also brings into sharp relief how few have been provided the opportunities to reach the top of their pro-fession and subtly reinforces the idea that most "normal" women would *not* choose a high-profile career. When a woman is presented as the "only one," she becomes the exception to the rule, separated from wider collective (femi-nist) action and, even, an unwilling purveyor of the stereotypes she may be seeking to challenge.[18] Time and again Presson Allen would discuss her efforts at creating on-screen women that were in possession of all the independence, strengths, and faults that have been associated with the male protagonists of the period. And yet, time and again, she would struggle against the same gen-dered expectations rife within the industry. There is an irritated wit in her instructions to those involved in *Family*, a television drama series she created and wrote the pilot for, to avoid endless representations of women merrily undertaking household chores. "Try to think of laundry as full frontal nudity," she remarked, "to be tolerated only in artistic context."[19] Too often, contended Presson Allen, male screenwriters "keep writing themselves. Or else they write fantasies of women."[20] And, in a direct challenge to the old stereotype of women being unable to write male characters, the same inter-view sees her argue that "male characters are easier to write."[21] Bold, brash, blunt, self-reflective—such comments helped to craft a vociferous and prom-inent public persona.

At the same time, however, film critics have made it clear that Presson Allen's publicly expressed views on feminist politics were, at best, evasive and, at worst, outright hostile. Francke observes that the screenwriter "claims to take little political interest in the representation of women in her films."[22] Other interviewers have noted a more strident enmity in her outlook. In his analysis of *Marnie* (1964), Presson Allen's first feature film assignment, Tony Lee Moral contends that she "avowedly jeered feminists."[23] Presson Allen's work on this film has long proved a source of debate. Moral and others note that Presson Allen was hired on the project after the previous screenwriter, Evan Hunter, challenged director Alfred Hitchcock on the notorious scene in which Mark Rutland (Sean Connery) rapes the female protagonist (played by Tippi Hedren). Presson Allen agreed to write the scene to Hitchcock's specifications; she saw it more as "a trying marital situation" than rape and, more generally, was said to have been "especially dismissive of feminist and theoretical approaches to film."[24]

Such statements might encourage a reading of Presson Allen's work as anti-feminist (or at least unconcerned with gender politics). But it should be remembered that her public persona hinged on a bluntness and bluster she also seemed willing to undercut when probed. Furthermore, like all creatives hoping to maintain a status within Hollywood, she was required to construct a public identity that would appeal to prospective collaborators. This was doubly true for women forced to navigate the highly gendered landscape of 1970s Hollywood. In her study of writer-director Nancy Meyers's Hollywood career, Deborah Jermyn discusses the endemic sexism of the 1970s. Women's opportunities for employment were likely enhanced should they market themselves as part of a male-female creative team; studios feared films that even subtly dealt with "women's lib" would prove off-putting for large swaths of the (male) audience.[25] As a consequence, there were reasons why a woman may choose *not* to announce any feminist intent in her work, and why there may be contradictions between her publicly crafted image and her creative output. One gets the sense that Presson Allen wanted to present herself as the consummate professional—very good at her job, a willing collaborator, and not particularly concerned with using her career as a political platform. And, as discussed later in the chapter, her screenplays demonstrate an attempt to create rounded, politically and psychologically complex female protagonists within creative milieus where such efforts were not always understood or actively encouraged.

Truly in Her Prime

Jay Presson Allen's screenplays teem with the characters generally associated with New Hollywood cinema. World-weary, cynical, sexually liberated, alienated, and, often, doomed protagonists wander the pages of everything from *The Prime of Miss Jean Brodie* to *Prince of the City*. "If New Hollywood films continue to be understood to concern such themes as alienation, cynicism, or loneliness," argues Aaron Hunter, "it makes sense to look at the writers who developed these themes."[26] Indeed, when one considers Presson Allen's scripts alongside those of writers such as Eastman, Tewksbury, and Leigh

Brackett (*The Long Goodbye*, 1973), any notion of a few superstar (male) directors leading American cinema's "renaissance" at this time becomes increasingly difficult to maintain. Though many of her most renowned screenplays are set in the past, there is a detached critique of issues such as political zealotry, charismatic leaders, traditional institutions—the family, marriage, and so forth—that feels very much of the New Hollywood. In the offhand wisecrack or shift in perspective, there is an insouciance with which Presson Allen can dismantle and confound expectations.

With a 1950s and early 1960s background in television and theater, Presson Allen experienced a career trajectory that bears similarities to many of New Hollywood's prominent creatives. Filmmakers including Arthur Penn, Mike Nichols, and Elaine May, born between the early 1920s and mid-1930s, had careers that began on the stage or the small screen. Quality television of the 1950s was important as both a training ground for prospective filmmakers—providing the opportunity to work with progressive, often socially conscious, material—and a meeting place for individuals who would go on to define the New Hollywood.[27] Arthur Penn, who collaborated with Presson Allen on stage plays in later years, directed one of her most well-received television plays, *Beg, Borrow or Steal* (1954). This story of a lawyer whose lavish expenditures lead him to embezzle, become guilt stricken, and plan his suicide only to be thwarted at the final hour by his heroic son-in-law demonstrated Presson Allen's interest in exploring avarice and emotional and psychological tension among America's wealthy (something continued in *Just Tell Me What You Want*). As one reviewer commented: "Jay Presson looks like a real up-and-comer in the Philco-Goodyear stable of serious writers. His [as would become a common trend, she was assumed to be a man] . . . 'Beg, Borrow or Steal' this week evoked pain, pity and embarrassment as only Philco-Goodyear . . . or your own psychoanalyst can."[28]

Presson Allen married the play and film producer Lewis Allen in 1955. By the early 1960s, Lewis was being touted as a Broadway and Hollywood "new wave producer" due to his support for experimental projects.[29] He had worked with the filmmaker Shirley Clarke and playwright Jack Gelber to bring Gelber's play *The Connection* (1961) to the big screen. In 1962, he produced the film adaptation of Jean Genet's play *The Balcony* with Joseph Strick as director. In the first of several professional collaborations throughout their marriage, Presson Allen translated the French script for the François Truffaut–directed *Fahrenheit 451* (1966), which Lewis produced. Throughout the 1950s and early 1960s, then, she was exposed to the kinds of socially conscious, experimental, art film–influenced material that is often discussed as having had an impact on New Hollywood filmmakers. It is also interesting to note that her first feature film credit was for *Marnie*, a production alternately celebrated as one of Hitchcock's most innovative and lambasted as incoherent, underdeveloped, and misogynistic. Moral contends that "*Marnie*, as an art film, . . . was part of a larger campaign by Hitchcock to be taken seriously as an artist."[30] Hitchcock had read an early version of Presson Allen's stage adaptation of Muriel Spark's novel *The Prime of Miss Jean Brodie* and apparently hired her because of "her handling of complex sexual motifs that were so crucial to the conception of *Marnie*, and because he felt she would bring a 'woman's point of view' to the project."[31]

Presson Allen worked closely with Hitchcock, discussing the characters, narrative, and visual concepts.[32] She made a significant contribution to the film's representation of gender and class.[33] For example, she added a number of scenes that explored the class backgrounds of Mark Rutland, the blue blood patrician from Philadelphia, and Marnie, a working-class woman from Baltimore. The alienation experienced by both during their upbringing "casts them as outsiders," a theme developed by Presson Allen during the screenwriting phase. She also introduced scenes of psychological turmoil (e.g., where Marnie recoils at the sight of red ink) and childhood trauma (Marnie killing a sailor).[34] According to Walter Raubicheck, one of Presson Allen's major contributions was the "addition of animal imagery" that offered allegorical fuel to the idea of Mark's predatory nature—he becomes the hunter with Marnie as his prey.[35]

Of course, that theme is made viciously manifest in the rape scene. Tania Modleski argues that, whereas in draft screenplays and in interviews, Presson Allen expressed politically conservative views regarding the pleasures of male dominance—even to the extent of women "fantasizing" about rape—the scene, as it appeared in the finished film, makes "us question the authority of the film's supposed hero and elicit the feminist interpreter's sympathy for its trapped and caged heroine."[36] It is emblematic of the slippery and complex ideological quandaries in so many of Presson Allen's screenplays. Her work on *Marnie* established a number of themes with which she would work throughout her New Hollywood career: outsiders (male and female), psychological turmoil, gender, and class relations.

Though Presson Allen may have been reticent to discuss gender politics, she undoubtedly created several of the New Hollywood era's most interesting female protagonists. From Jean Brodie (Maggie Smith) to Bones Burton (Ali MacGraw) of *Just Tell Me What You Want*, the women of Presson Allen's screenplays comprise a diverse assortment of charismatic and flawed (anti) heroines. *The Prime of Miss Jean Brodie* was itself based on a formally and thematically adventurous novel by Muriel Spark. Set in the 1930s and telling the story of a captivating, but woefully deluded, schoolteacher and the girls in her charge, *Brodie* takes a humorous scalpel to a series of emotional, psychological, and political relationships. The adaptation from novel to play to film saw a series of changes, in terms of form and content. Rather than experimenting with the complicated flash-forwards and flights of imagination in Spark's novel, the film followed a more conventional, linear narrative than even Presson Allen's stage version.

The film nonetheless explores some challenging and even provocative subject matter. Draft screenplays also indicate that Presson Allen was attempting to develop a rich visual iconography. Whereas the stage play had begun with a flash-forward—and a commentary from a grown-up version of one of Brodie's girls, Sandy—the film begins immediately at Marcia Blaine School for Girls. At this stage, we read that Brodie is "dressed in a conventional manner, but the colour of her dress, soft as it is, stands in strong contrast to the rest of the scene."[37] Distinguishing her from a world of gray conformity, Brodie's sartorial obsessions also become symbolic of dangerous political ignorance. At one point, Brodie recalls attending a Mussolini rally in Italy. "I myself mingled with such a crowd," she declares. "I wore my silk dress with the red poppies which is right for my colouring." The line, which is also present in Spark's novel, takes on added dramatic resonance thanks to script directions emphasizing the glow of her face in the light of the slide projector, the raising of her hand in a Roman salute. "Brodie," writes Presson Allen, "is irresistible, truly a seductress."[38] Clearly, the influence Brodie has over her "girls" is disconcerting—her seductive persona becoming akin to the "charismatic" and dangerous autocrat of the Mussolini and Hitler ilk. It will lead to one girl's death and all kinds of emotional and psychological trauma.

On the other hand, it is also this seductiveness that enables *The Prime of Miss Jean Brodie* to challenge its viewers. Brodie is the consummate antihero, sympathetic even as we become aware of her ethical and moral shortcomings. "She [Brodie] is magnificent," declare script directions as she reprimands the school's stuffy headmistress.[39] Brodie's enlightened views toward women's independence and sexual mores feel very much in keeping with a late 1960s and 1970s political climate. While the film, on the whole, eschewed explicit sex and violence, it did contain one scene of female nudity. Earlier drafts also contained graphic scenes of Mary, one of Brodie's charges who had fallen for her teacher's glossy ruminations on fascism and run off to Spain to fight in the civil war, "riddled with bullets," having been attacked by the very

Nationalist army she had intended to join. "Her face wears, in death, the very expression it wore most often in life, surprise," writes Presson Allen.[40] While the scene was eventually cut (we only hear of Mary's death), its grim irony is representative of *The Prime of Miss Jean Brodie* as a whole. The conflicting ideas and emotions present across the film question where our sympathies should lie: with a deeply flawed but captivating teacher, who instills independence in her "girls," while at the same time exploiting their fidelity and filling their heads with all kinds of fascist nonsense? Or with an uninspiring school establishment that, though ostensibly ridding itself of Brodie due to her fascist ideas, has made clear that there is no place for "modern" and "liberated" behaviors?

There are similarities between Jean Brodie and Sally Bowles, the female protagonist of Presson Allen's next screenplay assignment, *Cabaret*. Both have infectious personalities and appear able to impress their larger-than-life, often totally irresponsible worldviews on their more pedestrian acquaintances. Of course, both women are created within dire political circumstances, the creep of fascism providing a backdrop to their stories. Both appear blithely unaware of, or refuse to contend with, the true implications of these political developments. As studies of *Cabaret* have highlighted, the film was developed as an adaptation of multiple sources. In 1969, Allied Artists purchased the film rights to the stage musical *Cabaret* (1966) for $1.5 million.[41] The film was budgeted at $5 million, and veteran Broadway producer Cy Feuer was hired to produce. Feuer approached Presson Allen about writing the screenplay.

Apparently, one of the first topics of discussion between Feuer and Presson Allen was the need to go beyond the Broadway show and revisit *Cabaret*'s diverse source materials. This story of a young man (in the film he is called Brian Roberts, played by Michael York) arriving in Berlin at the turn of the 1930s and his subsequent encounters with the city's politics, culture, and a cast of eccentric characters—most famously, of course, the irrepressible Sally Bowles—was based on the experiences of British writer Christopher Isherwood and published in his *Berlin Stories* (1945). The stories were adapted by John Van Druten into the stage play *I Am a Camera* (1951), with a film version appearing in 1955. Then came the Broadway musical produced by Hal Prince, with a book by Joe Masteroff and music and lyrics by John Kander and Fred Ebb. Presson Allen's adaptation molded elements from these sources together and added new content. Feuer was keen that she dig into the original Isherwood stories for inspiration. They agreed that all but one of the musical performances would take place on the cabaret stage, thus eschewing the "integrated musical" format, popular since the 1940s, where musical numbers are woven into various scenes and settings, and characters—whether on city streets, on ships, in palaces, or atop mountains—might burst into song (something both Presson Allen and Feuer felt was too unrealistic for *Cabaret*).[42] Furthermore, they decided to present Brian as bisexual, a reference to Isherwood's experiences (by the 1970s he was openly gay), something altogether missing from the Broadway production.[43]

Presson Allen's *Cabaret* draft dated June 10, 1970, provides evidence of how she and Feuer envisioned the film's new approach and contained at least some key ideas and innovations that would make it into the finished film. The attention to visual detail is noticeable in the *Cabaret* script. Our introduction to Sally Bowles (Liza Minnelli) is instructive in this respect. The first reference to her is as "a very young girl with a shiny clean face, but wearing a soiled old kimono which she clutches with rather grubby little-girl hands, the fingernails of which are painted bright green." From the start, Sally is presented as a barrel of contradictions. She is desperate to appear sophisticated and worldly, but the descriptions of her "shiny clean face" and "grubby little-girl hands" clash with her childish attempts to feign experience. The "soiled old kimono" is soon joined by a "ridiculously long cigarette holder."[44] Like Brodie before her, she is a fantasist. Lost in a world of glitz, glamour, and "decadence," she has little understanding of the sinister political forces gathering around her. Presson Allen's 1970 draft actually featured Sally spouting anti-Semitic insults throughout, suggesting her to be not only ignorant of Nazism's threat but actively participating in the era's bigotry.[45] Most of these references were cut by the time the film reached cinemas—apparently on the request of Allied Artists, which wanted Sally to be more likable—and thus what might have been a highly challenging, problematic aspect of Sally's character was lost.[46] We are left with a stronger image of Sally as a naive young girl—complicit in the era's politics only through her seeming obliviousness.

Sally's first performance at the cabaret (known in the film as the Kit Kat Klub) introduces her in close-up: "exotic eyes, improbable lashes."[47] She could be from another planet—unencumbered by the reality of a country on the brink of implosion. Her ebullience reaches an early crescendo in a scene where she screams beneath a railway overpass. "I always scream when the train goes over," she informs Brian. "It's delicious." This moment is followed immediately by one in which the owner of the Kit Kat Klub is beaten by Nazis. "Soundlessly, the three set upon [him]," read the screen directions, "one holding him, the other two taking turns hitting his face."[48] We see an example of the careful attention played to aural motifs and structure. Sally's screaming provides a stark counterpoint to the "silent" beating—her histrionics, and perhaps the histrionics taking place at the Kit Kat Klub more generally, are a mask for, or distraction from, the political violence on the rise in Berlin.

Most historians agree that director Bob Fosse was unimpressed by Presson Allen's drafts and felt a lot of work was required. He commissioned screenwriter Hugh Wheeler to "improve the screenplay" and declared Wheeler's efforts to be "close to a total rewrite."[49] Analyses of the film have tended toward viewing *Cabaret* as a "Bob Fosse" film.[50] Of course, Fosse made some important decisions with his cinematographers, set designers, lighting technicians, editors, and others in order to enhance *Cabaret*'s visual spectacle. He is well known for having been the driving force behind the film's famous dance sequences. But, at the same time, he was working with structure and dialogue that did appear in the draft screenplays from 1970, screenplays that Presson Allen, Feuer, and to a lesser extent Fosse himself had discussed and worked on.

As with *Brodie*, the *Cabaret* screenplay demonstrates a careful attention to locations and interiors. When Sally and Brian enjoy a holiday with wealthy playboy Baron von Heune, detailed instructions on the salubrious décor are provided. The baron's home is described as having "great vaulted ceilings with beautiful great exposed beams . . . the rugs are eighteenth century French as are the chandeliers and colors." The bedroom provided for Sally is "pastel and gold baroque. It abounds in mirrors"; Brian's room contains photographs of the baron in military uniform as well as a closet "filled with carefully tended clothes."[51] In many ways, the directions offer a commentary on these two characters, perhaps as seen through the eyes of the baron: Sally the extrovert narcissist, Brian the starchy, repressed young man, uncomfortable with his sexuality. The baron tosses Brian a new sweatshirt, and we read that "there is something unspoken . . . covert . . . plainly seductive in his attitude toward Brian," one of many references to the sexual attraction between these two men.[52] Accounts of *Cabaret*'s production have noted that Feuer and Presson Allen were adamant that Brian's sexual desire for men should be emphasized. As the screenwriter put it in regard to previous attempts to elide Isherwood's sexuality: "It was a little late in the day for all that prissy business."[53] However, the film has also been criticized for constructing Brian in line with stereotypes of bisexuals (he does, after all, also sleep with Sally) as "on again, off again," "experimental," in possession of a "try anything" mentality.[54]

Presson Allen's contributions to *Cabaret* are manifold and detectable in the finished film. Scenes and characters were cut, curtailed, and/or changed, and certainly the script's dialogue was pruned during production. But *Cabaret* enabled her to demonstrate an ability to create well-developed characters, deal with challenging themes, and create complex narrative structures. "Closeup of wholesome, gentle-faced young man," she writes in what became one of *Cabaret*'s most iconic scenes. "The babe in the cradle is closing his eyes, the blossom embraces the bee"—the young man serenades his audience with lines from the Broadway standard "Tomorrow Belongs to Me." Then, "pull back to reveal the singing young man in brown Nazi uniform" and, shortly afterward, "the family joins the song, slowly rising to their feet. Then the rest of the people in the place join the singing. The music becomes stronger and less pastoral."[55] A chilling hymn to the quasi-mystical power of nationalist sentiment, one boy's crooning becomes a collective expression of bigotry, prejudice, and hatred. Of course, the scene was tweaked and modified during production, but the visual and emotional framework within which this scene operates is there in Presson Allen's script, testifying to her abilities as a dramatist and visual thinker.

The Battle Is On: Presson Allen and the New Hollywood

In a scene midway through *Just Tell Me What You Want*, an adaptation of Presson Allen's comic novel about corporate misdeeds, greed, and romantic entanglements among the East Coast jet set, Bones Burton sets upon her sometime lover Max Herschel (Alan King) with all the force that a purse can muster. The two had become estranged after Bones decided to marry another man; the wealthy Max had, as punishment, done everything in his power to sabotage her career. Now they come face-to-face in a swanky department store. "The battle is on," wrote Presson Allen in a 1978 draft screenplay.[56] A full-blown fight ensues—Bones chases Max across the shop floor, hurling a perfume bottle that smashes a display. Outside, as he attempts to enter his limousine, she pounces, walloping him again and again. A curious crowd begins to gather. Max is screaming. His chauffeur joins the fray, attempting to prize Bones from his employer. "When it appears the male protagonist has a henchman," wrote Presson Allen, "and a sinister black limousine, the fight is suddenly perceived as a class struggle."[57] The limo makes a hasty escape as Bones watches, cheered by a crowd of supporters.

Certainly, there is much in *Just Tell Me What You Want* that recalls the "battle of the sexes" themes of screwball comedies: feisty banter between would-be lovers, class relations, and so forth. But the female hero is as unconventional as those in Presson Allen's previous screenplays. A hard-nosed social climber Bones may be, but she is also this film's emotional core. In another context she might have ended up as little more than the acquisitive "mistress" stereotype. But her intelligence, her self-awareness, and her wit ensure that we root for her. When she finally marries Max at the film's denouement, it is through tough "negotiating"; she wants a film production company; she wants a few of his staff sacked. And only then, when Max retorts, "What's your real bottom line?" does she reply, "I want you to say you love me." Bones wraps things up: "Well that's it. That's how I got married. Didn't I tell you it was a romantic story?" All is fair in love and business, it seems, as the faces of the lovers fade into an image of yellow roses. Without wishing to strain any biographical connections, one might say that there is a touch of Presson Allen's public persona in Bones and that the film itself is also a sly allusion to her own struggles as a female creative in a male-dominated movie business.

Like the heroine of *Just Tell Me What You Want*, the New Hollywood career of Jay Presson Allen was built on negotiation. At a time when women screenwriters were denied the same opportunities as their male peers, she sustained regular employment and worked with many of Hollywood's most renowned creatives. In public she built a reputation for her wit and no-nonsense attitude toward screenwriting. Her publicly expressed views toward women in Hollywood and on-screen gender relations were contradictory, confounding, and sometimes hostile. But her screenplays—so frequently presenting psychologically complex female leads—were renowned for their rich, expansive, and diverse subject matter. She helped bring to the big screen some of cinema's most iconic characters: Jean Brodie, Sally Bowles, Marnie Holland, Fanny Brice (*Funny Lady*). From *Marnie* through to *Just Tell Me What You Want*, her work chronicled extraordinary lives and troubled minds adrift on a sea of political and social upheaval. Themes such as sexual repression, extremist ideologies, class and gender relations, and the dangerous power of charismatic leaders are ever present across her oeuvre. The highly seductive and deeply flawed characters of Brodie and Sally Bowles are surely two of 1960s and 1970s cinema's most memorable characters. Protagonists like Brice and Burton become entangled in romances encumbered with gender and class power relations. At the end of the 1970s, Press Allen began work on *Prince of the City*, which, in its character study of main protagonist Danny Ciello (Treat Williams), demonstrated her ability to work across an ever-widening array of themes, characters, and contexts. "My ear has been everywhere," she once said.[58] Whether it is the range of dialects and accents adopted in her films, or the historical contexts or shifts in perspectives, adaptability does appear to have been a defining feature. Identifying any singular outlook, let alone ideology, in Jay Presson Allen's oeuvre is difficult, to say the least. The screenplays—like her interviews—can elicit laughter, reflection, anger, and frustration, often within a short space of time. A "normal streak of greed" she might have had when it came to wangling a decent paycheck, but the New Hollywood also got its money's worth.

Notes

1   Paul Rosenfield, "The Prime Prose of Jay Allen," *Los Angeles Times*, October 5, 1982, C1.
2   Rosenfield, C1.
3   Ann Pinkerton, "Eye View: The Prime of Ms. Jay Allen," *Women's Wear Daily*, September 9, 1975, 12.
4   Dick Kleiner, "Big Screenplay Money Actually in Books, Plays," *Tennessean*, November 9, 1975, 29.
5   Marsha McCreadie, *Women Screenwriters Today: Their Lives and Words* (London: Praeger, 2006), 35.
6   I use "successful" to denote the number of screenwriting credits amassed by Presson Allen through the 1960s and 1970s. Certainly, writers such as Carole Eastman, Joan Tewksbury, and Elaine May enjoyed some success, but on fewer productions.
7   Lizzie Francke, *Script Girls: Women Screenwriters in Hollywood* (London: BFI, 1994), 95.
8   Helen Dudar, "The Prime of Jay Presson Allen, the Serious Screenwriter," *Washington Post*, October 18, 1981, L1.
9   Miranda J. Banks, *The Writers: A History of American Screenwriters and Their Guild* (New Brunswick, NJ: Rutgers University Press, 2016), Kindle; Steven Price, *A History of the Screenplay* (London: Palgrave Macmillan, 2013), 182–199.
10 McCreadie, *Women Screenwriters Today*, 35.
11 See, for example, Todd Berliner, *Hollywood Incoherent: Narration in Seventies Cinema* (Austin: University of Texas Press, 2010); Peter Krämer and Yannis Tzioumakis, eds., *The Hollywood Renaissance: Revisiting American Cinema's Most Celebrated Era* (New York: Bloomsbury, 2018).
12 Banks, *The Writers*, esp. 7–25, 178–184; Maya Montañez Smukler, *Liberating Hollywood: Women Directors and the Feminist Reform of 1970s American Cinema* (New Brunswick, NJ: Rutgers University Press, 2018), 33–76, Kindle.
13 Montañez Smukler, *Liberating Hollywood*, 64; Banks, *The Writers*, 179.
14 Montañez Smukler, *Liberating Hollywood*, 75–76.
15 Smukler, *Liberating Hollywood*; Banks, *The Writers*; Peter Krämer, "A Powerful Cinema-Going Force? Hollywood and Female Audiences since the 1960s," in *Identifying Hollywood's Audiences*, ed. Melvyn Stokes and Richard Maltby (London: BFI, 1999), 96–97.
16 Todd McCarthy, "Women in Film's Honorees: Weinstein, Tyson and 2 Allens," *Variety*, June 9, 1982, 6.
17 Patrick McGilligan, *Backstory 3: Interviews with Screenwriters of the 1960s* (Berkeley: University of California Press, 1997), 27.
18 Shelley Cobb, *Adaptation, Authorship, and Contemporary Women Filmmakers* (New York: Palgrave Macmillan, 2014), 36, 50.

19   Quoted in Stephen Zito, "New Grub Street-West," *American Film*, June 1, 1977, 20.
20   McGilligan, *Backstory 3*, 35.
21   McGilligan, 35.
22   Francke, *Script Girls*, 95.
23   Tony Lee Moral, *Hitchcock and the Making of Marnie*, rev. ed. (Plymouth, UK: Scarecrow, 2013), 194.
24   Moral, 41–52, 177–194; Walter Raubicheck, *Scripting Hitchcock:* Psycho, The Birds, *and* Marnie (Urbana: University of Illinois Press, 2011), xvii.
25   Deborah Jermyn, *Nancy Meyers* (New York: Bloomsbury, 2017), 30, 61.
26   Aaron Hunter, *Authoring Hal Ashby: The Myth of the New Hollywood Auteur* (New York: Bloomsbury, 2016), 165.
27   Peter Krämer, *The New Hollywood: From* Bonnie and Clyde *to* Star Wars (London: Wallflower, 2005), 73.
28   Gene Plotnik, "Philco Television Playhouse," *Billboard*, December 11, 1954, 12.
29   Jerry Gaghan, "Pair Matched in Arts Too," *Philadelphia Daily News*, October 28, 1963, 53.
30   Moral, *Hitchcock*, xiii.
31   Raubichek, *Scripting Hitchcock*, 13
32   Jule Selbo, "Jay Presson Allen," in *Women Screenwriters: An International Guide*, ed. Jill Nelmes and Jule Selbo (Basingstoke: Palgrave Macmillan, 2015), 752.
33   Moral, *Hitchcock*, 43.
34   Moral, 45–49.
35   Raubichek, *Scripting Hitchcock*, 108–110.
36   Tania Modleski, "Suspicion: Collusion and Resistance in the Work of Hitchcock's Female Collaborators," in *A Companion to Alfred Hitchcock*, ed, Thomas Leitch and Leland Poague (London: John Wiley, 2011), 180–183, electronic edition.
37   Jay Presson Allen, *The Prime of Miss Jean Brodie*, January 22, 1968, 1, British Film Institute Library, London. Unless stated otherwise, all script drafts consulted at the BFI.
38   Presson Allen, 101–102.
39   Allen, 92.
40   Presson Allen, 119.
41   Stephen Tropiano, *Cabaret: Music on Film* (Milwaukee: Limelight, 2011), loc. 489, Kindle.
42   Martha Shearer, *New York City and the Hollywood Musical: Dancing in the Streets* (New York: Palgrave Macmillan, 2016), 48.
43   Keith Garebian, *The Making of Cabaret*, 2nd ed. (Oxford: Oxford University Press, 2011), 136, Kindle.
44   Jay Presson Allen, *Cabaret*, June 10, 1970, 5, 6, 11.
45   Presson Allen, 6, 53.
46   Tropiano, *Cabaret*, loc. 579
47   Presson Allen, *Cabaret*, 13.
48   Presson Allen, 21.
49   Kevin Winkler, *Big Deal: Bob Fosse and Dance in the American Musical* (Oxford: Oxford University Press, 2018), 145.
50   Linda Mizejewski, *Fascism, Female Spectacle and the Making of Sally Bowles* (Princeton, NJ: Princeton University Press, 1992), 203.
51   Presson Allen, *Cabaret*, 70–71.
52   Presson Allen, 71.

53 "Cabaret: A Legend in the Making," documentary, *Cabaret: Special Edition*, directed by Bob Fosse (London: Freemantle, 2013), DVD.
54 Marjorie Garber, *Bisexuality and Eroticism in Everyday Life* (London: Routledge, 2000), 491–495.
55 Presson Allen, *Cabaret*, 98.
56 Jay Presson Allen, *Just Tell Me What You Want*, December 1978, 98, author's copy.
57 Presson Allen, 98.
58 Rosenfield, "The Prime Prose of Jay Allen," C1.

"We Knew and She Knew That She Was Barbra"

Streisand in the 1970s

NICHOLAS GODFREY

Barbra Streisand's rise to cinematic superstardom coincides with the New Hollywood period of the late 1960s and 1970s. Her debut film, *Funny Girl*, was the highest-grossing film of 1968, and *Hello, Dolly!* (1969), *On a Clear Day You Can See Forever* (1970), *The Owl and the Pussycat* (1970), *What's Up, Doc?* (1972), *The Way We Were* (1973), *Funny Lady* (1975), *A Star Is Born* (1976), and *The Main Event* (1979) all number among the most commercially successful films in their years of release.[1] And yet, despite her box office clout, she rarely figures in historical accounts of this period of American filmmaking. From the beginning of her cinematic career, speculation over the degree of creative control she wielded over her projects became a source of notoriety. Streisand's cinematic ascent also coincided with the burgeoning demands

63

of second-wave feminism and the emergence of feminist film studies. However, despite her status as the most prominent female star in 1970s Hollywood, Streisand is notably absent from major feminist film scholarship of the period. Where she does appear, the prevailing sense is that her star is too big, and too singular, to be contained within the discourses of New Hollywood or feminist film theory. Streisand's early cinematic career illuminates the discursive tension between notions of Old and New Hollywood, and the presence of women within them. Her industrial power, and the fact that she did not direct a film during this age of the auteur, complicates the critical construction of the New Hollywood as it has been historicized.

The New Hollywood is a period that has long been subject to a particularly gendered history. This has been challenged in recent years with concerted reappraisals of the truncated careers of directors like Barbara Loden and Claudia Weill, as in Maya Montañez Smukler's *Liberating Hollywood: Women Directors and the Feminist Reform of 1970s American Cinema* (2018).[2] This project corresponds to a wider body of scholarship that aims to recover women's contributions to film history: Julia Knight, Christine Gledhill, and J. E. Smyth, among others, have done much to illuminate the invisible contributions of women's labor in the motion picture industry. Such work presents a significant challenge to presumptions of auteurism, the critical construction that is itself central to the mythology of the New Hollywood. Aaron Hunter writes that "it would be difficult to overstate the intimacy of the relationship between auteurism and New Hollywood"; furthermore, auteurist histories of this period are typically dominated by specifically male filmmakers. Shelley Cobb notes of the relative scarcity of women film directors that "their conspicuousness functions to make manifest the gendered nature of authorship," a tendency that is particularly evident in the historiography of the New Hollywood.[3] In practical terms, the maverick individualist brand of auteurism functioned as a marker to differentiate the "new" youth films from the well-oiled machine of classical Hollywood, as conceptions of power shifted away from studios and producers and coalesced around directors. The fact that Streisand cannot be easily reconciled into any of these critical categories complicates this periodization.

Streisand's absence from most histories of the New Hollywood may be explained by the fact that she did not direct a film in the 1960s or 1970s. However, Warren Beatty too did not ascend to the director's chair until 1978 with *Heaven Can Wait* (sharing credit with Buck Henry), and yet the creative agency that Beatty wielded over his starring projects is central to histories of the period.[4] By contrast, most writing on Streisand can be categorized into straightforward biographies, or attempts to appraise her via marginal considerations, in relation to her Jewishness, or as a queer icon, but rarely as a major Hollywood power broker in her own right.[5] In recent years, Pamela Robertson Wojcik and Dominic McHugh have analyzed Streisand's early musicals in relation to broader industrial trends that were afoot during the period of her rise to Hollywood stardom.[6] Peter Krämer demonstrates how Streisand's extraordinary level of fame on Broadway and in the recording industry enabled her to broker unprecedented deals with her first three film roles, beginning with *Funny Girl*.[7] And yet, despite apparently emblematizing key components of the New Hollywood, Streisand cut a decidedly distinct cinematic figure.

From *Funny Girl* to *Funny Lady*

Streisand emerged to cinematic superstardom in 1968, between the release of *The Graduate* (1967) and *Easy Rider* (1969), but stands apart from those new youth films. She had begun her career in the early 1960s, first as a nightclub singer and then as a prolific recording artist and a star of stage and the television screen. As Krämer points out, Streisand was only twenty-three years old when Columbia announced it was putting the film adaptation of *Funny Girl* into production.[8] Streisand had already starred in the musical's Broadway production, which had opened the preceding year.[9] The film version of *Funny Girl* came in at a final cost of $14 million, at a time when the average Hollywood budget was $1.5 million and *Easy Rider* cost just $400,000.[10] By charting the rise to prominence of her biographical subject, the *Ziegfeld Follies* performer Fanny Brice, Streisand reiterates a metanarrative of the formation of her own stardom, a trope that recurs throughout her films of the 1970s. As Matthew Kennedy notes, by the late 1960s, Streisand was routinely commanding record sales in the millions, while her television specials had an audience of 70 million.[11] Joseph Morgenstern's 1969 *Newsweek* profile of Streisand opens, "By any standard but raw musculature, Barbra Streisand is the most powerful entertainer in America today."[12] And there was a sense in press coverage prior to the release of the film that Streisand already overshadowed the film; this despite the seemingly inevitable commercial logic that the movies were the only medium capable of representing a star of her magnitude, given her ascent from the stage to the television screen and now cinema. This was manifested in reports of on-set difficulties: Krämer notes that "during the production of *Funny Girl*, [Streisand] frequently argued with the

Hollywood veterans surrounding her (most notably the American film industry's most commercially successful and most celebrated director up to this
point, William Wyler), often getting her way."[13] The *Los Angeles Times*
reported that during the film's editing, director Wyler was threating to quit
the production "over 'monster' Streisand's many demands"; in private correspondence to the film's producer, Ray Stark (custodian of a considerable legacy as the son-in-law of the actual Fanny Brice), Wyler accused Stark himself
of orchestrating these stories to inflate his own reputation as the producer
who successfully steered the production through these creative disputes.[14]

None of this dampened the film's commercial prospects or its ability to
win over critics. Pauline Kael welcomed a star out of step with Hollywood's
prevailing sensibilities, writing that "Barbra Streisand arrives on the screen,
in *Funny Girl*, when the movies are in desperate need of her. The timing is
perfect."[15] Kael bemoaned the lack of bona fide movie stars circa 1968, the
year in which *Funny Girl* was joined at the top of the box office by the nar-
ratively and formally ambitious, and decidedly nonactorly *2001: A Space Odys-
sey*, in which the special effects take the front seat. Streisand continued her
filmic career in a series of lavish, old-fashioned musicals, directed by a suc-
cession of conspicuously Old Hollywood filmmakers like Wyler, Gene Kelly,
Herbert Ross, and Vincente Minnelli, figures who began their careers decades
earlier—in Wyler's case, in the 1920s—coinciding with the New Hollywood
moment when directors like Dennis Hopper were enjoying box office success
with the newly lucrative youth market and with considerably less budget
overhead.

While Streisand's choice of projects did not immediately cast her into the
company of her New Hollywood peers, her age was not the only dimension
of "newness" associated with her cinematic stardom. Many of the initial critical responses to *Funny Girl* made note of its star's "unconventional" physical appearance—a fixation that Krämer indicates was also present in coverage
of Streisand's initial stage performances earlier in the decade.[16] Streisand's big
screen debut came shortly after the ethnically marked Dustin Hoffman broke
into superstardom, directly addressing the youth audience in *The Graduate*.
Krämer writes, "If the Hollywood Renaissance was, among other things,
centrally concerned with ethnicity and youth, then it is worth noting that
hardly any important person in Hollywood was more ethnic and youthful
than Barbra Streisand."[17] The emergence of a range of young Jewish movie
stars in the late 1960s represents a major historical development. For context,
Vincent Brook and Neale Gabler have both noted that despite the long-
standing Jewish presence in Hollywood, from the 1920s onward, the major

motion picture companies consciously downplayed this both on and off the screen, via the widespread adoption of ethnically neutral pseudonyms.[18] Such sensitivity was exacerbated amid the Red Scare; Jon Lewis writes that the "residual, pervasive postwar anti-Semitism" of the House Un-American Activities Committee led to the "conflat[ion of] communism with Jewishness," pushing Hollywood to further disavow its Semitic origins and constitution, lest these facts prove politically and commercially inopportune.[19] This changed by the late 1960s, as the arrival of openly Jewish stars such as Woody Allen, Dustin Hoffman, Elliott Gould, and, indeed, Streisand, telegraphed their novelty in a transforming industry in which the presence of the chosen people was thoroughly entrenched, if not always visible.

The fact that the "new" youth films could be produced in tandem, and indeed economically compete with the more classically conventional Streisand musicals, suggests that the very hallmarks of differentiation that were later historicized as representing a New Hollywood may, in the context of their marketing, reception, and consumption, be understood as strategies of commercial opportunism. By 1967, *The Sound of Music* (1965) had surpassed *Gone with the Wind* (1939) to become the most commercially successful film of all time, yet the unexpected success of the considerably cheaper *Bonnie and Clyde* and *The Graduate* in the same year caused Hollywood to turn its attention toward college-age males. In May of the same year, Streisand was announced as the star of Fox's *Hello, Dolly!*, usurping Carol Channing from the Broadway production, and commanding an unheard-of million-dollar salary—all while Streisand's debut, *Funny Girl*, was still shooting.[20] The budget for *Hello, Dolly!* was estimated at $20 million—"the largest in Hollywood history," with a single set re-creating downtown Manhattan costing Fox $1.6 million.[21] Ultimately, *Hello, Dolly!* was one of the best-performing films at the North American box office for 1969, but its $15 million in rentals did little to offset its production budget as it was outperformed by films made at a fraction of its cost: *Butch Cassidy and the Sundance Kid*, *The Love Bug*, *Midnight Cowboy*, and *Easy Rider*.[22] This proved even more damaging as Fox was already reeling from the commercial failure of its expensive musicals *Doctor Dolittle* (1967) and *Star!* (1968), which made the cheap youth films all the more appealing by comparison. This did little to hamper Streisand, who signed to star in Vincente Minnelli's *On a Clear Day You Can See Forever* for Paramount before *Funny Girl* was released.[23] Her arrival as a major motion picture star was further consolidated when she won the 1969 Academy Award for Best Actress for *Funny Girl*, an honor she shared with Old Hollywood luminary Katharine Hepburn, for *The Lion in Winter* (1968)—the only time the award has been shared.

And while Streisand's choice of projects in the late 1960s and early 1970s partly characterized her as an old-style movie star, they also reveal a transforming Hollywood, as her most successful films were adaptations of presold theatrical productions (*Funny Girl*, *Hello, Dolly!*, *On a Clear Day You Can See Forever*, *The Owl and the Pussycat*), remakes (*A Star Is Born*), and a sequel (*Funny Lady*). *What's Up, Doc?* the third-highest-grossing film at the North American box office for 1972, traded in part on the auteur status of its director Peter Bogdanovich, as his follow-up to the widely acclaimed *Last Picture Show* (1971). All of these tendencies would come to the fore in 1970s Hollywood.

In a further significant move, in 1969, Streisand's management group, Creative Management Associates (CMA), founded the First Artists Production Company to produce projects specifically for its clients Streisand, Paul Newman, and Sidney Poitier, with Steve McQueen and Dustin Hoffman later joining. Streisand's agent throughout this period, Sue Mengers, first met the star in 1963 when she was in *Funny Girl* on Broadway. Mengers and Freddie Fields represented Streisand at CMA, with Mengers as Streisand's sole agent for much of the 1970s, alongside clients including Bogdanovich, Cybill Shepherd, and Faye Dunaway.[24] This relationship anticipates the way in which increasingly high-powered talent management agencies would recalibrate stardom in the 1970s. In an industrial sense, Streisand's close relationship with Mengers and Fields and the formation of First Artists point to Hollywood's broader realignment around a package model, as the binding legal power of contracts (and what is any film project other than a series of contracts and rights?) shifted from studios to agents.[25] After the Paramount Decree of 1948, the burden of financial responsibility was increasingly borne by independent producers, while studios consolidated their power around control of the distribution apparatus. After divorcement, writes Tom Kemper, "the Hollywood film business was relegated to a corporate division," and talent agencies developed as a parallel but deeply embedded corporate structure oriented around "strategies developed in the 1930s—packaging; assigning agents in a single firm to a particular studio; contractual guarantees of story approval; percentage points and freelance deals."[26] Emily Carman reveals the uniquely feminized importance of freelance stardom and creative agency in the studio system, prefiguring the later industrial changes in postclassical Hollywood, maligning "the scholarly neglect of independent stardom, and the failure of film historians to acknowledge the key role that women played in developing this industrial practice."[27] By the 1970s, Vincent Brook writes, "with talent no longer contractually bound for long stretches, as in the classical era, to a single studio, the industry dynamic was irrevocably altered, with above-the-liners

FIGURE 4.1 Barbra Streisand in *What's Up, Doc?* (1972)

and their agency underwriters now literally calling the shots."[28] Agent power was further consolidated with the formation of the superagency Creative Artists Agency in 1975. In the same year, International Creative Management was formed through the merger of CMA and International Famous Agency.

Undoubtedly, Mengers and Fields (and later Jon Peters) played a significant role in guiding Streisand's trajectory through 1970s Hollywood—as William Mann has pointed out, the Barbra Streisand star project had long been the product of a collective labor pool.[29] At the same time, the formation of First Artists as a visible vehicle for the formation of star-driven projects proved influential in its own right. Inspired by United Artists, which was formed in 1919 by D. W. Griffith, Mary Pickford, Douglas Fairbanks, and Charlie Chaplin, First Artists signaled the utopian dream of an artist-run company determining the destinies of its constituents; it later served as the inspiration for Francis Ford Coppola's Directors Company venture with Bogdanovich and William Friedkin, while anticipating the subsequent high-profile deals brokered with the likes of Orion Pictures and the Ladd Company.[30]

These names are central to the New Hollywood canon. Yet Streisand is rarely cast in their company, even as she joined the production of Bogdanovich's follow-up to the acclaimed *Last Picture Show*, the knowing screwball homage *What's Up, Doc?* (figure 4.1). Bogdanovich's reverence for classical Hollywood contributed to a cycle of nostalgia films: *The Last Picture Show* coincided with *Summer of '42* (1971) and *Carnal Knowledge* (1971) and foreshadowed *American Graffiti* (1973), films that struck paydirt right as the youth-centric cycle of *Easy Rider* imitators ran out of steam. Streisand made her own appearance in this cycle, appearing alongside her counterpart as the decade's most bankable male star, Robert Redford, in *The Way We Were* (1973). Streisand's casting and the characterization of Katie Morosky provide a distinctly ethnic resonance to this entry in the cycle, as the film incorporates the backdrop of Hollywood's Red Scare, a historical event with its own anti-Semitic dimension.

Even in the commercially volatile 1970s, Hollywood's output can be understood as a series of interlocking commercial cycles.[31] *The Main Event* may be industrially accounted for as a belated the response to the extraordinary commercial success of *Rocky* (1976), with the latter film's sequel also arriving in 1979. Interestingly, on April 3, 1973, *Variety* announced that Streisand would star in *Roller Skates* for Paramount, as a nascent roller cycle materialized with the likes of *Kansas City Bomber* and *Unholy Rollers* in 1972.[32] Streisand's film never entered production, and, indeed, it is the films that Streisand did *not* make throughout the 1970s that demonstrate her industrial clout as much as the films she did. In his book *Lost Illusions* (2000), David Cook contrasts Streisand with her ex-husband Elliott Gould, to demonstrate the danger of overexposure for movie stars in the 1970s. From *Funny Girl* in 1968 to *The Main Event* in 1979, Streisand appeared in eleven films. Over the same span, Gould has twenty-five feature film credits, which does not include television movie appearances. By appearing in less than a film a year throughout the 1970s, Streisand was able to retain her bankability as a star commodity. *Variety* reported in October 1973, "Barbra Streisand plans (as of now) to limit her film career to one pic every two years soon as she winds up current contractual obligations."[33] The prolific Gould's career faltered by mid-decade, so relentless had he been in his omnipresence. Streisand chose her projects carefully. For instance, her partner, the similarly multihyphenate business manager-producer-hairdresser Jon Peters, developed John Carpenter's voyeuristic serial killer screenplay *Eyes of Laura Mars* as a vehicle for Streisand, but when she rejected its violent premise, Faye Dunaway was cast instead, and Streisand contributed the theme song to the soundtrack.[34]

In the mid-1970s, Streisand also experienced some flops, and it is the subject matter of these films—the comedic criminal milieu of *For Pete's Sake* (1974) and the surreal dream life of a New York housewife in *Up the Sandbox* (1975)—that skewed closest to the typical terrain of the New Hollywood youth films. On the latter film, which was produced by First Artists and Streisand's Barwood production company (which would also handle *A Star Is Born*), *Variety* concluded its review by asking, "What on earth went wrong with this picture."[35] Notably, however, *Up the Sandbox* was the sole Streisand film to attract the attention of emerging feminist film criticism in Marjorie Rosen's *Popcorn Venus* and Molly Haskell's *From Reverence to Rape* (both 1973). Rosen writes of the film that "the actress has never been more interesting, suggesting that she and modern 'small' roles were made for each other"—an impression that was not shared by audiences, as the film yielded the smallest box office of any of Streisand's films to date.[36]

The film and the dissatisfied wife and mother portrayed by Streisand within it explicitly and didactically iterate the demands and dilemmas of second-wave feminism, which Streisand ensured would also underscore the dynamics of *A Star Is Born*. Haskell places the film and its contradictions in material terms, labeling it a work "about women's liberation or about the world; and the tendency to overlook the importance of class—the fact that both are expressions of that very confusion by women (upper-middle class, educated) who enjoy a greater freedom of choice than they have ever had before. And the confusion as to what is true and what conditioned in a woman's (or a man's) nature, how much we can and want to change ourselves while preserving some of the values of sexual difference and opposition; what, finally, will be the consequences and the by-products of the mutations we seek."[37] Pamela Wojcik finds similar tensions inherent in Streisand's more conventional musicals of the period, in which "the major contradiction in Streisand's persona is that between two modes of desire—the first, romantic longing, and the second a drive for freedom and independence."[38] While *Funny Girl*, *On a Clear Day You Can See Forever*, and *The Way We Were* end with the breaking of the heterosexual union, asserting the independence of the Streisand protagonist, Rosen is troubled that *Up the Sandbox* concludes with "an uncharacteristic about-face in the final minute of the movie [as the protagonist] decides abruptly, joyously, to tie herself down with a third baby."[39] Yet viewed within the context of the New Hollywood, when Streisand's Margaret jumps in a taxi at the film's conclusion, we cannot be sure that she is not planning to take leave and join Shirley Knight somewhere on the open road, as the latter's protagonist in *The Rain People* (1969) also experienced existential crisis prompted via pregnancy. Where the earlier film charts a cross-country road trip, Streisand's *Sandbox* spans a series of elaborate fantasy sequences on the streets of New York, in a similar manner to *Move* (1970), which starred Streisand's then husband Gould. That *Up the Sandbox* failed to find critical purchase further reveals that the burgeoning New Hollywood brand of ennui remained conventionally limited to the masculine domain.

While audiences rejected the ambivalent *Up the Sandbox*, Streisand landed monster hits with her return to the musical in both *Funny Lady* and *A Star Is Born*. And while *Funny Lady* was a direct sequel to Streisand's cinematic debut, *A Star Is Born* relitigated extratextual components of the 1968 film in fascinating ways, evoking once again the rise to fame of its star, while her off-screen persona colored press coverage of the film's production.

A Star Is Born

A Star Is Born is the film that represents the peak of Streisand's fame and influence in the 1970s, while complicating preconceived notions of film authorship in 1970s Hollywood. Yet like Streisand's cinematic debut, it survived a troubled production before eventually achieving commercial success. The project originated with its high-profile scribes Joan Didion and John Gregory Dunne—the latter of whom had earlier documented Streisand's role in *Hello, Dolly!* in his insider account of Richard Zanuck's 20th Century Fox, *The Studio* (1969). Didion and Dunne's concept was to update the 1937 and 1954 installments of the *Star Is Born* narrative to a contemporary setting, transplanting it from Hollywood's dream factory to the rock and roll scene. Indeed, the film's excess of substance abuse aligns more with the social realist project of many New Hollywood films than with the baroque evocations of the past in *Funny Girl* and *Hello, Dolly!*

The project came to Streisand via her agent Sue Mengers having already lost director Mark Rydell, but it was producer Peters who fixated on the production, convincing Streisand to join.[40] Replacement director Jerry Schatzberg soon left the project, which was subsequently shopped to Bob Fosse, Hal Ashby, Sidney Lumet, and Robert Altman, while Peters himself was considered as director.[41] On the prospect of the inexperienced Peters directing the film, an unnamed industry source speculated: "It doesn't matter . . . it would be nice if the picture was good, but the bottom line is to get her to the studio. Shoot her singing six numbers and we'll make $60 million."[42] This account comes from *Dog Day Afternoon* (1975) screenwriter Frank Pierson, who was doing rewrites at the time on *A Star Is Born* and was subsequently hired as its director. The fact that Pierson had only a handful of television directorial credits and a single feature, *The Looking Glass War* (1970), to his name perhaps led to his being perceived as a pliable presence between the strong creative poles of Streisand and Peters. Sure enough, the project was not without conflict. According to Pierson, Streisand initially rejected his offer for her to collaborate on rewrites with him, but she later took control of the edit from the director, recalling the *Los Angeles Times'* earlier report of post-production turmoil on *Funny Girl*. For his part, Pierson took the unusual step of launching a public battle over the film's authorship, penning tell-all missives in *New West* and *New York* magazines in November 1976 weeks before the film's release, painting Streisand as obtuse and indecisive.[43]

Despite its troubled production and contested authorship, *A Star Is Born* became the second-highest-grossing film of 1976, taking $37 million at the box office, trailing only *Rocky*. There was no doubting the film's provenance: *Monthly Film Bulletin* wrote: "It would be highly misleading if this remake entered the reference books as Frank Pierson's *A Star Is Born*, for the film belongs totally to Barbra Streisand. She is star, executive producer and prime mover, part-composer of two songs . . . provider of 'musical concepts' and provider of her own extravagant wardrobe."[44] And for some, Streisand overwhelmed the film itself. Roger Ebert took issue with the very thing that Kael had earlier celebrated in *Funny Girl*—Streisand's arrival, fully formed; in his review of the same film from 1968, Ebert had dubbed her "a born movie star."[45] Now, of *A Star Is Born*, Ebert wrote, "There's just no way, after all the times we've seen Streisand and all the ways she's imprinted herself on our minds and tastes, for us to accept her as a kid on the way up, as an unknown who hitches her destiny to a star. Even in her first rags-to-riches movie, even in *Funny Girl*, we knew and she knew that she was Barbra Streisand."[46] Ebert's quote proves that Streisand remained a star first and foremost, and one who outshone the cinematic text of *A Star Is Born*, a risk that was present from *Funny Girl*. Dominic McHugh has demonstrated that even from her earliest films, the theatrical source material was liberally adapted to accommodate, and accentuate, Streisand's existing star persona.[47] And textually, while her musicals routinely follow their protagonists through a process of becoming, Wojcik stresses that "Streisand is always already a star."[48] As her industrial power increased throughout the 1970s, Streisand's categorization typically remained that of star rather than creative agent in her own right. In his book *Final Cut*, former United Artists production head Steven Bach writes of that studio's desire in the late 1970s "to enhance its product with star names, and there was no name more celestial than that of Barbra Streisand."[49] The studio attempted to develop several projects with Streisand, but she was determined to bring her own passion project to the table: *Yentl* (1983), its gender-bending premise representing a potentially risky commercial proposition. Yet Bach writes, "A far greater problem with *Yentl* than its subject was its intended director: Barbra Streisand. Who was also the intended producer and had written (or was writing) the script. The songs she had left to Alan and Marilyn Bergman and composer Michel Legrand, but the functions of star, director, screenwriter, and producer seemed at least one too many, even for so protean a talent as Streisand's . . . a big-budget musical from a first-time director seemed doubly unlikely at UA, still suffering through the looming unknowns of the shortened *Heaven's Gate*."[50] And while Michael Cimino's infamous directorial excesses on that film would ultimately both cost Bach his job and spell the end of the United Artists studio, *Heaven's Gate*'s reappraisal is complete, with its director's dithering on set now considered the hallmark of eccentric genius, whereas Streisand's reputation continues to be shrouded in an aura of "difficulty." Streisand later turned such rhetoric on her detractors in her 1992 speech accepting the inaugural Dorothy Arzner Directors Award from the Women in Film advocacy group, saying, "If [a man] acts, produces and directs, he's called multi-talented. If [a woman] does the same thing, she's called vain and egotistical."[51]

Conclusion

None of this troubled Streisand's fans when it came to the box office. David Cook's list of the most bankable stars of the 1970s, drawn from the pages of *Variety* and *Motion Picture Almanac*, lists Streisand among the top 10 box office–drawing performers for 1972, 1973, 1974, 1975, 1977, 1978, and 1979—often the only woman appearing on the lists otherwise dominated by Clint Eastwood and Robert Redford.[52] This is auspicious company, as Eastwood and Redford are perhaps the two performers who most successfully made the transition to the director's chair over this period, while keeping their star power intact. Sylvester Stallone, too, consolidated his career as the director of the string of *Rocky* sequels, while Woody Allen made his transition from funny guy to Oscar success story while banking on the kind of critical goodwill that eluded Streisand for much of the 1970s. Streisand is, of course, not the only woman star to wield creative power in Hollywood at this time: of the sixteen subjects of Maya Montañez Smukler's *Liberating Hollywood*, all but three began their careers as performers before transitioning to direction.[53] *Alice Doesn't Live Here Anymore* (1974) is typically regarded as an outlier in director Martin Scorsese's body of work, rather than a job-for-hire instigated by its star, Ellen Burstyn, in search of her next hit after the success of *The Exorcist* (1973).

Yet by sheer weight of numbers, Streisand is the irrefutable star of the 1970s. In the popular imagination, her trajectory runs parallel to the New

Hollywood, but never intersects it. Given the unmatched scale of her commercial success throughout this decade, Streisand's continued marginalization in histories of the period reveals much about active critical condescension toward particular genres, and particular kinds of movie stars. Her creative demands were typically characterized in highly gendered terms, diminished further by the fact that she did not direct herself in the age of the hypermasculine auteur. Furthermore, Streisand was at the peak of her powers at the very time early feminist film critics were beginning to reveal the inequities of representation on-screen, and the long-standing marginalization of so-called women's genres.[54] Such complex and intersecting strands make it difficult to situate Streisand within the narrow paradigms of Old or New Hollywood, or in those of auteurist or feminist film theories. Yet it is precisely by reappraising Barbra Streisand's movements through 1970s Hollywood that we can obtain a richer understanding of the complexity of this period, and the role that women played in shaping new configurations of industrial power that would come to the fore in the subsequent decades.

Notes

1   David A. Cook, *Lost Illusions: American Cinema in the Shadow of Watergate and Vietnam 1970–1979* (Berkeley: University of California Press, 2000), 497–505; Peter Krämer, *The New Hollywood: From Bonnie and Clyde to Star Wars* (London: Wallflower, 2005), 106–109.

2   Julia Knight and Christine Gledhill, *Doing Women's Film History: Reframing Cinemas, Past and Future* (Urbana: University of Illinois Press, 2015); J. E. Smyth, *Nobody's Girl Friday* (New York: Oxford University Press, 2018); Maya Montañez Smukler, *Liberating Hollywood: Women Directors and the Feminist Reform of 1970s American Cinema* (New Brunswick, NJ: Rutgers University Press, 2018).

3   Shelley Cobb, *Adaptation, Authorship and Contemporary Women Filmmakers* (Basingstoke: Palgrave Macmillan, 2015), 5.

4   Peter Biskind, *Easy Riders, Raging Bulls: How the Sex-Drugs-and-Rock 'n' Roll Generation Saved Hollywood* (New York: Simon & Schuster, 1998); Peter Biskind, *Star: How Warren Beatty Seduced America* (London: Simon and Schuster, 2011).

5   William J. Mann, *Hello Gorgeous: Becoming Barbra Streisand* (Boston: Houghton Mifflin, 2014); Ethan Mordden, *On Streisand: An Opinionated Guide* (New York: Oxford University Press, 2019); David E. Kaufman, *Jewhooing the Sixties: American Celebrity and Jewish Identity—Sandy Koufax, Lenny Bruce, Bob Dylan, and Barbra Streisand* (Waltham, MA: Brandeis University Press, 2012); Neal Gabler, *Barbra Streisand: Redefining Beauty, Femininity, and Power* (New Haven, CT: Yale University Press, 2016).

6   Pamela Robertson Wojcik, "The Streisand Musical," in *The Sound of Musicals*, ed. Steven Cohan (London: BFI, 2010), 128–138; Dominic McHugh, "'I'm Once Again the Previous Me': Performance and Stardom in the Barbra Streisand

Stage-to-Screen Adaptations," in *The Oxford Handbook of Musical Theatre Screen Adaptations*, ed. Dominic McHugh (New York: Oxford University Press, 2019), 423–443.

7   Peter Krämer, "'A Triumph of Aura over Appearance': Barbra Streisand, *Funny Girl* (1968) and the Hollywood Renaissance," in *The Hollywood Renaissance: Revisiting American Cinema's Most Celebrated Era*, ed. Peter Krämer and Yannis Tzioumakis (New York: Bloomsbury Academic, 2018), 53.

8   Krämer, "'A Triumph of Aura over Appearance,'" 53.

9   Matthew Kennedy, *Roadshow! The Fall of Film Musicals in the 1960s* (New York: Oxford University Press, 2014), 61.

10 Krämer, "'A Triumph of Aura over Appearance,'" 57, 67.

11 Kennedy, *Roadshow!*, 61.

12 Joseph Morgenstern, "Superstar: The Streisand Story," reprinted in *Film 69/70*, ed. Joseph Morgenstern and Stefan Kanfer (New York: Simon and Schuster, 1970), 236.

13 Krämer, "'A Triumph of Aura over Appearance,'" 66.

14 Kennedy, *Roadshow!*, 146.

15 Pauline Kael, *Going Steady* (Boston: Little, Brown, 1970), 133.

16 Krämer, "'A Triumph of Aura Over Appearance,'" 55–56.

17 Krämer, "'A Triumph of Aura Over Appearance,'" 66.

18 Vincent Brook, "Still an Empire of Their Own: How Jews Remain Atop a Reinvented Hollywood," in *From Shtetl to Stardom: Jews and Hollywood, The Jewish Role in American Life*, vol. 14, ed. Steven J. Ross (West Lafayette: Purdue University Press, 2017), 7; Gabler, *Barbra Streisand*, 5.

19 Jon Lewis, *Hollywood v Hard Core: How the Struggle over Censorship Saved the Modern Film Industry* (New York: New York University Press, 2002), 7, 12.

20 Kennedy, *Roadshow!*, 64–65.

21 John Gregory Dunne, *The Studio* (London: W. H. Allen, 1970), 145, 170.

22 Krämer, *New Hollywood*, 107.

23 Krämer, "'A Triumph of Aura over Appearance,'" 54.

24 Andy Lewis, "Review: Peggy Olson Meets Ari Gold in Bio of 1970s Super Agent Sue Mengers," *Hollywood Reporter*, September 14, 2015, https://www.hollywood reporter.com/bookmark/sue-mengers-streisand-agent-bio-822849.

25 See Paul McDonald, Emily Carman, Eric Hoyt, and Philip Drake, eds., *Hollywood and the Law* (London: British Film Institute/Palgrave, 2015); Peter Labuza, "Putting Penn to Paper: Warner Bros.' Contract Governance and the Transition to New Hollywood," *Velvet Light Trap*, no. 80 (Fall 2017): 4–17.

26 Tom Kemper, *Hidden Talent: The Emergence of Hollywood Agents* (Berkeley: University of California Press, 2010), xiii.

27 Emily Carman, *Independent Stardom: Freelance Women in the Hollywood Studio System* (Austin: University of Texas Press, 2016), 143.

28 Brook, "Still an Empire of Their Own," 10.

29 See Mann, *Hello Gorgeous*.

30 Biskind, *Easy Riders, Raging Bulls*, 206.

31 See Richard Nowell, "Hollywood Don't Skate: US Production Trends, Industry Analysis, and the Roller Disco Movie," *New Review of Film and Television Studies* 11, no. 1 (2013): 73–91; Peter Stanfield, *Hoodlum Movies: Seriality and the Outlaw Biker Film Cycle (1966–1972)* (New Brunswick, NJ: Rutgers University Press, 2018).

32 Anon., "Streisand on Rollers," *Variety*, April 4, 1973, 7.

33   Anon., "Film Reviews," *Variety*, October 31, 1973, 26.

34   Richard Harland Smith, *"Eyes of Laura Mars," Turner Classic Movies*, http://www
      .tcm.com/tcmdb/title/4554/Eyes-Of-Laura-Mars/articles.html.

35 · Arthur D. Murphy (Murf), *"Up the Sandbox," Variety*, December 20, 1972, 18.

36   Marjorie Rosen, *Popcorn Venus: Women, Movies and The American Dream*
      (London: Peter Owen, 1975), 359.

37   Molly Haskell, *From Reverence to Rape: The Treatment of Women in the Movies*,
      2nd ed. (Chicago, IL: University of Chicago Press, 1987), 368.

38   Wojcik, "The Streisand Musical," 133.

39   Rosen, *Popcorn Venus*, 359.

40   Jon Burlingame, *"A Star Is Born*': How Does the Music in the Previous Films Stack
      Up?," *Variety*, October 5, 2018, https://variety.com/2018/film/news/a-star-is-born
      -previous-films-judy-garland-barbra-streisand-1202969451/.

41   Nancy Griffin and Kim Masters, *Hit and Run: How Jon Peters and Peter Guber
      Took Hollywood for a Ride* (New York: Touchstone, 1997), 41

42   Frank Pierson, "My Battles with Barbra and Jon," *New West*, November 22, 1976,
      https://web.archive.org/web/20150716005847/http://barbra-archives.com/bjs
      _library/70s/new_west_battles_barbra_jon.html.

43   Pierson, , "My Battles with Barbra and Jon."

44   Geoff Brown, *"A Star Is Born," Monthly Film Bulletin* 44, no. 566 (1 January 1977): 53.

45   Roger Ebert, *"Funny Girl," Chicago Sun Times*, October 18, 1968, https://www
      .rogerebert.com/reviews/funny-girl-1968.

46   Roger Ebert, *"A Star Is Born," Chicago Sun Times*, December 24, 1976, https://www
      .rogerebert.com/reviews/a-star-is-born-1976.

47   McHugh, "'I'm Once Again the Previous Me.'"

48   Wojcik, "The Streisand Musical," 132.

49   Steven Bach, *Final Cut: Dreams and Disaster in the Making of* Heaven's Gate
      (London: Pimlico, 1996), 388–389.

50   Bach, *Final Cut*, 390.

51   Barbra Streisand, "Women in Film Speech," June 12, 1992, https://www.barbra
      streisand.com/news/women-film-speech/.

52   Cook, *Lost Illusions*, 339.

53   See Montañez Smukler, *Liberating Hollywood*.

54   See Haskell, *From Reverence to Rape*; Annette Kuhn, "Women's Genres," *Screen* 25,
      no. 1 (1984): 18–29.

5

I Know Why

Maya Angelou and the Promise of 1970s Hollywood

MAYA MONTAÑEZ SMUKLER

By 1968, when Maya Angelou began work on *Blacks, Blues, Black!* for public television station KQED in San Francisco—the first television project she exerted creative authority over as writer, producer, and host—she was forty years old and already had an expansive and multifaceted career and a personal life that would provide rich and complex material for seven best-selling auto-biographies.[1] During the 1970s, Angelou was prolific and critically acclaimed as an author and poet, as was her productivity and recognition in the perform-ing arts—in theater, television, and film—as a writer, director, producer, and performer. In 1971, Angelou was one of the few Black women to have written an original screenplay for a major motion picture, *Georgia, Georgia* (1972), for which she also wrote the soundtrack.[2] Also in 1971, it was announced that Angelou would adapt and direct her best-selling autobiography, *I Know*

Why the Caged Bird Sings, published in 1969, as a feature film.[3] In 1973, she costarred with Geraldine Page in the Broadway production of *Look Away*, for which Angelou received a Tony Award nomination. In 1974, she participated in the American Film Institute's inaugural Directing Workshop for Women, where she directed and wrote her first film, the short *All Day Long*. In 1975, Angelou became a member of the Directors Guild of America, becoming the first Black woman to join the union in the Directors category. Also during 1975, she was one of four alternating interviewers for the series *Assignment America*, produced by New York City's public television station Channel 13, WNET. In 1976, she directed two short films for the series *Visions* on KCET/PBS. And in 1977, Angelou joined the cast of the miniseries *Roots*, broadcast on ABC; that same year she was a guest on *The Richard Pryor Special* that aired on NBC, cowriting the sketch in which she appeared.

This chapter examines Angelou's film and television work during the late 1960s and through the 1970s, specifically the projects in which she participated as writer, director, and/or producer.[4] I argue that Angelou engaged in and lived the politically radical values of feminist Pan-African solidarity as she simultaneously pursued a career as a producer of mainstream media in the late 1960s and through the 1970s, however challenging this combination was.[5] Racism and sexism in the entertainment industry during these years were enormous and often impenetrable barriers. Angelou was a rare example of a Black American woman artist who had succeeded in building a body of work that included local and national public television, network television, and educational and commercial filmmaking, in addition to her literary and theater work. Her presence as a Black woman in the entertainment industry was radical; and her determination to change popular film and television's representations of gender, race, and sexuality was revolutionary, in the productions she completed and especially evidenced by those projects she was unable to bring to completion on her terms.

Born Marguerite Johnson, in 1928 in St. Louis, Missouri, Maya, a nickname given by her brother Bailey, began her career as a performer in her early twenties working as a nightclub dancer and singer in San Francisco. In 1953, she joined the cast of *Porgy and Bess* as a featured dancer on its tour across Europe. Her creative work and political coalition building became a more focused practice around 1959 when she was living in New York City. Angelou joined the Harlem Writers Guild; she was the northern coordinator for Dr. Martin Luther King Jr.'s Southern Christian Leadership Conference; she was a founding member of the Cultural Association for Women of African Heritage; and she appeared in Jean Genet's play *The Blacks* with Louis

Gossett Jr., James Earl Jones, Abbey Lincoln, and Cicely Tyson. Between 1962 and 1965, she worked and lived in Africa (Cairo and Ghana) where her connection to Pan-Africanism and anti-colonialism and her identity as a Black woman—in Africa and in the United States—became defined by her lived experience abroad. Angelou returned to the United States in the mid-1960s, to a country in an emergency state of nation-changing anti-racist activism entrenched in violence.

The civil rights and feminist movements that define the 1960s and 1970s challenged Hollywood's institutionalized racism and sexism, insisting that mainstream film reflect more realistic and meaningful stories made by, about, and for people of diverse races and ethnicities and all women. Eithne Quinn maps the emergence of the Black Hollywood Renaissance in the 1960s, led by African American artists who were prominent activists in the civil rights freedom movement and whose cinematic work foregrounded a Black liberation political aesthetic.[6] Ruth Feldstein examines how prominent Black women performers, such as Diahann Carroll, Lena Horne, Abbey Lincoln, Cicely Tyson—and, adding to the list, Ruby Dee and Diana Sands—whose work traversed film, television, theater, and music, as entertainers engaged Black activism within popular culture platforms creating representations of Black second-wave feminism as part of the projects in which they were involved.[7]

However, Black filmmaking in Hollywood, specifically the role of director, was dominated by men. The first three Black directors who made feature films for major studios were Gordon Parks Sr. (*The Learning Tree*, Warner Bros.–Seven Art, 1969), Ossie Davis (*Cotton Comes to Harlem*, United Artists, 1970), and Melvin Van Peebles (*Watermelon Man*, Columbia, 1970). Black women directors during these years, who were producing narrative films in the United States, often starting with short films and then moving into longer formats and features, such as Kathleen Collins, Julie Dash, Alile Sharon Larkin, and Jessie Maple, would build their careers outside of Hollywood, working in different creative roles and as part of a variety of independent production cultures, including, for some, film school.[8]

Angelou's ambition to write, produce, and direct film and television during these years is situated within this historical turn of Black cinematic production. She was part of a generation of African American women writers, who, like Toni Morrison and Alice Walker, began their literary careers in the early 1970s and shaped Black second-wave feminism in ways that overlapped commercial media and social justice politics. Activism that was mobilizing within the media industry during this era challenged the institutionalized racism and sexism that defined the entertainment industry; however, these movements frequently failed to recognize the necessity of intersectionality within their own reform platforms. The fight for racial justice within Hollywood prioritized better employment for men of color; feminist reform focused on improving the hiring of white women in positions of creative and financial power.[9] Angelou would find herself navigating these gender and racial divides as they manifested during these years.

Public Television, a Starting Place: *Blacks, Blues, Black!*

In February 1968, Dr. King had asked Angelou, then living in New York City, to lead a fundraising tour on behalf of the Poor People's Campaign being planned by the Southern Christian Leadership Conference. Angelou recounts, in the final chapters of her sixth autobiography, *A Song Flung Up to Heaven*, how on April 4, her fortieth birthday, as she prepared for her party, her close friend Dolly McPherson called to tell her that King had been murdered.[10] Angelou describes how during the weeks following King's death, her close friend James Baldwin "pried me lose from my despair" by taking her to dinner at Jules and Judy Feiffer's home. Judy would recommend Angelou to editor Robert Loomis of Random House, as an author to pursue, and Loomis would spend some time convincing Angelou to write her first memoir, *I Know Why the Caged Bird Sings*. Exactly at this time, Angelou would be offered the opportunity to write, produce, and host *Blacks, Blues, Black!* a ten-part series for San Francisco public television channel KQED that focused on the relationship between African and Black American culture and history.[11] Angelou frames the conclusion of the memoir as a time of tremendous loss met with professional and creative opportunity. Both the book and the television series would mark a turning point for her maturity as a multimedia artist and her growth as a public figure within a commercial marketplace.

The previous year, President Lyndon Johnson had formed the National Advisory Commission on Civil Disorders to investigate the protests and civil uprisings that had taken place across the United States in 1967. The commission's findings, known as the Kerner Report, were released to the public on February 29, 1968. Crucial to the commission's findings was that the news media had failed to report sufficiently on the events as they expressly related to historical and systemic racism that informed the realities of inequality and injustice experienced by Black Americans. As Allison Perlman argues, the release of the Kerner Report contributed to the work of the Black Freedom

Movement to reform local television's racist and discriminatory hiring and programming practices, specifically stations located in the American South.[12] The timing of the report and the murder of Dr. King, just months apart in 1968, bolstered the mission of National Education Television (NET) to produce programming that represented more accurately, and through different perspectives, the experiences of race and racism in the United States.[13] It was within this historical moment, when social activism, politics, and public television's need for innovative and topical programming were all responding to a nation in crisis, that Angelou was presented with the opportunity to move into broadcasting.

A funding recipient of NET, KQED's *Blacks, Blues, Black!* fell in line with the Kerner Report's mandate for better and more equitable television programming; notably, the series' producers cited the report in their proposal.[14] The program revolved around Angelou as the host, and on her first television showcase she was already a star: "The program series is only possible because of the unique talents of the producer and host for the series, Miss Maya Angelou. . . . Except for her sex, Miss Angelou would be known as a Renaissance Man."[15] The show's format was described as similar to a Black studies program celebrating and exploring "Negro history, art, culture, and society [that] will be examined from the inside by Blacks and for Blacks."[16] Crucial to the series was the target African American audience, and while white audiences were expected to benefit from the show greatly, "for the first time, [the Bay Area Black community's] attitudes will be reflected openly and fully in a public media, unaltered and untouched by white interpreters and without white interposition."[17]

The KQED budget was small, and the station's interests were ambitious.[18] Correspondence suggests the show came together quickly. In April 1968, Gerald G. Marans, KQED's associate director of programming, had given word that plans for the project should move forward.[19] A few months later, in June, the station hosted a reception for "Miss Angelou, a resident of Ghana and a citizen of the United States."[20] On July 8, 1968, the first episode aired on KQED, Channel 9.[21]

Blacks, Blues, Black! is a stylistically complex television series and a culturally rich media text constructed of layers of literary reviews and historical references, visual collage in photos, illustrations, footage, and field interviews with local business owners, educators, and students of all ages. Every episode featured music and dance, from Africa and America, performed on the set, with Angelou, wearing a different exquisite African print dress, regularly joining in. As host, Angelou steered the segments by singing, reciting poetry, and discussing topical subjects such as the education of Black young people, the history of racism and violence in the United States, the African slave trade, and profiles of African American entrepreneurs.

"Maya just doesn't stand in front of the color camera for a solid hour and lecture," observed John Stanley of the *San Francisco Sunday Examiner and Chronicle*. "She is conscious of pace and mood and is continually injecting some device . . . to illustrate her points. She is low-key and effective."[22] Angelou is eloquent and dynamic. She fumbles her lines in a conversational way, suggesting that she is not reading from cue cards, notes, or a teleprompter. And still she has an expert command of the screen as she lists global statistics, recites lines of verse, and frames sociological debates. The low-budget production value of public television in 1968 forced each episode to utilize the set—and the television frame—to its fullest capacity, filling it with musicians, dance troupes, poets, a live audience, and African art borrowed from neighboring university collections. Guests and topics registered on a national and global scale, but Angelou's attention was predominantly local to California, presumably because of budgetary restraints and to adhere to the short production schedule. Dancers Blondell Breed and Danny Duncan joined Angelou throughout the series, performing role-plays and interpretive dance sets.

Angelou was clear in her intentions with the series, explaining to local press at the time of its premiere: "I'm not here to win a popularity contest. I want to stimulate Black people. I want to show underprivileged Black children can be motivated."[23] *Blacks, Blues, Black!* provided Angelou with tremendous creative freedom that allowed her to explore a range of topics pertaining to Black culture—African and American—and to experiment with forms of presentation that were allowable in public television, and expected of KQED. Unfortunately, feature filmmaking and network television would not be as nurturing an environment.

Georgia on My Mind

In 1969, Random House published the first of Maya Angelou's seven autobiographies, *I Know Why the Caged Bird Sings*. The book chronicled Angelou's childhood years growing up in Stamps, Arkansas, and the traumas of racism and sexual assault she experienced as a girl; it also described her beloved grandmother, brother, uncle, and teacher, who encouraged and supported her. The memoir was a bestseller and was nominated for the National Book Award in 1971. In 1971, *Variety* announced that Maya Angelou would write and direct the screen adaptation of her autobiography for the production company

Kelly-Jordan Enterprises. The article emphasized a historical first: "The belief is that it will be the first feature film directed by a black woman."[24] Business partners Quentin Kelly, who was white, and Jack Jordan, who was African American, marketed their company as focused on Black films—in content and filmmakers.[25]

In April 1972, Kelly and Jordan ran a full-page advertisement in *Variety* announcing the company's three upcoming productions. *Honeybaby, Honeybaby*, starring Diana Sands in the performer's final film before her death of cancer at age thirty-nine in 1973, would be directed by Michael Schultz, his second feature film. *Night In . . . Night Out (Story of an Obsession)*, written, directed and co-starring Bill Gunn, was originally released as *Ganja & Hess* but was reedited and rereleased by the producers. The third title, *I Know Why the Caged Bird Sings*, was to be written and directed by Maya Angelou. The ad also congratulated Sands on her "projected" Academy Award performance in *Georgia, Georgia*, highlighting positive blurbs from reviews in an effort to create a media buzz.[26] *Georgia, Georgia*, written by Angelou, who also wrote songs for the film's soundtrack, and directed by Stig Bjorkman, who was Swedish, was the second theatrical feature film produced by Kelly and Jordan.[27] For this small, independent production company, much was resting on the picture's box office success to promote the subsequent titles in production, and Sands, an Emmy and Tony Award nominated actress and critically acclaimed for her screen roles in *A Raisin in the Sun* (1961) and *The Landlord* (1970), was crucial to its marketing.

Georgia, Georgia stars Diana Sands as Georgia Martin, a famed and glamorous American singer on a European concert tour. She is accompanied by her loyal and overbearing gay manager, Herbert (Roger Furman), who worships the star and is single-minded about her success, and by her domineering surrogate stage mother, Mrs. Alberta Anderson (Minnie Gentry), whose traditional values regarding women's sexuality and female independence and her hatred for whites stifle the protagonist, while her selfless care and affection provides comfort. The three are locked in an abusive codependent bond. When the trio stops over in Stockholm, Georgia falls in love with a white American expatriate photographer and Vietnam veteran (Dirk Benedict) struggling with his own emotional and sexual traumas. At the same time, Mrs. Anderson connects with a group of African American Vietnam defectors who convince the older woman to persuade Georgia to use her stardom to rally support for their cause. Georgia is elated about her new love, but the interracial romance unhinges her entourage, and the film ends in a haunting final scene.

Georgia, Georgia was reviewed widely, and most critics were ecstatic to see Angelou, the acclaimed author, turn her talents to screenwriting, recognizing her significance as one of the first Black women to write an original script for the screen. Sands in the lead role received enormous praise. The majority of reviews also cited an inconsistent script and a miscast director, who, as a white Swedish man with only one (Swedish) film to his credit, was ill-equipped to interpret the intricate story of an African American woman, adored by everyone but struggling to love herself. The film prompted a range of critical response, from Black and white reviewers, generating some debate.

Gail Rock from *Women's Wear Daily*, noting how a film that is "full of promise" fell short, still stood up for *Georgia, Georgia* and its potential, calling it "one of the most interesting and thoughtful attempts to bring a discussion of black identity to the screen, and Ms. Angelou's material deserves a little more careful production than it gets here."[28] The *New York Amsterdam News* featured opposing reviews of the film by two critics. Rosa Guy, a close friend of Angelou's, praised the screenwriter for presenting an "American dilemma": "What is the responsibility of those Blacks who have 'made it' to the unknown strugglers, hopelessly ensnared in the on-going battle to maintain a sense of decency and high morality against the American power structure?" Clayton Riley gave a counterpoint, finding the characters thinly drawn, writing that while Sands "is a gem of constant brilliance . . . [she does] battle with a screenplay by Maya Angelou, that is often grossly written and wildly uneven."[29] Peter Bailey, associate editor of *Ebony* magazine, writing in the *New York Times*, was intrigued by the film's portrayal of the relationship between the strident Mrs. Anderson, who disapproves of her charge's interracial affair, and Georgia, who strives to distance herself from Black identity and Black politics. "I found what I saw interesting and provocative," Bailey explained. "I left the theater feeling that several important questions about [Angelou's] characters were still unanswered." For him, Bjorkman was "not that up on what complex Black women like Georgia Martin and Alberta Anderson are all about." His wish was that Angelou had written *and* directed the film.[30]

Angelou expressed strong feelings as to where the production, and specifically Bjorkman, failed in bringing her script to the screen. "I knew I should have directed it," said a disappointed Angelou months after the film's release. "The director, being European, was once removed; being Swedish, was twice removed."[31] Kelly and Jordan had justified Bjorkman's hiring because the producers "wanted a man who could bring a new perspective to Americans and an American problem."[32] Of course, hiring an African American woman, for the first time in history, to direct her own script would have provided a never before seen "new perspective." But still, Angelou, at least in the press, was open to criticisms, admitting that the script was uneven: "I can see that now, myself. But it was my first film and those kinds of mistakes I will avoid next time."[33]

Angelou's work during this time was invested in exploring heterosexual relationships, social and romantic, in the context of race—racial identity and empowerment—and the impact of racism on African Americans, through the perspective of a Black female character. Her handwritten treatment of the script and the finished film are very similar, including the film's shocking ending. However, what stands out in her descriptive notes setting up the story is the struggle and quest for love. One treatment draft, entitled "Georgia: A Movie Treatment by Maya Angelou," begins with: "Man is born in love naturally and naturally born to love. . . . In *Georgia* we see immediately two people whose need for love are [sic] so great they feel they must deny its demands."[34] For her, the film was an expression of something personal. "The film says something specific about my life," she confessed. "I haven't had a substantial relationship with a Black American man in 21 years."[35]

Visions of Women Directors

Angelou was still slated to write and direct *I Know Why the Caged Bird Sings* for Kelly-Jordan Enterprises in 1974, although the film had been in static pre-production going on four years.[36] That same year, it was reported in *Variety* that Quentin Kelly and Jack Jordan had ended their partnership, with Jordan resigning.[37] As her feature film deal stalled, Angelou encountered opportunities to direct short films in the nonprofit sector, where the budgets were small but so were the financial pressures, opening up a creative space with less interference. In 1974 she was accepted to the first year of the American Film Institute's Directing Workshop for Women (DWW).[38] The following year Angelou was a participant in *Visions*, an anthology drama series produced by Los Angeles public television station KCET, which would be broadcast nationally on PBS. Both production initiatives were designed to address the rampant hiring inequities in the film and television industry. The number of working women directors during the 1970s was abominable. In 1979, the Women's Steering Committee of the Directors Guild of America published this statistic: between 1949 and 1979, 7,332 feature films were made and released by major distributors. Women directed 14, or 0.19 percent, of those 7,332 films.[39] All the women represented in this data set were white.

The DWW was an example of a feminist intervention to support women seeking opportunities to direct, primarily feature films and scripted television for the three major networks. Workshop participants had established careers in some part of the media industry but had not yet directed a studio feature film. Angelou and her cohort, which included performers Ellen Burstyn, Lee Grant, Lily Tomlin; producer Julia Phillips; studio executive Nessa Hyams; and independent filmmakers Karen Arthur and Juleen Compton, were expected to make two short films, on videotape, for a budget of $300, which could be used as calling cards as they pursued the profession. Angelou, whose celebrity status and list of accomplishments and credits by 1974 made her a high-profile and highly qualified candidate (she would be elected to the organization's Board of Trustees in 1975[40]) was the only African American participant, and the only woman of color accepted that year. The DWW, in its early years, struggled to recognize the connection between gendered and racial discrimination, and while the program set out to confront sexism, it failed to make race and ethnicity equal priorities.[41]

The *Visions* anthology series was produced by veteran television executive Barbara Schultz. The program invested in up-and-coming artists, foregrounding stories that focused on gender, race, sexuality, and national identity, portrayed in ways that were often considered controversial for network television and mainstream feature films. The running times for the films were under ninety minutes, and the budgets were around $200,000. Schultz considered it important to seek out new writers. "It was discovery time," she said of the 3,000 unsolicited manuscript submissions the production received. "We found very exciting people, some that I'm certain will become major figures." Alexis De Veaux, an African American woman, whose scripts, *Tapestry* and *Circles*, Angelou directed, was one of the new writers. Schultz described De Veaux, a participant in Budd Schulberg's Frederick Douglass Writers Workshop in Harlem, as "one of the most remarkable young talents I have ever come in contact with."[42]

Although these three films are smaller, in scope and format, than *Georgia, Georgia*, Angelou continued to explore Black women's interiority in each of them. Her DWW film *All Day Long* (1975), which she wrote and directed, follows middle schooler Jimmy B (Marc Copage), who lives with his Aunt Gloria (Ketty Lester), who is in her thirties and is beautiful, loving, confident, and lonely. When it is revealed that Buddy Boy (Andre Edwards), an older teen who befriends Jimmy B, has had an affair with Gloria, the aunt must make amends with her disappointed nephew. The filmmaker acknowledges Gloria's need and desire for physical and emotional love and gives her space, within the cinematic frame, to express joy and sadness.[43] *Tapestry* (56 minutes) and *Circles* (22 minutes), which were broadcast together, are separate stories that overlap thematically.[44] In *Tapestry*, Jet (Gloria Jones Schultz), a law student, struggles to reconcile her aspirations to build a career rooted in social justice work with the expectations of her peer group consumed by relationships and lifestyle choices. Retha (Tamu), in *Circles*, clashes with her pious and traditional-minded grandmother in a battle of self-determination when the young woman is offered a chance to travel with her dance troupe to Africa. In both films, Angelou and De Veaux examine the legacy of generational conflict and family history shaped by religious views, framed by feminist themes of professional empowerment and personal agency, in stories led by Black female protagonists.[45]

Network Television and the Broadcast Blues

By the late 1970s, Angelou had moved away from feature film production (not by choice) and expanded her broadcast experience to include not only public television but also network programming. She sold the rights to *I Know Why the Caged Bird Sings* to Tomorrow Entertainment in 1977, and the book was made into a television movie for NBC, airing in 1979, with Angelou as cowriter but not director. The cast featured leading African American actresses Diahann Carroll, Ruby Dee, Esther Rolle, and Madge Sinclair and introduced Constance Good. The experience was a difficult one for Angelou, who battled with co-screenwriter Leonora Thuna and was greatly disappointed that she did not get the chance to direct.[46] "I wanted so badly to direct the film . . . if you butt your head against a stone wall long enough, at some point, you realize the wall is stone and that your head is flesh and bone. So I gave it up."[47]

Angelou's next project, another television movie, *Sister, Sister*, was produced for Twentieth Century-Fox, where she was under contract. Starring Carroll again, with Rosalind Cash and Irene Cara, as the Lovejoy sisters, the telefilm traced the fissures within a Black family bonded and broken by its relationship with the Black church and a legacy of Black migration between the South and North. During a time when television dramas featuring an African American cast were rare, anticipation for *Sister, Sister* was high. The program was completed in 1979 and sat on the shelf at NBC until finally airing in 1982. "Black drama remains the invisible man for all seasons on commercial TV," lamented Howard Rosenberg, advocating for the program in the *Los Angeles Times*, "especially when it comes to stories about middle-class blacks."[48] Angelou had fought with the director, John Berry, over script and producing credits.[49] Finally, when the movie was set to be broadcast, the white conservative Mississippi-based Coalition for Better Television launched a boycott of the show, claiming that it portrayed "negative stereotyping of Christian people."[50] Support from viewers and critics poured in, and the movie's ratings took a well-deserved bump from the controversy.[51]

A Busy Decade of Unproduced Projects

While the 1970s were a prolific and ambitious era for Angelou in her pursuit of a career in writing, directing, and producing film and television, and her portfolio exploded with projects across every media platform, still, directing a feature film was impossible. Throughout this decade, she was in a constant state of announcement: her name was often in the press with the promise of being hired to direct feature films. In March 1972, she told the *New York Times* that she was going to direct a film by Alex Haley, who was a close friend.[52] Jim Cleaver, writing for the *Los Angeles Sentinel* in July 1975, announced that Angelou was set to direct a film titled *Justice*, "within a matter of weeks," starring television actress Mittie Lawrence as a Black female lawyer, karate expert, and concert pianist.[53] In January 1976, the American Film Institute's "member news" reported that Angelou had to leave the Board of Trustees' meeting early to catch a flight to Rome where she had been offered a film to direct.[54] In June 1977, *Variety* announced that she would write the screenplay for a feature film on the life of civil rights activist Fannie Lou Hamer, to be played by Della Reese, with producer Frank Evans negotiating for theater director and actress Vinette Carroll to direct.[55] That same year, Angelou was in the running to direct episodes of the miniseries *Roots*, but she was thought to be not experienced enough, and the pressures of scheduling and production costs removed her from consideration.[56] Her determination and creative energy were relentless, as were the obstacles in the way of her employment. Speaking to the *Los Angeles Times* in 1976, Angelou expressed her desire to make films: "I need very much to be taken seriously in film. I need to have someone who trusts me trusting myself to risk the money. I know I will have to do a number of Z (as opposed to B) pictures. I don't mind."[57] One can only wonder what Z films Angelou was being offered at the time—or, rather, what movies she considered to be Z films. What is clear were the financial constraints and anxiety she experienced—and, perhaps more accurately, caused in those hiring—as a first-time African American woman filmmaker.

During these years, Angelou consistently discussed her creative work, as an African American woman artist who had lived and worked abroad in Africa and Europe, at the intersection of gender, race, and socioeconomic class, geographic location, and national identity. Her film and television work focused on Black culture and frequently centered on a Black female protagonist; as a public figure and artist, she demonstrated great skill at infusing commercial media with political meaning that registered deeply with both Black and non-Black audiences. As the 1970s came to a close, Angelou prepared to leave Hollywood for Wake Forest University in North Carolina, where she would become a full-time faculty member. "It's a very rough place," she admitted. "I won't say I'm not coming back. You can't rule that out."[58] In fact, she would return many times to the film and television industry as a performer, writer, and finally as director in 1998 when she made her debut, *Down in the Delta* (Showtime Networks). Maya Angelou's inability to realize her full potential during these formative years in Hollywood points directly to the industry's racist and sexist value system that would not, during a historical period of great change and upheaval, invest in the opportunity for a Black woman filmmaker to try, fail, and quite possibly succeed.

Notes

Portions of this chapter appear in Maya Montañez Smukler, *Liberating Hollywood: Women Directors and the Feminist Reform of 1970s American Cinema* (New Brunswick, NJ: Rutgers University Press, 2019).

1 All of Angelou's autobiographies were published by Random House: *I Know Why the Caged Bird Sings* (1969), *Gather Together in My Name* (1974), *Singin' and Swingin' and Gettin' Merry Like Christmas* (1976), *The Heart of a Woman* (1981), *All God's Children Need Traveling Shoes* (1986), *A Song Flung Up to Heaven* (2002), and *Mom & Me & Mom* (2013).

2 Other screenplays by Black women writers that were produced during these years include Ruby Dee's *Uptight* (1968), cowritten with Jules Dassin and Julian Mayfield; Lorraine Hansberry's adaptation of her play *A Raisin in the Sun* (1961); and J. E. Franklin's adaption of her play *Black Girl* (1972).

3 George Gent, "Black Women Take Roles as Directors," *New York Times*, November 17, 1971, 40.

4 Angelou's archival collections are held at the New York Public Library Schomburg Center for Research in Black Culture and Special Collections and at Z. Smith Reynolds Library, Wake Forest University. Due to the COVID-19 pandemic, access to these collections was limited. Special thanks to Tanya Zanish-Belcher and her

colleagues at Wake Forest University for providing digital materials. Additional thanks to Hayley O'Malley for sharing her insights regarding these special collections.

5 For an examination of Angelou's memoirs demonstrating the author's duality as a revolutionary Black artist and a mainstream feminist, see Cheryl Higashida, *Black Internationalist Feminism: Women Writers of the Black Left, 1945–1995* (Urbana: University of Illinois Press, 2011).

6 Eithne Quinn, *A Piece of the Action: Race and Labor in Post–Civil Rights Hollywood* (New York: Columbia University Press, 2020).

7 Ruth Feldstein, *How It Feels to Be Free: Black Women Entertainers and the Civil Rights Movement* (Oxford: Oxford University Press, 2013).

8 For example, see chapters in this collection by Virginia Bonner (on the L.A. Rebellion) and Nicholas Forster (on Jessie Maple); also Jacqueline Bobo, ed., *Black Women Film & Video Artists* (New York: Routledge, 1998); Allyson Nadia Field, Jan-Christopher Horak, Jacqueline Najuma Stewart, eds., *L.A. Rebellion: Creating a New Black Cinema* (Oakland: University of California Press, 2015); L.H. Stallings, *The Afterlives of Kathleen Collins: A Black Woman Filmmaker's Search for New Life* (Bloomington: Indiana University Press, 2021); Christina N. Baker, *Black Women Directors* (New Brunswick, NJ: Rutgers University Press, 2022)

9 For histories of gender and race in 1970s Hollywood, with emphasis on directors, see Montañez Smukler, *Liberating Hollywood*; Quinn, *A Piece of the Action.*

10 Maya Angelou, *A Song Flung Up to Heaven* (New York: Random House, 2002), chap. 29.

11 *Blacks, Blues, Black!* is an extraordinary cultural and historical text. All ten episodes were preserved by archivist Alex Cherian, Bay Area TV Archive at San Francisco State University, with support from the Library of Congress and became available online in 2014 (https://diva.sfsu.edu/collections/sfbatv).

12 Allison Perlman, *Public Interests: Media Advocacy and Struggles over U.S. Television* (New Brunswick, NJ: Rutgers University Press, 2016), chap. 2.

13 Perlman, 57.

14 KQED proposal, page 2, *Blacks, Blues, Black!*, box 2, folder 8, Maya Angelou Film and Theater Collection (MS597) (hereafter MAFTC, ZSR), Wake Forest University, Winston-Salem, North Carolina.

15 KQED proposal, 4.

16 KQED proposal, 2.

17 KQED proposal, 3.

18 For a history of KQED, see James Day, *The Vanishing Vision*, 45, UC Press E-Books Collection, 1982–2004.

19 Letter from Adele Davidson to Maya Angelou, April 8, 1968; letter from Gerald G. Marans to Maya Angelou, April 10, 1968; letter from Jonathan C. Rice to Maya Angelou, May 10, 1968, box 2, folder 10, MAFTC, ZSR.

20 *Blacks, Blues, Black!* publicity release, June 27, 1968, box 65, folder 5, MAFTC, ZSR.

21 "Tonight's Best Bets on Television," *San Francisco Examiner*, July 8, 1968, 33.

22 John Stanley, "Television: Blacks, Blues and 24 Robbers," *San Francisco Sunday Examiner and Chronicle*, August 4, 1968, 16.

23 Dwight Newton, "Will Blacks Still Like Her Next Week?," *San Francisco Sunday Examiner and Chronicle*, July 21, 1968, 5.

24 "'L. S. Fields' ('Derby') Really Quentin Kelly; Quits Group W for Pix," *Variety*, July 28, 1971, 1, 31.

25 Frank Segers, "Quent Kelly Enterprises Succeeds Two-Tone Producing Partnership; No 'Head-Busting' of Whites," *Variety*, November 20, 1974, 3.

26 "Congratulations Diana Sands," *Variety*, April 5, 1972, 23.

27 "'L. S. Fields' ('Derby') Really Quentin Kelly."

28 Gail Rock, "Flicks: 'Georgia, Georgia,'" *Women's Wear Daily*, March 13, 1972, 14.

29 Rosa Guy and Clayton Riley, "'Georgia, Georgia' Reviewed by Amsterdam News Critics," *New York Amsterdam News*, March 25, 1972, D4.

30 Peter Bailey, "A Black Woman with White Fever," *New York Times*, March 26, 1972, D13.

31 Jane Julianelli, "Maya Angelou," *Harper's Bazaar*, November 1972, 124.

32 Bailey, "A Black Woman with White Fever," D13.

33 George Goodman Jr., "Maya Angelou's Lonely, Black Outlook," *New York Times*, March 24, 1972, 28.

34 "Georgia: A Movie Treatment by Maya Angelou," p. 1, Manuscript (1 stenographer's notebook and 2 legal pads), box 65, folder 7, MAFTC, ZSR.

35 Goodman, "Maya Angelou's Lonely, Black Outlook," 28.

36 "3 Kelly-Jordan Pix; Add Exorcism to 'Ganja'; Diana Sands' Finale," *Variety*, April 17, 1974, 4.

37 Segers "Quent Kelly Enterprises Succeeds Two-Tone Producing Partnership," 3.

38 For histories on the DWW, see Philis M. Barragán Goetz, "Breaking Away from Reverence and Rape: The AFI Directing Workshop for Women, Feminism, and the Politics of the Accidental Archive," *The Moving Image: The Journal of the Association of Moving Image Archivists* 15, no. 2 (Fall 2015): 50–71; Jan Haag, "Women Directors in Hollywood," 2007, http://janhaag.com/ESTheDWW.html; Montañez Smukler, *Liberating Hollywood*, chap. 3.

39 Letter to signatories from Michael Franklin regarding employment statistics, June 20, 1980, "DGA Clipping File," Margaret Herrick Library, Los Angeles, CA.

40 "AFI Member News," *American Film*, October 1, 1975, 73.

41 The DWW's selection of so few women of color during the program's first years is described by Jan Haag, who speculates that because the workshop received federal funding, the lack of racial diversity could have been negligible in accordance with Title VII of the Civil Rights Act, in correspondence with Barragán Goetz, "Breaking Away from Reverence and Rape," 57, 61n60.

42 Cecil Smith, [no title], *Los Angeles Times*, July 20, 1975, S2.

43 For a study of *All Day Long*, see Hayley O'Malley, "All Day Long," *Black One Shot*, *ASAP Journal*, September 24, 2020, https://asapjournal.com/16-3-all-day-long-hayley-omalley/. Special thanks to archivist Emily Wittenberg and librarian Robert Vaughn at the Louis B. Mayer Library, AFI, for providing access to *ALL DAY LONG* (1975) ©American Film Institute.

44 "Tapestry and Circles," *Visions*, KCET, December 30, 1976, Archive Research and Study Center, UCLA Film & Television Archive, University of California, Los Angeles.

45 Some descriptions here build on Maya Montañez Smukler, "'The Tapestry' and Maya Angelou Behind the Camera," *Screen Slate*, March 4, 2021, https://www.screenslate.com/articles/tapestry-and-maya-angelou-behind-camera.

46 Howard Rosenberg, "Angelou and Baldwin Speaking Out Again: Writer Making Inroads in TV, a 'White' Industry," *Los Angeles Times*, April 27, 1979, E1.

47 Howard Taylor, "She Wants to Change TV's Image of Blacks," *New York Times*, April 22, 1979, D35.

48 Howard Rosenberg, "NBC Delays Showing 2 Black Productions," *Los Angeles Times*, April 24, 1981, G1.

49 For a discussion of Angelou's difficulties making *Sister, Sister*, see Paul du Feu, *In Good Company: A Story in Black & White* (Edinburgh: Mainstream Publishing, 1991), chap. 12.

50 Sally Bedell, "Advertisers Asked to Drop Coming NBC Movie," *New York Times*, June 3, 1982, C22; Ida Peters, "Preempting of 'Sister, Sister' Draws Flood of Irate Calls," *Afro-American*, June 26, 1982, 11.

51 Stanley G. Robertson, "'Sister, Sister': An Overnight Success in the Nielsens," *Los Angeles Sentinel*, June 17, 1982, A3.

52 Goodman, "Maya Angelou's Lonely, Black Outlook," 28.

53 Jim Cleaver, "Kleaver's Klippins: In Open Admiration of Maya Angelou," *Los Angeles Sentinel*, July 10, 1975, A7.

54 "AFI Member News," *American Film*, January 1, 1976, 63.

55 "No Back-Seat Fannie," *Variety*, June 29, 1977, 3.

56 Curt Davis, "Maya Angelou: And Still She Rises," *Encore American & Worldwide News*, September 12, 1977, 28–32, in *Conversations with Maya Angelou*, ed. Jeffery M. Elliot (Jackson: University Press of Mississippi, 1989), 71.

57 Beth Ann Krier, "Maya Angelou: No Longer a Caged Bird," *Los Angeles Times*, September 24, 1976, A12.

58 Wayne Warga, "Author! Author! Another Phase for Maya Angelou," *Los Angeles Times*, November 5, 1981, G27.

Part 2

Text

_____

6

Women Editors in New Hollywood

Cutting Down on the Raging Bullshit

KAREN PEARLMAN

> It's time to stop imagining that "it's really the director" who does the editing.
>
> **SU FRIEDRICH**, "Edited By: Women Film Editors"

In his salacious "tell-all" book about New Hollywood, *Easy Riders, Raging Bulls* (1999), author Peter Biskind elevates stoned sexual predators of the 1960s and 1970s American movie industry to the status of saviors of cinema, detailing multiple sensational examples of excess and tacitly positioning these as the signs of individual genius.[1] Given the deep mythology in Anglo-European culture that "genius" is generally accompanied by bad behavior,[2] this association of personal and professional self-indulgence with genius is commonplace, and the idea of "New Hollywood" as an entity or movement is deeply entangled with it.[3] However, this chapter will suggest that the cocktail of good ideas and bad behavior is not actually what gets movies made.

The chapter begins with a very brief discussion of some misapprehensions about "authorship" that attribute aspects of filmmaking to directors in New Hollywood that are actually demonstrably being done partly or wholly by others. It then asks, what do editors, particularly the women editors of New Hollywood, actually do that is misapprehended? What do editors do to shape movement as part of the generation of a film's form and style, and how could this work be understood as a mode of thinking not "only or merely" technical?[4] Drawing on a decades-long theoretical and practical body of work on editing, I will argue that film editors' work shapes the movement of story, movement of emotion, and movement of images and sound into coherent and compelling cinematic structures and rhythms.[5] Further, these structures and rhythms are not inevitable and are not intrinsic to the script or shot materials; rather, they are the culmination of thousands of decisions that editors make about how the pieces will come together. They are therefore expressions of the editor's attitudes and ideas in movement—the edits are the editor's "thoughts."[6]

Some examples of significant passages of films shaped by women editors of New Hollywood are then analyzed, briefly, to substantiate the argument that their work is creative and intellectual participation in the generation of films and to provide some detail of their specific strategies and actions in *making* the films on which they worked. In conclusion, I propose that an understanding of the actual work of editors allows us to see a finished film not as an expression of one man's mind but as the distributed creative cognizing of a community of practice, in this case the community of women editors who may have, by saving various movies, *actually* "saved Hollywood."[7]

The Authorship Problem

There are, of course, many strong theoretical challenges to the "director as author" idea.[8] However, in postwar Europe the long-standing mythologizing of genius as a trait of individual artists combined with the clear need for ways to see cinema as an art form rather than a fairground attraction to create a fertile cultural ground for the notion that films have individual authors. When Alexandre Astruc declared, in 1948, that a new form of cinema was emerging and that the "film-maker/author writes with his camera as a writer writes with his pen,"[9] he tapped into what Dana Polan calls deep cultural "auteur desires."[10]

Andrew Sarris famously compacted this idea (and Truffaut's follow-ups on it in *Cahiers du Cinéma*) into the "auteur theory." Sarris's timing was good. The Hollywood studio system was, in the early 1960s, once again in transition. The industrial methods of movie making had been disrupted (by a successful antitrust lawsuit), so this new idea about individuals making movies rather than studios making them was able to work its way into the growing cracks in the system. Interestingly, the critical adoption of the idea by Sarris (in 1962) to the American/Hollywood context preceded the first English translation of Astruc's manifesto (in 1968) by six years. I would like to suggest that, perhaps because the idea of director as auteur had already taken hold and become popular, there are some ideas in Astruc's essay that were overlooked but which could be useful.

The first is that Astruc clearly conceived of the camera as pen and the director as the author who wields it as a *metaphor*. Astruc writes: "I would like to call this new age of cinema the age of camera-stylo (camera-pen). This metaphor has a very precise sense."[11] Thus, from the outset, a suggestive metaphor, not a statement of fact, and Astruc is clear about the limits of his metaphor. Although cinema may be as flexible as written language, he does not see it as a written language but as an art of movement: "Its primary function is to move."[12]

This points to a significant role in authorship for anyone who deals with movement in the cinema and composing it. This could be actors (who devise their own expressive movement), cinematographers (who move the camera and are responsible for the capture of moving images), even designers (who create the space in which movement occurs). However, I will limit this chapter's discussion to editors as choreographers, composers, and conductors of movement.[13] I will take Astruc's idea about movement as a "primary function" of film and consider how editing shapes this movement, to show, that yes, cinema is an art, but no, it is not an art authored solely by an individual director.

Agency and Visibility in Shaping Movement

Editing as an expressive technique is largely taken for granted.
—Valerie Orpen, *Film Editing: The Art of the Expressive*

It is not unusual to hear "good" editing described as "invisible." The American Cinema Editors Guild, for example, celebrates mastery of the "Invisible

Art."[14] However, unless the film is invisible, the editing is not actually invisible.[15] We may not see edits, but we see the flow of movement (moving pictures, a movie). This flow of movement has been designed, shaped, and ultimately determined by the editor, and unfortunately, calling editing "invisible," even if meant as praise, occludes the creative input of the editor—the editor who, in New Hollywood, was significantly more likely to be a woman than was the director or cinematographer. In order to remove the invisibility cloak from around the editor's shoulders, two things are necessary: first, an understanding of what editors do, and second, some ways of *seeing* what they create.

What Editors Do

Editors are responsible for piecing together the flow of three kinds of movement in a film. These are the movement of events, movement of emotions, and movement of image and sound.[16] Editors shape these flows through a process of making decisions about which shot to use, where, and for how long, which is a deceptively simple description of the complex cognitive process of responsive and generative creative work that three-time Academy Award–winning editor Thelma Schoonmaker calls "the art of decision making."[17] Editors often describe their decision-making processes with variations on the word "intuitive,"[18] which is a catch-all word for knowledge and ability that has been acquired through implicit learning and experience.[19] However, "intuitive" does not mean there is not a wealth of expertise at work; it simply means that much of the expertise is embodied, embedded or enactive and therefore functioning at a preconscious level.

A short list of the kinds of expertise editors refer to under the umbrella term "intuitive" might include the following:

- Interpersonal expertise in recognizing and responding to a director's partially or inexactly articulated "desires"[20]
- Expertise in design of appropriate story shapes for the context of a particular production
- Sensory/aesthetic expertise in perceiving potential rhythms and dynamics of timing, pacing, and trajectory phrasing inherent in uncut material[21]
- Memory expertise that supports the "search and retrieval" of specific material from among many hours of possible options[22]
- Expertise of "kinaesthetic imagination" deployed when considering which options to select and try out from the material[23]

- Choreographic expertise that supports the shaping of movement from moment to moment, and overall, into satisfactory phrasing of events, emotions, and visual/aural experiences
- Finally, what might be called "technical" expertise, which refers to editors' embedded mastery of tools of editing—be they the scissors and glue of the 1920s, the motorized flatbeds of the 1970s, or the digital editing software widely in use since the late 1990s.

Unfortunately for editors, the only instance of this expertise that is actually visible in action is their "technical" expertise of operating the gear. The rest of it takes place in a speedy, unspoken domain of distributed cognition whereby ideas are generated and realized through the entanglement of brains, bodies, filmed material, and context.[24] That only the interaction with tools is visible leads to what Raymond Williams would call a division along "class lines" of editors' expertise, whereby editing is associated with "operation of the technology itself" and this creates an opportunity for "doubt whether such workers were truly part of cultural production."[25]

Indeed, in America, anyone involved in the direct handling of tools on a filmmaking set is referred to as a "technician," a "class" that leads to exclusion from authorship claims in both the cultural and the legal domain.[26] The question that arises is how to peel away the occluding mask of invisibility and actually see the editor's professional dexterity with tools and hands as itself a "form of cognizing,"[27] part of the thinking, the ideation, the creative and intellectual work required to make a film.

My proposal here is that if we can *see* the editing, maybe we will be able to comprehend the creative complexity involved. Thus, I turn now to articulating some ways of seeing the editing and its significance to realization of films in the work of women editors in New Hollywood. The following very brief case studies look at what editors do to shape movement of events, emotions, images, and sound into compelling and coherent structures and rhythms.

Movement of Events in *Bonnie and Clyde*

As a movement, New Hollywood is often marked as commencing with *Bonnie and Clyde*.[28] The story, characters, and many aspects of the production process on this film were disruptive to "old" Hollywood systems; however, one detail that is particularly relevant to our discussion is that *Bonnie and Clyde* was the first Hollywood film on which an editor has a front credit. A front credit signifies creative input, and it is not coincidental that Dede Allen was the first editor to receive it: her creative fingerprints are all over *Bonnie and Clyde*.

The final scene of the film, the dramatic shoot-out, with fifty shots in sixty seconds, is often heralded as a feat of editing prowess. However, this final scene is also the logical yet surprising culmination of carefully designed and stylized flows of events. By comparing the first scene, which opens the film "like a slap in the face,"[29] and the last scene, we can begin to see that a stylistic logic has been designed across the whole.

As film journalist Mark Harris notes, "Allen cut *Bonnie and Clyde* with an eye and ear for accelerating pace of the story, making the building of its panicky momentum her priority."[30] This flow, or what director Arthur Penn calls giving the film the "complexity of music,"[31] is created by a series of decisions about order of shots, order of scenes, and how sharply sliced the edges of movement trajectories are from one moment to the next, one scene to the next, one sequence to the next and over the whole. The choices to start scenes on close-ups, to cut midmotion, and to jump from extreme wide shots back to close-ups were revolutionary at the time and have since been assimilated—"films became very different" after *Bonnie and Clyde*.[32]

These edgy techniques are Allen's. Talking about an earlier film in which she began developing them, Allen says: "I had a crisp way of editing, even then. I was already beginning to cut in a certain way. I remember cutting from something like a wallet to a car. Bang. It was unusual then; everybody does it now. Rossen was very fond of that style. When it was later referred to in *Time* magazine, he took credit for it. I think he thought he invented the style. I definitely think I had an influence on him as a director."[33] Allen's "crisp" way of editing would have disrupted and rearranged, rewritten, in a sense, the script in *Bonnie and Clyde*. This is important in part because it points to something that is recognizable as a form of authorship, which is the "writing" or sequencing and structuring of plot events. Indeed, the statement "the editor writes the last draft of the script" is a well-worn film industry truism.

Like most truisms, this one masks some complexities. In this case, it is worth noting that there are multiple drafts of most, if not all, feature films. These may all be written by the credited "authors" but are more likely to have been through drafts by multiple, often uncredited authors. Even the "shooting script" of a film is not really considered a final or definitive version of what will be filmed. As noted on the blog of the popular screenwriting software Celtx: "Shooting scripts are guaranteed to change—constantly."[34] These changes have to do not only with the problems of challenging logistics of shooting but also with the creative interpretation of character, dialogue, and movement by actors (who could be considered authors of their own performances).[35] Thus, the script is considered a draft, as is the shooting of the production, where multiple ideas, variations, and vicissitudes of performance, directing, design, and framing are captured on camera.

Filmed materials arising from these complex and multiply authored processes arrive in the edit suite as hundreds of separate pieces that could have innumerable possible structures and flows. The editor makes multiple drafts to find the final version of these. She assembles the material this way and that, crafting something that could not have been present in even the most polished and definitive of written scripts: actual movement. One might say, then, given that cinema is an art of movement, the editors *actually* write the film and that all the previous drafts are blueprints or materials from which the film will be created.

For our purposes, since many scripts (including that of *Bonnie and Clyde*) are available online, and films can be watched and rewatched easily, it is instructive to notice the re-visions of the script the editor has shaped in response to the affordances of the filmed material. It is beyond the forensic opportunities of this chapter, or indeed what most archives would afford, to identify all the many changes the ideas go through from draft to draft of script to shoot, and draft to draft of edited versions, but comparing the final film to the script is one way to *see* the editor's embedded and embodied expertise at work. Editors make dozens of decisions a day about which shot, where, and for how long in response to the filmed material, not the script. The editor's "authorship," then, is the imprinting of an affective, sensory style on the film's actual movement, not its planned or hoped-for movement. This process is expertly responsive to the possibilities of the movement in the material, the patterns it could make. These possibilities are, for all practical purposes, innumerable, given that any frame of any shot could theoretically connect with any other frame of any other shot, and there are twenty-four frames per second in each shot and hundreds of shots. So, these possibilities are chunked down and filtered through the editor's own kinesthetic sensibility and those of their collaborators and context. Editing, in other words, is distributed thinking, an instance of creative ideas arising in a distributed cognitive system.

Allen, in particular, is drawing on all these forms of expertise, and what *Bonnie and Clyde* displays is mastery of the synthesis of movement of events, emotions, images, and sounds into a novel but appropriate story shape for the content and context of the particular production. What makes Allen's expertise exceptional in this instance is her capacity to see beyond the standard "appropriate" story shape and to recognize that she is at the entryway to a new context that demands a new "appropriate." She slips through that doorway with what looks like ease but is actually expertise, and the success of *Bonnie and Clyde* holds that doorway open for others.

Movement of Emotion in *Jaws*

Another way of "seeing" the editing and its significance to shaping the screen experience is to recognize that editing shapes cycles of tension and release in a film viewer and to notice the cycles of tension and release in one's own viewing experience. When audiences go on a ride with the rise and fall of tension in a film, they are riding in a vehicle being driven by the editor.[36]

Take, for example, the "Amity Beach—Day" scene in *Jaws*[37], edited by Verna Fields. In this scene, the police chief, Brody (Roy Scheider), knows there is a shark lurking, but he has been coerced into staying silent so he will not scare the tourists at the opening of the summer season. As an audience, we too know the shark may be lurking—we have the same knowledge Brody has, and thus also the same tension: Will the shark attack, and should Brody not be preventing it? No one else on the beach knows what we and Brody know, of course. As a result, this scene has the classic ingredients for suspense, which Hitchcock famously describes as knowing a bomb is under the table and not knowing when it will go off.

The scene portrays one event: the shark attack. The single event unfolds in a classic arc of preparation, action, and recovery,[38] within which there are multiple smaller cycles of tension and release—little scares, false alarms that each ratchet up the tension of the preparation toward the climactic action. Each of these cycles and the rhythm of the whole scene are designed, timed, and shaped by Fields. The loose and effervescent play of people on the beach contrasted with Brody's rigid watchfulness is the "preparation," the building of tension toward the scene's central action. The unseen attack, seeping blood, and the highly visible panic is the scene's "action." The aftermath, the bloody, tattered flotation device washed onto shore is the "recovery," the point at which the film gathers and compresses its energy back into a moment of quietude before the next event.

Fields's work was not to decide on that arc per se but to shape its rise and fall in time and movement: to decide how long each of these phases runs for, what elements are within each phase, and from whose perspective. In editing the scene, Fields has deviated from the script in a number of important ways to create and sustain the tension of fearing something bad could happen and hoping that it will not. Comparing the shooting script to the final scene reveals multiple changes to those things that can be scripted.[39] The scene on-screen starts later than in the script, and it contains fewer distinct actions and different dialogue to the scene on paper. Without access to the uncut material, we cannot determine which of these changes occurred in shooting and which in editing. However, there is something that can definitely be assigned to the "authorship" of Fields, which is the flow of movement across time and its consequent impact on our embodied tension and eventual release when watching. Fields had to choose how long to hold us in dread, where to go in the meander around the beach, and which shots to cut in to isolate Brody from the carefree people at play.

Fields is widely credited for her solution to the multiple mechanical shark malfunctions the production experienced. Her solution is elegant: instead of shots of the shark, use the shark's point of view. When she does this in the beach scene, she positions that point of view very precisely: she withholds the shark's perspective until just before the attack. Brody, the police chief who is burdened with guilty apprehension, knows the shark may attack, but we in the audience think that no one else does—until we see the shark's point of view. As soon as we experience the shark watching the unsuspecting swimmers, our understanding of the whole trajectory of the scene changes. We realize we are not the only ones who know there is a shark that may attack: the shark knows, too.

Fields uses this device of the shark's point of view to "turn" the scene tonally from suspense to dread. When it comes in we suddenly find ourselves knowing something Brody doesn't. The knowledge, however, does not make us more powerful. Instead, we are, like the innocent swimmers, stripped of any protective power Brody's watchful gaze may have had. Our tension levels rise beyond Brody's, but we experience this tension as though we are underwater ourselves—unable to protect, to warn.

None of this specific tension and perspective is in the script, of course; it is in our experience, and our experience is what is shaped by the editing. If all the script was "covered" (meaning every shot described was taken, usually from more than one angle), then Fields made choices about the material that radically and significantly deviate from the script by shortening and compressing it.[40]

What is more likely is that the script was not "covered." Exigencies of the shoot, the weather, temperaments, sand in the dolly tracks, or a malfunctioning mechanical shark, among the thousands of possible things, probably led to quick decisions about what to shoot instead, since the original plan was untenable in some way. In this case, which is more common than one might think, the editor is in fact writing the scene without the benefit of a script. She is solving problems, crafting tension and release out of her faculties of kinesthetic imagination (her capacity for imagining flows). Her sensory/aesthetic expertise for perceiving potential rhythms and dynamics of timing, pacing, and trajectory phrasing inherent in uncut material is strongly at play,[41] as is her choreographic expertise, which supports the shaping of movement from moment to moment and overall into satisfactory phrasing of events, emotions, and visual/aural experiences.

Shaping of movement of emotions is, like all aspects of film editing, an instance of distributed cognition. Fields is cognizing, making decisions, and creating flows with the material that is there, her own kinesthetic sensibility, Spielberg's hopes, and the studio's expectations. And she is thinking, fleetly, in motion, about her intended audience, how far we want to go and how to take us on the ride.

Movement of Image and Sound in *Alice Doesn't Live Here Anymore*

The final example is a very brief scene in *Alice Doesn't Live Here Anymore*[42] edited by Marcia Lucas. In the scene, Alice and her son, Tom, drive away from their home, hitting the road to try to make their way, support themselves, pursue Alice's dream of being a singer, and just get out of New Mexico and back to California (which is a culturally significant move toward "freedom" in America in the 1970s). The scene as written stipulates only that there will be aerial shots and the Elton John song "Tiny Dancer" on the radio to which Alice and Tom will sing along.[43] In fact, there are aerial shots, but there are also shots in the car and shots of the dusty roadside Americana that Alice and Tom are passing through. An Elton John song is playing, but it is "Daniel," not "Tiny Dancer," and Alice and Tom do not sing along.

The deviations from the script's shot design are clearly decisions made in response to the material available from the shoot (which probably also deviated from the script). However, it is once again the less concrete aspects of the deviation that make Lucas's artistry palpable. Her crafting of the counterpoint between close interiors and distant exteriors—the movement over time, in a decelerating rhythm from impersonal wide shots to intimate close-ups, distinguishes her work from the script's design. Lucas makes sharp visual and audio cuts, leaping from interiors of Alice and Tom, with background music and playful mom-kid car stuff, to extreme high angles of highways and the audio equivalent of a crash-cut abruptly halting the music and shoving in the roar of passing traffic instead.

As the scene progresses, back and forth from car interiors to high-angle highway, the playing around in the car gets less playful, more still, with just the smallest edge of irritation creeping into the tone. The towns Alice and Tom pass get dustier, the crash-cuts to traffic roar and long concrete ribbons of highway become more and more ironic. No longer are they happy and carefree in their car, impervious to the outside world. The music is fading, and the enormity of the roads is impinging. By the end of the scene Tom is asleep, his neck exposed vulnerably; the music is gone altogether, along with their feeling that the world may be theirs to explore.

I have chosen this scene as an example of the movement of image and sound that is clearly using the affordances of shots and sounds to convey an emotional journey as well as a physical one. It is a simple event—driving away—that becomes an emotional arc from possibility to vulnerability, and this occurs not on dialogue or exposition but simply by the design, the editor's responsive and creative design, of the movement of image and sound.

New Hollywood as a "Movement"

Having examined the ways in which editors shape the flow of movement in a film, and the significance of this to shaping the audience experience, I turn now to another sense of the word "movement" that could be applied when thinking about what these editors created, and that is movement in the sense of "a film movement." The very fact, I will argue, that New Hollywood can be seen as a movement relies on editors. Without them, there would have been no New Hollywood.

New Hollywood was not the only film movement going on in the 1960s and 1970s, but it was the only one identified as a "movement" that engaged, as its name implies, directly with Hollywood. The directors identified with New Hollywood are often described as having an adversarial relationship with Hollywood production companies, financing systems, producers, and unions that were intent on retaining power and control.[44] In light of these "battles," the directors become "heroes" on a journey to elevate and individuate filmmaking. At the same time, however, they made use of the Hollywood structures. Unlike their counterparts in New York at the time, loosely known as American Independents, they got financing for multimillion-dollar budgets, and their films were distributed through the Hollywood system's marketing structures.

One key to this balancing act of independence and industrial positioning is, I propose, editors. The directors lauded as saviors of Hollywood repeatedly had their films saved by editors. The story of how Marcia Lucas "saved" *Star Wars* has been widely reported.[45] The film *Jaws* owed such a considerable debt to Verna Fields's "saving" of the story from the chaotic, dramatically overbudget, and problem-plagued shoot that she was actually featured in the marketing materials and publicity tours of the film.[46] The editing of *Bonnie and Clyde* was specifically singled out by its positive reviewers for praise.[47] The point being that all these films, and many more, made money and would not have done so had they not been "saved" by editors. Had they not been successful, the directors would not have been able to make another film, at least not through the Hollywood structures. They may have become great, albeit relatively obscure filmmakers anyway, but their movement would not have been called New Hollywood and may not, indeed, have been called anything at all.

The presence and expertise of women in edit suites is part of what makes these directors' relationship to Hollywood possible, but it is not actually part of what makes "New Hollywood" new. It is part of what makes it Hollywood. Editing in early Hollywood was heavily populated with women, and editing is one of the very few places in the film industry where at least some women were able to sustain a presence through midcentury Hollywood.[48] Like the women before them, women editors in New Hollywood worked for and were paid by production companies, they were union members, and they delivered their final work according to specifications of production companies. By managing to deliver work that satisfied both production companies/investors and the directors who were trying to claim their independence of vision within the industrial system, these women present a challenge to the idea that films are individually authored. However, that they were women also, at the time, afforded neat logistical and linguistic ameliorations of the challenge—ameliorations that it is now possible to challenge and overturn.

The logistical dodge of any authorship claims by editors has traditionally been to valorize editors' invisibility, their propensity for working long hours alone in dark spaces,[49] and their ability to produce "invisible" edits. Describing their work as invisible—in process and in product—neatly occludes any visible threat their methodical expertise might make to an authorship claim by a highly visible enfant terrible. This probably worked well because, logistically, saving a film in editing is rarely dramatic; in fact, it happens all the time. It takes place slowly, quietly, in small, dark, often airless rooms, with painstaking and expert attention to the nuances, moment by moment, of the composition that is coming together. As noted, little, if any, of the editor's expertise beyond the actual handling of the film pieces is visible to an observer in the edit suite, and frequently the editor is deliberately masking some of their authority and decision-making power so that directors and producers think it is only their own influence and insight that have shaped the final film, not the editor's.

This diplomatic handling of often competing priorities and massive egos is generally considered part of the editor's job and expertise. It contributes to their invisibility and is often seen as something that women are likely to do better than men. Quentin Tarantino, for example, specifically says that "he wanted a woman who would 'nurture' both him and his movie, rather than 'shove their agenda or win their battles with me.'"[50] Thus, when Spielberg, Bogdanovich, and Lucas referred to Verna Fields as "mother cutter,"[51] they were ameliorating any threat her skill may have presented to their authorship claims by referring to her nurturing role in saving the film from sinking, not her authority in steering it to safety. The incursion I would like to make into this debate is not to dispute mothering, collaborating, or even providing a "womblike" space,[52] but to reclaim those words from any pejorative imputations and instead to understand them as descriptors of expertise. In the first instance this requires severing the erroneous connection of fathering to authoring.

Describing the idea of an auteur as the French theorists originally envisioned it, Robert Stam notes that they thought a film "would resemble the person who made it, not so much through autobiographical content but rather through the style which impregnates the film with the personality of the director."[53] The misapprehension that requires correcting here is that impregnation is the action that causes style to be born. Perhaps, like other terms used by the original French proponents of the idea of director as auteur, impregnation has also been misrecognized. One would think that it goes without saying that producing life is an intrinsically synthesizing process generally requiring at least two. It should come as no surprise, then, that the same can be said of a film's style once the cloak of invisibility is lifted from the editor's work. From there it is easy to see that in fact film style does not just require two; it requires, as Hilary Clinton famously declared about raising children, "a village,"[54] in this case a village of designers, cinematographers, sound editors, composers, producers, and indeed, a village culture or fertile ground on which a film movement can grow.

Associating authorship with fathering and suggesting that authoring can be a solo act is not just a mangling of the biological metaphor; it is a patriarchal misapprehension of the director-editor relationship and the actual work of making film. While the editor may be diplomatic, dedicated, invisible, or other feminized descriptors, she is also an author, and films necessarily have multiple authors doing the thinking, having the ideas, and expertly realizing them on-screen. The director and editor are both, at least, authors, with the editor in this case being the author of the film's final flow of movement of events, emotions, images, and sounds. In shaping this flow, directors give direction, not instruction,[55] and editors make decisions that create, as we have seen, the temporal and dynamic flow of the movie, decisions that may "save" the movie by bringing it to life.

Notes

1   Peter Biskind, *Easy Riders, Raging Bulls: How the Sex-Drugs-and-Rock 'n' Roll Generation Saved Hollywood* (New York: Simon & Schuster, 1998).
2   See Peter Kivy, *The Possessor and the Possessed* (New Haven, CT: Yale University Press, 2001).
3   See Rebecca J. Sheehan, "'One Woman's Failure Affects Every Woman's Chances': Stereotyping Impossible Women Directors in 1970s Hollywood," *Women's History Review* 30, no. 3 (2021): 483–505.
4   Karen Pearlman, John MacKay, and John Sutton, "Creative Editing: Svilova and Vertov's Distributed Cognition," in *Apparatus: Film, Media and Digital Cultures of Central and Eastern Europe* 6 (2018), http://www.apparatusjournal.net/index.php /apparatus/article/view/122/306.
5   See Karen Pearlman, *Cutting Rhythms, Intuitive Film Editing*, 2nd ed. (London: Focal Press, 2016); Karen Pearlman, "On Rhythm in Film Editing," in *The Palgrave Handbook of the Philosophy of Film and Motion Pictures*, ed. Noël Carroll, Laura T. Di Summa, and Shawn Loht (Cham, Switzerland: Palgrave Macmillan 2019), 143–164.
6   Karen Pearlman and Jane Gaines. "After the Facts: These Edits Are My Thoughts," *[In]Transition* 6, no. 4 (2019): 1–7, http://mediacommons.org/intransition/after-facts.
7   See Biskind, *Easy Riders, Raging Bulls*.
8   See, for example, Karen Pearlman and John Sutton, "Reframing the Director: Distributed Creativity in Film Making Practice," in *A Companion to Motion Pictures and Public Value*, ed. Mette Hjort and Ted Nannicelli (Malden, MA: Wiley-Blackwell, 2022); Paisley Livingston, "On Authorship and Collaboration," *Journal of Aesthetics and Art Criticism* 69, no. 2 (Spring 2011): 221–225; Sondra Bacharach and Deborah Tollefsen, "We Did It: From Mere Contributors to Coauthors," *Journal of Aesthetics and Art Criticism* 68, no. 1 (Winter 2010): 23–32; Berys Gaut, "Film Authorship and Collaboration," in *Film Theory and Philosophy*, ed. Richard Allen and Murray Smith (Oxford: Oxford University Press, 1997) 149–172; and so on back to Pauline Kael, "Circles and Squares," *Film Quarterly* 16, no. 3 (Spring 1963): 12–26.
9   Alexandre Astruc, "The Birth of a New Avant Garde: La Caméra-Stylo," in *Film Manifestos and Global Cinema Cultures: A Critical Anthology*, ed. Scott Mackenzie (1948; repr., Berkeley: University of California Press, 2014), 604.

10 Dana Polan, "Auteur Desire," *Screening the Past* 12 (2001): 1–9, http://www
    .screeningthepast.com/2014/12/auteur-desire/.

11 Astruc, "The Birth of a New Avant Garde," 604.

12 Astruc, 605.

13 Kate Amend, "'Our Art Is Sometimes Called Invisible': Kate Amend on What It
    Means to Be a Film Editor," *Sundance Institute*, 2016, https://www.sundance.org
    /blogs/artist-spotlight/our-art-is-sometimes-called-invisible—kate-amend-on-the
    -art-of-editing.

14 American Cinema Editors, "Invisible Art/Visible Artists," Event Announcement,
    n.d., accessed April 3, 2021, https://americancinemaeditors.org/invisibleart/.

15 Pearlman, *Cutting Rhythms*.

16 Pearlman, *Cutting Rhythms*; Pearlman, "On Rhythm in Film Editing."

17 Quoted in Hamish Anderson, "The Woman behind Martin Scorsese," *Elle*,
    November 2011, 5, https://www.elle.com/culture/movies-tv/a12336/thelma
    -schoonmaker/.

18 See Gabriella Oldham, *First Cut: Conversations with Film Editors* (Berkeley:
    University of California Press, 1992); Gabriella Oldham, *First Cut 2: More Conver-
    sations with Film Editors.* (Berkeley: University of California Press, 2012); Declan
    McGrath, *Editing and Post-production Screencraft* (Crans-Pres-Céligny: Roto-
    vision, 2001).

19 Terry Atkinson and Guy Claxton, *The Intuitive Practitioner: On the Value of Not
    Always Knowing What One Is Doing* (Buckingham: Open University Press, 2000).

20 Polan, "Auteur Desire."

21 Pearlman, "On Rhythm in Film Editing."

22 Karen Pearlman, "Documentary Editing and Distributed Cognition," in *A
    Cognitive Approach to Documentary Film*, ed. Catalin Brylla and Mette Kramer
    (London: Palgrave Macmillan, 2018): 303–320.; David Kirsh and Paul Maglio, "On
    Distinguishing Epistemic from Pragmatic Action," *Cognitive Science* 18, no. 4
    (1994): 513–549.

23 Dee Reynolds, *Rhythmic Subjects, Uses of Energy in the Dances of Mary Wigman,
    Martha Graham, and Merce Cunningham* (Hampshire: Dance Books, 2007); Karen
    Pearlman, "Editing and Cognition beyond Continuity," *Projections: The Journal for
    Movies and Mind* 11, no. 2 (2017): 67–86.

24 See Pearlman, "Documentary Editing"; Pearlman, MacKay, and Sutton, "Creative
    Editing."

25 Raymond Williams, *Culture* (London: Fontana, 1981), 115.

26 Williams, *Culture*.

27 John Sutton, "Distributed Cognition, Domains and Dimensions," *Pragmatics and
    Cognition* 14, no. 2 (2006): 238.

28 Arthur Penn et al., 1967, *Bonnie and Clyde*, https://www.imdb.com/title/tt0061418
    /?ref_=fn_al_tt_1. Note on this unusual referencing style: I am establishing a
    referencing system for film that acknowledges films are never sole authored. As in
    this instance, the director's name is followed by "et al.," and an IMDB link points to
    the full credits of the film.

29 Roger Ebert, quoted in David Meuel, *Women Film Editors: Unseen Artists of
    American Cinema* (Jefferson NC: McFarland, 2016), 118.

30 Mark Harris, quoted in Meuel, *Women Film Editors*, 122.

31 Quoted in Meuel, 123.

32 Meuel, 107.

33 Quoted in Patrick McGilligan, "Dede Allen," in *Women and the Cinema: A Critical Anthology*, ed. Karen Kay and Gerald Peary (New York: Dutton, 1977), 203.

34 Celtx, n.d., accessed May 22, 2021, https://blog.celtx.com/understanding-script-revisions/.

35 See Gaut, "Film Authorship and Collaboration."

36 See Pearlman, *Cutting Rhythms*, chap. 4.

37 Stephen Spielberg et al., 1975, https://www.imdb.com/title/tt0073195/?ref_=fn_al_tt_1

38 See Meyerhold in Paul Schmidt, *Meyerhold at Work* (New York: Applause, 1996); Pearlman, *Cutting Rhythms*.

39 Carl Gottlieb, *Jaws* (Screenplay), 1975, https://indiegroundfilms.files.wordpress.com/2014/01/jaws-final-numbered.pdf.

40 See Gottlieb, *Jaws*.

41 Pearlman, *Cutting Rhythms*; Pearlman, "On Rhythm in Film Editing."

42 Martin Scorsese et al., 1974, https://www.imdb.com/title/tt0071115/?ref_=fn_al_tt_1

43 See Robert Getchell, *Alice Doesn't Live Here Anymore* (screenplay), 1974, https://cinephiliabeyond.org/martin-scorseses-alice-doesnt-live-here-anymore/.

44 See Biskind, *Easy Riders, Raging Bulls*.

45 See, for example, "George Lucas' Brilliant Ex-Wife Was Secret Weapon in 'Star Wars,'" *New York Post*, December 18, 2015, http://nypost.com/2015/12/18/george-lucas-brilliant-ex-wife-was-secret-weapon-in-original-star-wars/; Jim Nelson, "How Marcia Lucas (and Smart Editing) Saved Star Wars," *Jim Nelson* (blog), 2019, https://j-nelson.net/2019/12/how-marcia-lucas-and-smart-editing-saved-star-wars/; Gregory Wakeman, "The Secret Weapon of 'Star Wars' Was George Lucas's Ex-Wife Marcia," *SFGate.com*, March 1, 2021, https://www.sfgate.com/streaming/article/star-wars-george-lucas-marcia-editor-wife-15991031.php.

46 Meuel, *Women Film Editors*.

47 Pauline Kael, "Bonnie and Clyde: Arthur Penn's Iconic Gangster Film," *New Yorker*, October 13, 1967, https://www.newyorker.com/magazine/1967/10/21/bonnie-and-clyde; Roger Ebert, "Bonnie and Clyde," *Chicago Sun Times*, September 25, 1967, https://www.rogerebert.com/reviews/bonnie-and-clyde-1967.

48 Kristen Hatch, "Cutting Women: Margaret Booth and Hollywood's Pioneering Female Film Editors," in *Women Film Pioneers Project*, ed. Jane Gaines, Radha Vatsal, and Monica Dall'Asta (Center for Digital Research and Scholarship, Columbia University, 2013).

49 Karen Pearlman, "Intuition and Collaboration: Editing and the Vulcan Mind Meld," *Lumina: The Australian Journal of Screen Arts and Business* 1, no. 11 (2013), 51–58.

50 Quoted in Girish Shambu, "Hidden Histories: The Story of Women Film Editors," *Criterion Collection*, September 2019, https://www.criterion.com/current/posts/6582-hidden-histories-the-story-of-women-film-editors.

51 Meuel, *Women Film Editors*.

52 Anderson, "The Woman behind Martin Scorsese."

53 Robert Stam, *Film Theory: An Introduction* (Malden, MA: Blackwell, 2000), 84.

54 Hillary Rodham Clinton, *It Takes a Village* (London: Simon and Schuster UK, 2012).

55 See Pearlman and Sutton, "Reframing the Director."

Elaine May's
Awkward Age

JAMES MORRISON

Elaine May's films of the 1970s are awkward in many senses of that word, most of them salutary. Mary Cappello's pioneering, capacious cultural study of the concept provides a suggestive backdrop for thinking about May's work: "A situation could turn 'awkward,'" Capello writes, "if some truth about it were revealed."[1] Among the few Hollywood films of the decade directed by a woman—eight in total, of which May directed three—May's movies revel in a certain dislocated quality, a discomfiting sense of being out of place. Knowing and sophisticated, they concern characters who are to varying degrees naive, gauche, blundering, backward, benighted, inarticulate. Excruciation, embarrassment, and annoyance are among their dominant comic notes. *A New Leaf* (1971) and *The Heartbreak Kid* (1972) in particular place awkward women in central roles—the graceless and gawky botanist played by May herself in *A New Leaf*, and the whiny newlywed played by her daughter Jeannie Berlin in *Heartbreak Kid*—while *Mikey and Nicky* (1976) features a portrait of an emotionally troubled prostitute (Carol Grace) in scenes so relentless and prolonged that they can make viewers recoil. Yet the director expresses complex feelings for these characters, making them crucially indicative of each film's distinct sensibility. While the men in May's films also toil under the banner of awkwardness, theirs is of a different stripe—more often odious and blameworthy rather than sympathetic and strangely redemptive.

May's route into film comedy differs from that of male contemporaries like Mel Brooks and Woody Allen, despite parallels among them. All three forged roots in live performance. Brooks debuted on the postwar Borscht Belt circuit soon after World War II, while Allen began to appear soon afterward in the same high-profile venues for stand-up comedy in New York and San Francisco as such other figures of the day as Lenny Bruce and Mort Sahl. In the 1950s, May worked with the Compass Players, a precursor to the legendary improvisational comedy troupe Second City in Chicago. With Mike Nichols, also a member of that company, she formed a duo that toured the same clubs as Allen, Bruce, and Sahl, culminating in a Broadway run in 1960. All three also made their mark as writers before becoming directors. Brooks and Allen, however, both devised distinctive comic personae, the manic Jewish everyman in Brooks's case, the neurotic nebbish in Allen's, that figured decisively in the development of their film comedy.

May never developed or inhabited such a persona. In her sketch work with Nichols, she played nagging mothers, breathy ingenues, or uptight by-the-book functionaries of impersonal bureaucracies, like the funeral director who trades on clients' grief with smarmy courtesy to get them to purchase services, or the unyielding telephone operator who tortures a hapless caller over a lost dime. As a member of the duo, she always adopted a greater array of roles than Nichols, who almost always played some version of a bumbling milquetoast or a rakish naïf. From her debut as a film actor in *Enter Laughing* (1967), directed by Brooks's comedy partner Carl Reiner, through all her performances of the 1970s, May assays a rich variety of parts, from the sweet-spirited daughter of a fallen theatrical family (*Enter Laughing*), to the hostile, psychobabble-prone jilted wife in *Luv* (1967), the clumsy, moneyed botanist in *A New Leaf* (her first film as director), or the forbearing, suspicious but imperturbable spouse in *California Suite* (1978).

May's work retains this range throughout her career, but the legacy of her experience in live performance is most visible in her films at the level of style, in her preference for spontaneity over polish, and in her commitment to the comedy of excruciation. The excitement of comic improvisation resides in part in the prospect of spur-of-the-moment inspiration, the sudden burst of the perfect ad-lib, but it also turns on the ever-present possibility of failure—the awkward moment when the impromptu duet stalls, when one partner's invention short-circuits the other's response. May earned a reputation in her work with the Compass Players for deliberately avoiding easy setups for her partners in improvisation, even blocking their options for building on a sketch's theme by throwing impossible curveballs as a practical joke, until this intentional self-sabotage became part of the comedy.[2] Most connoisseurs of improv comedy would likely admit that the bombs can be funnier than the hits because the whole exercise, like a tightrope walk, courts failure so dramatically that it comes as a cathartic stimulation when it finally arrives. Though May's films are all scripted, each of them explores effects akin to both the lightning-bolt eurekas and the agonizing fails of improv.

Similar attitudes inform May's cinematic technique. Conventional wisdom counsels that film comedy benefits from a zero-degree style that will not impinge on the material. The genre has rarely been considered a bastion of cinematic virtuosity. Even exceptions like Buster Keaton and Jacques Tati are exceptions in specialized senses, their bravura residing more in a kind of spiritual choreography of matter, the synchronized, precisionist movements of bodies and objects through cinematic space, than in any particular manifestations of camerawork. Directors from Leo McCarey to Jerry Lewis, Brooks, and Allen (until Allen's bid starting with *Annie Hall* [1977] for a more sophisticated style), among many others, have used the license of comedy to resort to obviously crude technique as part of the gag.

May does something of the kind too, though some of the more pronounced examples might indicate directorial foundering, as similar moments could for any filmmaker.[3] A scene at the beginning of *A New Leaf* is a clear example of deliberate tackiness for comic effect: after Henry (Walter Matthau) learns that he is out of money, he wanders through the street, followed by a wobbly handheld camera while corny, sad music and grating bird cheeps play on the soundtrack. Many such moments permeate May's films, but what really defines her work is a certain dialectic between emphatically "awkward" technique and sudden swerves into elegance. The entire last scene of *Mikey and Nicky* is a remarkable example, as Mikey and his wife cower in their well-appointed living room while a desperate Nicky, fearing assassination, pounds on the front door, begging for entry. Though not a marked departure from the rest of the film in content, the scene could only be called "comic" on a very broad definition; in fact, it stands among the most devastating climaxes in American film of the 1970s. In texture, though, it seems almost part of a different film, with saturated colors, molded lighting, and stately, symmetrical framings replacing the grainy look, jerky camera, rough cuts, off-center images, and overall vérité stylings of much of the rest of the film. (A different cinematographer, Lucien Ballard, is credited for this scene than for the rest of the film, credited to Victor Klemper.) The more jagged dominant style of the film makes its way back in through sharp cuts to Nicky on the porch and the approaching hit man outside. An extreme example, this one parallels many throughout May's films, linking the veins of excruciation in the material with a complex dynamic of film form.

The satirical tendencies of May's films extend to a series of fascinating exercises in style that mount an intricate dialogue with the work of men whose films define the era—her former partner Nichols and screenwriter Neil Simon in *The Heartbreak Kid*, for example, or John Cassavetes in *Mikey and Nicky*. This deconstructive exploration amounts to a trenchant critique of prevailing cinematic practices. Interlaced with the brilliantly executed set pieces of all three films are elements of blunt inelegance or seeming clumsiness—the very aspects that members of the critical establishment like Pauline Kael cited to label May's films simply bad, even before the debacle of *Ishtar* (1987) effectively ended her career as a film director in the next decade.[4] Ultimately, May reworks "awkwardness" as a transformative condition, a productive vehicle to counter the dominant order and to articulate a distinctive style and voice of her own.

The truncated shape of May's career imparts a near-perfect symmetry. As Jonathan Rosenbaum notes, her films all involve betrayals between pairs, the heterosexual married couples of the first two, *A New Leaf* and *The Heartbreak Kid*, and the male duos of the next two, *Mikey and Nicky* and *Ishtar*.[5] Equally notable is that the first two derive from prior sources, the next two from original scenarios. Both adaptations cull simple premises from the short stories they are based on. In the first, from Jack Ritchie's "The Green Heart" (1963), a wealthy lothario spends himself into pennilessness, then hastily marries an heiress with the intention to bump her off as beneficiary of her fortune. In the second, from Bruce Jay Friedman's *Esquire* story "A Change of Plan" (1966), a newlywed falls in love with another woman on the second day of his honeymoon. The procedure in both cases is to treat the basic idea as a prompt, a springboard for improvisation, building on it in a series of comic riffs, with the tone and development bearing little relation to the source.

Narrated in the first person by the lothario, Ritchie's story gives him an arch, sly voice that places the reader in a conspiratorial relation to his plot. *A New Leaf* is also angled through Henry's point of view, but it is crucial to the film that we see him as oblivious, inept, and deluded, not clever and resourceful. Part of the strategy is to undermine Henry's perspective, in keeping with May's overweening theme across all four films of male cluelessness. Yet her first two films are not simply about "outrages perpetrated [by men] against vulnerable women."[6] In both cases, the women are also denied easy sympathy. One of the central jokes in *A New Leaf* is that Henry barely conceals his murderous scheme, being obliged to find and marry an heiress within a week, making it even more obvious. This in turn throws Henrietta's gullibility into sharp relief. Though the film takes Henrietta's vulnerability for granted and points up her sweetness, it keeps her at a distance by centering Henry's point of view, and it rarely misses an opportunity to highlight her own lack of awareness, her naively trusting and credulous character, her overall manner of being severely out of it. In the first scene in which she appears, we see her before Henry notices her at a fancy brunch. She is placed in the background of the shot, seeming barely cognizant of her surroundings. Alone at her table, her glasses as always about to slip off her nose, her face tipped down in a withdrawn attitude, she sports an unreadable, daydreamy grin. In this initial view, the film treats her insular state as a joke, and the main comic spurs throughout the film are Henry's misplaced sense of indignity—misplaced due to his own selfishness and duplicity—and Henrietta's galling stupidity.

Henrietta's dominant character trait is passivity, an unfortunate one at first glance for the lead in one of the few films made by a woman in the New Hollywood. Her usual expression is serenely blank, and when she reacts at all to goings-on around her, it is with a sense of vacant faux composure. When the dining table is pulled back to reveal a multitude of crumbs massed in her lap, she is nonplussed—this obviously happens all the time—yet still feebly dithering, at a loss about how to proceed, until Henry gallantly brushes the crumbs away. Exasperation and annoyance, Henry's stocks-in-trade, are entirely lacking from Henrietta's admittedly limited spectrum of response, so much so that Henry's one inconvenience is having to downplay them in her company, to match her equanimity. When she tries to don a Grecian nightgown with Henry's tepid assistance, the comedy derives not from frustration but from its absence, as they both keep calmly repositioning the intricate garment over and over without finding the right armholes. Even in the end, when Henrietta clings to a branch in a river amid turbulent rapids that will bear her swiftly over a waterfall if she lets go, she remains placid and uncomplaining, waving mildly to the shore as Henry shouts his instructions.

Yet this passive, even masochistic person is not exactly just another marcher in the parade of objectified women that wends its way through Hollywood history. For one thing, the world of the film is essentially sexless. Almost every account of May in person accents her beauty; none of her film performances do.[7] In these roles, she occupies the alternative line of abject cinematic womanhood, subject to injury by virtue of alleged homeliness rather than ostensible beauty—the Shelley Winters type, one could say, rather than the Marilyn Monroe model. In either case, in May's work, it is the projection itself that is key. The violence Henrietta is prone to is not the erotic contemplation of an implicitly sadistic male gaze but the foreseeable function of an order in which human relations are instrumental. Henrietta's stance overall is of one who would just as soon be a casualty of such a system than a perpetuator of it, if those be the choices. The most jarring images in the film, both shots in its mode of resolute tackiness, show Henrietta subject to direct physical abuse: Henry's vision of her being carried off by a gorilla, or his lifting her up by the hair in the climactic scene to keep her from drowning. These moments of calculated ugliness are stranded at the film's wrenching tonal divide between the acrid and the sweet, virtually daring the viewer not to share Henry's grotesque fantasies of violence.

With the writer-director in the role, it does make a difference that Henrietta is her own creation to an important extent. Certainly, the film never implies that Henrietta wants to be derided or stolen from, only that she knows she is and understands why, to a point—an understanding, conveyed in touches of May's performance like those fey darting glances, that seems almost existential by the end, when it becomes strangely piercing. The final sequence, after Henrietta's rescue, goes so far as to suggest that Henrietta has suspected Henry's plot all along. "I know this is not exactly what you planned, Henry," she says as they slump together on the riverbank, her intonation giving some indication of meaning more than she says. The last shots of Henrietta are among the most telling in the film. At an ungainly high angle, we look down at her upturned face, streaked with water from her near-drowning, from a vantage point not far from Henry's, whose likely reaction of recoil inflects the shot. Her self-effacement gone, Henrietta adopts an importuning attitude, demanding that Henry pledge his commitment, her eyes wide, her tone flat yet urgent and unyielding as she presses her face insistently forward. An awkward moment, awkwardly filmed: Henrietta is at her most annoying and her most lovable at the same time, and there is no choice but to assent to her behest, as even Henry does. Her quiescence has proved to be a kind of conviction after all, and this belated realization earns her our respect in the end.

Lila, the bride of *The Heartbreak Kid*, is a close relation to Henrietta in more ways than one. As noted earlier, the character is played by Jeannie Berlin, May's daughter, who bears a striking resemblance to May. For another thing, like Henrietta, Lila is viewed in the story from an increasingly unsympathetic male perspective, that of her groom, Lenny (Charles Gro-din). (Lila's male counterpart is also a close relation to Henry in *A New Leaf*, another odious man whose repellant scheme falls easily into place.) Yet, cast in this ironically marginal position, Lila also occupies the emotional core of the film. The viewer's access to this core and Lenny's remoteness from it are crucial to the film's odd temper—distinct from that of *A New Leaf* in that sweetness is all but banished and acridness made paramount. The film's comic set pieces, like the famous scene of Lenny's confession to Lila over a honeymoon dinner that he has met another woman, play from many slants as more harrowing than humorous. The more in touch with Lila a viewer gets, the less "funny" the whole thing seems—and the more one connects to the film overall, which encourages us against the odds to reach Lila as closely as possible from the distance at which the basic conceit must place her. This strategy is what ultimately gives the movie its unexpected gravity.

The film shows the couple to be an imperfect match from the start. A few quick shots take them from an inauspicious meeting through an unpromising courtship to the eve of their wedding, culminating in an awkward make-out session that recalls notable Nichols and May routines on the same theme, with uncomfortably intertwining limbs and a general sense of the indignities of embodiment and intimacy. The first third of the film shows Lenny and Lila as they move through the dazed paces of their wedding, embark on their honeymoon, drive south from New York to Florida, stop in fleabag motels for bouts of uninspired sex along the way, and finally check in to their hotel in Miami Beach. Compressed as they are, these scenes acutely convey the pressures of time. After the high of the wedding, presented as a poignant but vaguely crass affair, these scenes document the quick lapse into predictability, tedium, and disappointment in Lenny's realization that they will be together, as Lila keeps saying to his chagrin, "for the next forty or fifty years." Repeatedly, quick shifts of light place Lila's body in unflattering views, which we are prompted in passing to see Lenny register furtively.

Throughout the car trip, one unwieldy shot follows another as the camera gawks from the back seat, peers through side windows with sun spilling in, rams itself too closely into the actors' faces, especially Lila's, hovers above the glare-riddled, reflection-smeared windshield. At first the couple's attempts at buoyancy make them seem touchingly obtuse, despite the film's inability to find any but these clumsy angles from which to view them, especially Lila. They sing a grating duet of the same pop song they danced to at the wedding (the Burt Bacharach–Hal David number "Close to You") or the TV commercial jingle for Coca-Cola ("I'd Like to Teach the World to Sing"). From

Lenny's standpoint, the mood shifts from hopeful expectancy to stunned dis-illusionment, then temporarily back, as Lenny tries half-heartedly to get into the spirit of being married. Meanwhile, Lila's contentment proves non-infectious, as she holds an off-note too long in singing, calls out in the midst of lovemaking for Lenny to affirm how wonderful it is, scurries to the too-proximate john to go "pee-pee," pushes a postcoital Milky Way candy bar into Lenny's unreceptive face, teases him about being a grouch, gobbles a sloppy egg salad sandwich at the IHOP and then pushes that too into Lenny's mortified mug. She is always trying to bring him in, to share with him, but it is the sour notes of Lenny's perception of this that condition the overall mood, not the blither tones of Lila's happiness or her touching efforts to abandon inhibition, speak her needs directly, or enter into a sense of intimacy with her new husband, all of which register mainly in the first instance as Lenny sees them—as unbearable pressures, terrible infringements on his autonomy. The exception is a sudden, heartbreaking moment of pause after Lenny has answered Lila's expressed need for reassurance with the testy objection that sex is "all new to me." The camera holds on Lila as she replies, "It's new to me too," her tone soft and patient, but laced with a quiet inflection that suggests she had not expected to have to point this out. It is the one example up to that moment when we glimpse directly a Lila who is something other than Lenny's peevish projection.

All the while, the film continues to emphasize Lila's particular suscepti-bility to unfavorable regard. In contrast to that pregnant pause, shots of Lila tend toward the askew, from the first shot when the two meet in a bar, the camera's off-center placement making Lenny's head obscure her face. The next shot shows the two of them sitting in a restaurant, Lenny smiling with smug indulgence as Lila laughs excessively about we know not what—the elision of the source of her laughter heightens its disproportion, but when the laugh-ter subsides, Lila says affectionately, appearing to credit Lenny for an empathy that is otherwise nowhere evident, "How did you know that?" Here again, the film poses Lila's tender regard of Lenny as a counterpoint to his (and by extension the film's) inability to view her kindly. Over and over, we see her in garish light, half off-frame, blocked within the composition, or with her unruly hair hanging in her face, with little bits of egg salad strewn across her lips, with her sunburned skin covered in a mealy, lumpy lotion that resem-bles nothing so much as the egg salad writ large and spread over her whole body. When Lenny meets Kelly (Cybill Shepherd), the shiksa he dumps Lila for, she too is seen indirectly, in steep, low-angle point-of-view shots in which the glare of the sun blots her out. This fantasy of an idealized sex object free of human faults is the exact counterpoint to the relentless projections of Lila as a figure of disgust and revulsion—all for anticipating a mutual commitment and hoping for human closeness.

In May's world, such hopes and expectations tend to be dashed because they are inevitably shaped by a masculinized ethos that privileges decisive action and use value, prefers pretty surfaces to emotional depths, aligns satisfaction with an ego-driven pleasure principle and immediate gratification, and places feeling at a distance, cast in terms of feminized kitsch. How enduring can a love be that is celebrated via a Burt Bacharach tune or an advertising ditty—yet what other ways are there to honor it? Nichols and May's sketches were known for their shrewd observations of pretentiousness and cant on the contemporary scene, their unforgiving takes on modern mores, their skewering of current outlooks and the novel jargons of whatever trends were pushing hardest, their characters mostly caricatured products and enthusiastic consumers of just such transient social fads or up-to-the-minute discourses.[8] May's films give the characters more dimension, but the ways that needs and wants get commodified in this context place these characters endlessly at the racking cross-purposes that are what the films are mainly about. A salesman of sporting equipment "novelties," Lenny talks and acts like a soulless schmoozer in almost any situation, his efforts to persuade Kelly's family of his honorable intentions amounting to little but the slogans of an obvious huckster. At the dinner table with them, when he tries to acknowledge anything like intangible worth, he sounds ridiculous: "There's no lying in that beef, there's no dishonesty in those potatoes, there's no deceit in the cauliflower."

Though associated with Lenny in a glib formulation, the heartbreak of the title is Lila's, and the scene in which it materializes stands at the heart of the film. The scene's audacity is to place Lila's intense emotion against Lenny's shallow embarrassment, juxtaposing the former in all its searing pain with the "comedy" of the latter and challenging us to identify with Lila against the film's own seeming grain. The visual rhetoric is consistent, Lila viewed from sideward angles as Lenny shrinks away from her, casting uneasy glances around the restaurant as if to deny involvement in the excruciating scene unfolding, even as Lila clings to him, moaning desperately. In performance, Jeannie Berlin's rendering of Lila's anguish is brilliantly unsparing. Though still shaded with "comic" touches, it is extreme enough to reverberate in its profound discomfort for the remaining half hour of the film. Lenny gets what he wants: Lila disappears, he marries Kelly. In this final stretch, marking Lila's absence and Lenny's trivial tenacity, the film assumes a tinny, desolate ambience, filled with detached long shots and chilly snowscapes, the swaggering theme song taking on an ever more strident yet empty vibe. In the last shot, following a wedding that echoes at every turn the one that starts the film—albeit substituting Christian rites for Jewish ones—Lenny bears exactly the same sad, abysmal, vacant look he did after his first night with Lila, even though she is now safely consigned to the past.

This vacant look has a notable precedent. It directly recalls the expression of Benjamin (Dustin Hoffman) in the last shot of *The Graduate* (1967), Mike Nichols's second feature. The parallels do not end there. The theme song of *The Heartbreak Kid* (with suitably banal lyrics by Sheldon Harnick, May's ex-husband) echoes the Simon and Garfunkel songs in *The Graduate*, though it is jaunty and bland rather than moody and arty. Both feature an elfin-sounding male tenor, and both are used for similar kinds of punctuation in the films. The plot of Nichols's film also involves a complicated sex triangle, with the male character, on resolving to leave one female partner, obliged to travel north to claim the other one, a journey rife with overtones of stalking that Nichols disregards and May highlights. In both cases, the bond with the alternative partner is successfully sealed but followed by the ironic, melancholy anticlimax signaled by the blank looks. In both cases, the dominant point of view is the man's, though *The Graduate* is incomparably more sympathetic to Benjamin (a role Charles Grodin turned down) than *The Heartbreak Kid* is to Lenny.

This difference upends the whole comparison, giving the ironies of May's film a much greater force and pungency. In *The Graduate*, Benjamin is viewed as the victim of an older woman (Anne Bancroft) who is cast as predatory. His subsequent escapades as he pursues her daughter instead, though not so different in kind from Lenny's "change of plan," are viewed as cute, romantic, noble, and justified. For all its revisionist New Hollywood posturing, *The Graduate* remains a rom-com while *The Heartbreak Kid* leaves that genre in shreds. The viewpoints of women characters may be curtailed in May's films, but this should be understood as an objective correlative to the patriarchal attitudes that subordinate them in reality, and in relation to the woman's point of view—May's—that guides the films and their uncompromising breakdowns of toxic masculinities.

Although the script of *The Heartbreak Kid* is credited to Neil Simon, it bears none of the usual marks of his authorship. Situational and character-based, the comedy is discomfiting rather than soothingly programmatic, without a single Simon-esque one-liner. As inherited from Friedman, the plot could tilt toward Simon's characteristic boys-will-be-boys indulgence from plays like *Come Blow Your Horn* (1961), *The Star-Spangled Girl* (1966), or indeed the Walter Matthau–Elaine May episode of *California Suite* in its film version. Certainly, Simon's version would have promoted the insouciant kid above the heartbreak, but May's direction subverts this option while bringing out the Jewish themes that are, as usual in Simon, effaced in the script, painting Lenny as a self-hating Jew seeking WASP legitimation. The credits read, "Neil Simon's *The Heartbreak Kid*, An Elaine May Film" (all on the same screen), and it's been said that Simon was so proprietary of authorship that he demanded not a word of his script be altered in filming. In one interview, Simon himself notes this demand but irately emphasizes May's many changes, all of which he criticizes—especially what he characterizes as a completely rewritten ending and the casting of the very Jewish Jeannie Berlin as Lila instead of Simon's preference, the Waspy Diane Keaton.[9]

If May's first two films put a critical spin on the Nichols and Simon branches of 1970s American film comedy, her next film turns to an outlying variant, dispensing with much of the comedy along the way and producing her most vigorous and direct examination of male obliviousness and cruelty. Few critics failed to note the affinities of *Mikey and Nicky* with the work of its costar, John Cassavetes, who by then had been making a remarkable series of films as a pioneering independent for fifteen years, and whose work was ushered more into the mainstream as the New Hollywood ascended. May's film shares the raw, adamant intensity of Cassavetes's work, as well as the mercurial, stuttering rhythms, though its blending of jolts of crudity with an overarching sophistication places it squarely in the line of May's work. Malignant male behavior is also a principal Cassavetes theme, especially in films like *Husbands* (1969), *A Woman under the Influence* (1974), and *The Killing of a Chinese Bookie* (1976)—the last of which plays like variations on themes from May's film. Yet May's more complex structures of feeling differ from the cool suspension of judgment that defines Cassavetes's treatment, much as Cassavetes's staunch commitment to individualism—his ultimate celebration of people being "themselves," or trying to be—stands against May's conceptions of characters within larger social contexts, who still might not know who they are.

Their very names connoting something infantile, Mikey (Peter Falk) and Nicky (Cassavetes) are two-bit gangsters who carry out nebulous deeds for a crime syndicate while carrying on (as we learn near the end of the film) standard middle-class lives. Holed up in a cheap hotel room, Nicky fears the syndicate has put a contract out on him for some shadowy transgression, and he calls his old friend Mikey to help, even though he suspects from the start that Mikey is complicit in the hit. As in many of Cassavetes's films, the characters are removed from their everyday lives, but in Cassavetes this is often so that we can see them in their essence, stripped of extraneous determinants, while May emphasizes how their circumstances, assumptions, and social conditionings continue to dictate their behavior even apart from their ordinary contexts. As the two rove the city at night, dogged by the would-be assassin, we are with them alone for most of the film, observing how their interwoven pasts, their familial histories, their social roles, and their ways of thinking about women have made them who they are.

Despite the tonal contrasts, the film may be closer to May's earliest work with Nichols than any of her other films. She worked on the script as early as her days with the Compass Players, and critics often note the echo of Nichols's name in the film's title.[10] The structure is essentially a series of quasi-improvisatory duets, including several adventitious encounters—Mikey's efforts to get cream from a local diner where the counterman refuses to sell it to go, or their conflict with a bus driver who will not let them exit the bus through the front door—closer to Nichols-and-May territory in their treatment of frustrations in confrontation with fatuous, power-hungry, by-the-book peons than anything in the previous two films (except perhaps Henry's colloquy in *A New Leaf* with an unsympathetic lawyer [William Redfield] who strikingly resembles Nichols).

As it turns out, Mikey *is* secretly working with the hit man, as Nicky suspects, but this is never really treated as a plot point or exposed as a narrative revelation. We either know from the start or figure it out somewhere along the line, with no fanfare or any particular assistance from the narration. To an extent deeper than in May's previous movies, betrayal here goes without saying in relationships predicated on mutual need but with no allowances for it. What gives the film its special charge is its capacity to reveal so much that is appalling about the men's behavior while also crediting their ambivalent love for each other, without that point in their favor letting them off the hook. Not surprisingly, the characters' ways of treating women are singled out for particular attention and shown to be especially vile. Women appear only on the periphery, but the men treat them, whether wife or prostitute, according to their own trumped-up self-images—Nick with a pseudo-slick version of oleaginous "charm," Mike with a creepy, deferential earnestness, both equally fake—and neither views women as anything but nuisances or, at best, necessary conveniences. We see the women's responses to them more starkly than they do: Nick's ex-wife (Joyce Van Patten) has left him because she recognizes his negligence and misogyny, yet still represses helpless tears as she says goodbye to him. Mike's wife (Rose Arrick) tries to stroke his ego while accommodating his insecurities and carefully skirting any triggers to his anger. The encounter with the prostitute, meanwhile, is excruciating enough the first time, with the woman enacting a prim, high-toned, zonked-out modesty, sharply on the lookout for petty slights to her dignity while heedless of the enormous ones that shape the whole transaction. It is nearly unbearable the second time, when the same awkward dynamic nightmarishly repeats itself, but the repetition seems necessary to make the point that the men's behavior is, at its root, compulsive. This perception too brings little in the way of forgiveness. The fact that they cannot help it is no excuse, and the film can only watch with a kind of bemused, strangulated pity as the terrible fate they could not help either plays itself out.

Awkwardness arises when someone tries to face something. In Cappello's definitive treatment, awkwardness—despite the bad rap it gets across the board—points up constructive prospects more often than not. It is a "detour" that must often be taken to get to the right place, a sometimes painful way station to arrive at an actual understanding instead of a superficial one, a preparatory vehicle, a requisite condition, for grasping certain kinds of truths. According to Cappello, awkwardness "bares"—it breaches, stalls, and falls, doings that might indeed sound futile or destructive unless they happen to breach rules that should not stand, stall outcomes best deferred, or fall into grace. Finding elegant detours through the still largely male domains of the New Hollywood, Elaine May seizes upon awkwardness as a route to bare little-seen realities. Her characters may not wish to face the uncomfortable truths about themselves, but she does, and we might—however awkward it may turn out to be.

Notes

1   Mary Cappello, *Awkward: A Detour* (New York: Bellevue Literary Press, 2007), 56.
2   Janet Coleman, *The Compass: The Improvisational Theatre That Revolutionized American Comedy* (Chicago: University of Chicago Press, 1990), 167.
3   For an incisive account of May's learning to direct on the job and detailed production histories of all three films considered here, see Maya Montañez Smukler, "Hollywood Can't Wait: Elaine May and the Delusions of 1970s American Cinema," in *ReFocus: The Films of Elaine May*, ed. Alexandra Heller Nicholas and Dean Brandum (Edinburgh: Edinburgh University Press, 2019), 41–62.
4   Writing in the *New Yorker*, in a column following a pan of Barbara Loden's *Wanda*, Kael calls the film "almost implausibly bad." Pauline Kael, "Eric Rohmer's Refinement," *New Yorker*, March 20, 1971, 140.
5   Jonathan Rosenbaum, *Essential Cinema: On the Necessity of Film Canons* (Baltimore: Johns Hopkins University Press, 2008), 365–366.

6   Coleman, *The Compass*, 111.

7   See Coleman, *The Compass*, 65–67, and, most recently, Manohla Dargis's *New York Times* profile describing May as "a slight, beautiful woman." Manohla Dargis, "The Marvelous Ms. Elaine May," *New York Times*, January 22, 2019, sec. C, 1.

8   In his recent work on Nichols, without denying the caricatured nature of the representations, Kyle Stevens emphasizes the "realism" of the pair's improvised dialogue. Kyle Stevens, *Mike Nichols: Sex, Language, and the Reinvention of Psychological Realism* (New York: Oxford University Press, 2015), 27–28.

9   John Joseph Brady, *The Craft of the Screenwriter* (New York: Simon and Schuster, 1981), 329–331.

10 Coleman, *The Compass*, 65.

8

"She's a Professional, Now"

Girlfriends, Creative Labor, and the Challenge of Feminist Professionalization

ABIGAIL CHEEVER

The quotation in this chapter's title is taken from a moment near the end of Claudia Weill's *Girlfriends* (1978), in which Susan Weinblatt (Melanie Mayron) is reprimanded by the gallerist presenting her first photography exhibit. Susan and her roommate, Anne Monroe (Anita Skinner), the film's titular girlfriends, are recent college graduates and aspiring artists—Susan is a photographer and Anne is a writer—struggling to establish themselves in New York City's creative marketplace. Seven minutes into the film, Anne decides to marry her boyfriend, Martin (Bob Balaban), and the movie explores how each woman, but particularly Susan, negotiates her life after Anne's marriage. *Girlfriends* suggests Susan's show is the successful conclusion of a narrative of professionalization, but this quotation implies her status is more tenuous. Fighting first with Anne and then with her own boyfriend, Eric (Christopher Guest), Susan forgets to approve the arrangement of her photographs and then complains that the gallerist, Beatrice (Vivica Lindfors), has not hung *Bar Mitzvah Boy*, a photo the audience watches Susan shoot at the beginning of the film. Beatrice, in turn, chastises Susan—"Why didn't you come by last night to check it? I told you to do that, Susan. . . . This is your exhibition"— and warns that she "better grow up . . . if [she's] going to stay in this business." When her assistant Charlie (Kristoffer Tabori) offers Susan mild reassurance in response to Beatrice's disapproval, she rebukes him as well: "Don't patronize her, Charlie. She's a professional, now."

Beatrice's use of the term "professional" to describe a photographer is notable here. Sociologists typically reserve this term for occupations meeting specific criteria that then allow those occupations near monopolies over certain types of expert labor—as with doctors or lawyers, who must be licensed to practice legally but gain significant autonomy over their operational practices as a result. But the growth of colleges and universities in the decades after World War II expanded its use as occupations began to require undergraduate degrees and sought the prestige that attends professional status. In 1978, sociologists Barbara Ehrenreich and John Ehrenreich coined the phrase "the professional-managerial class" (PMC) to describe this growing population of educated workers whose labor would not necessarily meet sociological definitions of the professions but had become a key demographic in postwar American life. Their definition included "culture producers"—such as photographers, writers, artists, and filmmakers—as part of the PMC and suggests a sociological backdrop for Beatrice's use of the term.[1] Beatrice likely intends "professional" adjectivally rather than literally, characterizing qualities a person might bring to any occupation rather than a designation in and of itself, and demonstrates the term's application to this expanded stratum. Yet even as the viewer understands Beatrice's meaning, her phrasing, with that tentative and contingent "now," draws attention to Susan's failure fully to warrant it. Allowing interpersonal conflict to distract her, Susan violates a central principle of professional ideology, which demands the subordination of personal concerns to professional obligations. An analogy from the medical profession, the imaginary ideal around which postwar professional ideology is arguably constructed, illustrates Susan's mistake: one would not want surgery from a doctor distracted by private turmoil. Of course, analogizing a surgical procedure to a gallery arrangement likewise illustrates the complications of categorizing creative occupations alongside doctors and lawyers. No one will be hurt if *Bar Mitzvah Boy* is not exhibited. Yet "professional" is the term Beatrice deploys and then undermines to characterize Susan's creative labor, and the tension between the professional and the personal suggested in this moment runs throughout *Girlfriends*'s representation of Susan's occupational development.

In what follows, I argue that *Girlfriends* imagines what I term a "feminist professionalization," one that reinscribes the individuated and subjective within labor typically characterized as depersonalized and objective. At first glance, to imagine that any professionalism could be feminist might seem implausible. Midcentury professional discourse emphasized impersonal and disinterested labor based in formalized and abstract knowledge; by comparison, feminist ideologies were fundamentally concerned with the notion that "the personal is political": that individual experiences, articulated and shared, might foment widespread structural change. If professionalism is defined against individuated personhood—if it subjugates the personal and subjective to the abstract and objectified—how can it be reconciled with second-wave feminism, which prioritizes the personal experiences and material conditions of populations overlooked in claims to a so-called universal? More immediately, *Girlfriends* arguably appears more invested in its characters' emotional rather than creative labor, which may explain why scholars frequently focus on Susan and Anne's friendship rather than their occupational development and consider the film in relation to Hollywood's brief "New Woman" cycle.[2] It may seem counterintuitive to prioritize Susan's work life when the film itself appears more invested in her interpersonal relations. Yet those stories are fundamentally intertwined. Narrativizing the aspirations of a white, college-educated, cisgender female photographer, *Girlfriends* explores a lived reality behind abstract theorizing about the professional-managerial class and documents the challenges faced by women starting out in newly professionalizing occupations with long-standing hostility, both individual and structural, toward women's participation. As Susan struggles to secure a degree of professional autonomy—arguably the central goal of PMC labor—*Girlfriends* models a reconciliation between the professional and the personal and imagines a professionalization that is both appropriate to aesthetic labor and productive of female participation.

The primary instruments of this reconciliation are modernist aesthetics of form. Responding to discourses that suppress the impulse to self-expression beneath the discipline of formal structures, *Girlfriends* emphasizes the personhood of the artist in relation to the aesthetic object as it charts

Susan's career from the production of her photographs to their exhibition. Photographic discourse in the 1960s and 1970s was dominated by formalist aesthetics; those principles, influentially elaborated by John Szarkowski, the director of photography at the Museum of Modern Art, maintained that a photograph should "seem as objective and inevitable as the snapshot in the family album. . . . [in which] personal vision is here disguised as objective fact."[3] Its production demands the subordination of the specificities of the artist to the formal exigencies of the medium. Yet *Girlfriends* reconsiders the place of the individual and subjective—the personal—first to Susan's photographs in and of themselves and then to the elusive process whereby those photographs become visible within a creative marketplace. The film recenters the personal at each stage of Susan's professional development: first, in the formal components that constitute her photographic aesthetic and then in networks of female mentoring and support that legitimate and institutionalize that aesthetic in a gallery show. At each stage, *Girlfriends* imagines a professionalism in which what Gloria Steinem describes as the "mutuality of our life experiences as women" serves as a corrective to the exclusion of women's creative labor from the aesthetic marketplace and is central to women's occupational advancement.[4]

In so doing, the feminist professionalization for which *Girlfriends* advocates starts to seem less like the formalist discourses that dominated the institutionalization of photography during the 1960s and 1970s and more like the auteurist discourses that provided a theoretical imprimatur to the industrial and aesthetic changes broadly known as the New Hollywood. The discourse of auteur theory as popularized and elaborated by Andrew Sarris is defined by the dynamics of individuals and institutions and prioritizes the personal and subjective within Hollywood films. Recent scholarship has explored how auteurism influenced the new operational realities that emerged in the wake of the classical studio and enabled the rise of professional-managerial authority.[5] As Derek Nystrom observes, "Many New Hollywood practitioners deployed the discourse of auteurism as an assertion of professional-managerial class prerogative," as a tool to secure a measure of directorial autonomy as the industry recalibrated during the 1970s.[6] In *Girlfriends*, that professional autonomy is a goal realized through networks of female support that remind Susan (and, to a lesser extent, Anne) to "take yourself seriously," "take care of yourself," and "know what's best for you," both professionally and personally. For filmmaker Claudia Weill, professional autonomy required she not "forget [she's] professional" as she moved from *Girlfriends* to her second film, the studio-produced *It's My Turn* (Columbia,

1980).[7] *Girlfriends* suggests the inseparability of the individual and subjective from the disinterested and objective at all stages of creative labor and suggests a key revision to the most famous slogan of women's liberation: "the personal is professional." Yet the film overlooks the crucial centrality of that second element—the political—and, in so doing, suggests one source for the long-standing challenges faced by women working in New Hollywood.

The Impersonal Is Professional

Girlfriends begins with a pre-titles scene of creative production that under-scores the complicated relation between formalist aesthetics and personal dynamics that reappears throughout the narrative. The film opens in a tight close-up of Anne, lying down and from behind, while a figure moves across the image and a camera shutter is heard. In response to Anne's disoriented questions—"What are you doing? It's still dark in here"—Susan whispers, "It's dawn. This light is fantastic." Irritated, Anne turns on a light and demands, "You can't take pictures of me asleep when I'm awake, right?" She then asks: "Did you dream again? Did you have a bad dream?" The opening titles then present a series of photo booth images of the women and prefigure the film's style, which draws from Weill's documentary work to deploy an ostensibly neutral and passive camera that captures quotidian moments from which meaning is constructed syntagmatically.[8] The scene also illustrates Susan's model of creative production, one based around the transmutation of sub-jective experience into aesthetic objects. Susan's need for personal solace ("Did you dream again? Did you have a bad dream?") drives her intrusion upon Anne's privacy, but in the moment that need is transformed into a search for aesthetic value ("This light is fantastic"). This model will be recognizable to anyone familiar with what T. S. Eliot famously described as the "process of depersonalization" through which "art may be said to approach the condi-tion of a science." Defining art-making as "a continual self-sacrifice, a con-tinual extinction of personality," Eliot understands the artist's "surrender of himself as he is at the moment" as the production of "something which is more valuable"—the aesthetic artifact.[9] While personal motivations might lead Susan to pick up the camera, formal exploration compels the actual shots. Depersonalization is central to modernist aesthetic discourses, in which the artist has "not a 'personality' to express, but a medium . . . in which impres-sions and experiences combine in peculiar and unexpected ways."[10] That it emerges in an independent film from 1978 suggests the extent to which those discourses had been institutionalized in the colleges and universities that enabled the expansion of the professional-managerial class.

John Szarkowski understands such institutionalization as crucial for post-war photographic history. From his position as MoMA's director of photography from 1962 to 1991, Szarkowski "espoused a formalist theory that held the attention of the photography world" and operated as the intellectual apparatus that justified the institutionalization of art photography in universities, galleries, and museums.[11] "The dramatic escalation of photograph education" during the 1960s in the form of bachelor's and master of fine arts degrees, Szarkowski argues, produced "photographers of originality and achievement," but a crucial secondary product included "the creation of an appreciative audience" on which fine arts museums and galleries depend.[12] As the leading curator for that audience, Szarkowski favored artists who imagine photography as "a method of exploration" rather than "a mode of self-expression."[13] In his exhibits on Eugène Atget, Walker Evans, and Garry Winogrand, the photograph appears simultaneously as a detailed record of a specific moment and an aesthetic object abstracted through formal elements particular to the medium.[14] Szarkowski's curatorial reach is apparent when Susan hangs a poster from his Atget exhibit on her wall and demonstrates her internalization of formalist discourse when one of her pictures of Anne is purchased by a magazine. "You won't believe it," she announces. "You're going to be famous and I'm going to be famous!" When Anne objects, "But I'm half naked," Susan responds dismissively: "No, you're not naked, Anne. They loved the lighting. That was their favorite one." The photograph is not a private image of Anne in revealing nightclothes; it is a formal exploration of light and shadow. By comparison, when Anne and Martin show honeymoon slides from Morocco, a naked picture of Anne appears among shots of mosques and landscapes, and Susan looks away. This, *Girlfriends* insists, is a photo of Anne naked—and then shows one of Martin to underscore the point.

That Susan and Szarkowski might share an aesthetic speaks generally to the authority of institutions such as MoMA to shape taste, but it also speaks specifically to the lived experience of Claudia Weill, whose biography suggests a highly privileged, liberal arts trajectory circa the 1960s—one designed to produce a PMC career, at least for its male students. Undergraduate classwork in photography at Radcliffe College brought Weill to a prestigious summer photography fellowship with Walker Evans at Yale University.[15] Weill's work with Evans suggests a source for Susan's version of the "snapshot aesthetic," an approach drawn from amateur photography that privileges documentary subject matter and benefits from "the snapshot's directness and authenticity."[16]

Deceptively informal, Susan's photographs center the main figures within open frames, capturing faces candidly and conveying the immediacy of lived experience. This style corresponds to her practice, which favors spontaneity and unpredictability. A well-timed corny joke prompts a laugh from the Bar Mitzvah boy and disrupts the formality of a posed handshake with Rabbi Aaron Gold (Eli Wallach); a sneezing fit provides the opportunity to capture the fleeting vagaries of human experience. "Oh, that's going to be very flattering," Martin objects, when he realizes he is being photographed, but Susan is indifferent to her subjects' vanity. Her camera's objective vision disguises the individuated and motivated gaze operating behind it.

Szarkowski elevated this vernacular aesthetic, in which photographers such as Walker Evans reject "an exaggerated concern for the autographic nature of a personal style" in pursuit of "art that would seem reticent, understated, and impersonal."[17] In so doing, he suggests the deep compatibility of formalist and professional ideologies, renders formalist aesthetics intelligible to professional paradigms, and, intentionally or inadvertently, facilitates the inclusion of "cultural producers" within the PMC. Like the "impersonal" photographs that Szarkowski favors, professional labor is also "marked by 'disinterestedness,'" as Talcott Parsons explains: the "professional man is not thought of as engaged in the pursuit of his personal profit, but in performing services to his patients or clients, or to impersonal values like the advancement of science."[18] Those "impersonal values"—embodied in the Hippocratic oath, pledges made on admittance to a state or federal bar, and abstract commitments to advancing knowledge—commit professionals to an activity in and of itself, rather than its manifestation in a particular client or assignment. They also define and potentially circumscribe a professional's participation in the marketplace by requiring their labor to meet a standard beyond individual profit. "Creative producers" also have such values—the aesthetic principles that define a practice and determine what counts as artistically compelling. When Szarkowski celebrates photographs as "disinterested or objective, in the sense that they describe issues that one might attempt to define without reference to the photographer,"[19] he aligns photographic aesthetics with professional knowledges that "transcend the particular circumstances and subjective preferences of the groups that produce it."[20] The artist and the professional internalize similar ideologies and produce similarly objectified products as a result.

Yet even as *Girlfriends*'s early scenes subordinate the personal to the exigencies of form, those moments deliberately refocus the viewer's attention on the artist whose vision has been disguised within that "disinterested or objective" artifact. The film's representation of Anne's wedding provides a crucial

FIGURE 8.1 Anne's wedding in Susan's photograph (*Girlfriends*, 1978)

case in point. Rather than a scene or scenes depicting the wedding directly, *Girlfriends* shows a montage of eleven of Susan's photographs with the photographic and cinematic frames aligned, suggesting the shared vantage point of the two cameras (figure 8.1). The images are candid and improvisational, suggesting the "naïve and chaotic composition and apparently perfunctory craftmanship" evoked by the photo booth shots from the opening credits.[21] At the same time, a cinematic voice-over draws deliberate attention to the absent photographer. The viewer hears Anne and others urging Susan to appear in the pictures, but Susan declines: her presence is acknowledged through its visual absence. As the voice-over continues with toasts to Anne's happiness, the image track shifts to a forty-five-second shot of Susan alone and from behind, painting the red wall she and Anne planned for their new apartment. The formal organization of the photographs is sublimated into the physical body of the photographer through editing; an imperfectly patched hole in the plaster suggests the unacknowledged wound of Anne's departure from what was intended as a shared space.

A similar technique appears in a later wedding photograph that suggests a perspective on marriage that approaches critique (figure 8.2). The depth and diagonal composition present the young girl clearly while blurring the bride and emphasize the separation of the two figures, suggesting both similarity and difference: the time that elapses between childhood and sexual maturity. Further, the anonymity of the bride, in comparison to the specificity of the child, invites the viewer to imagine she could be looking at the young girl's

FIGURE 8.2 Child and bride (*Girlfriends*, 1978)

distant future. The child's frank gaze into the camera invites the viewer's identification even as it renders her expression opaque: Is the child excited?
Curious? Disdainful? Bored? It also demands that the viewer consider the
photographer, the direct recipient of that unexpectedly forthright counter-
gaze. Here, the photographer is acknowledged if not explicitly represented
within the picture; the child's gaze locates not an abstract and objectified
recipient of her look but a specific and individuated photographer that *Girlfriends* shows quite literally engaged in the process of development. The viewer
is invited to consider how the photograph's significance changes when it is
not, as Szarkowski observes, as "objective and inevitable as the snapshot in the
family album. . . . [in which] personal vision is disguised as objective fact," but
rather is understood in undisguised relation to the experience of its maker.[22]

The Professional Is Networked

From a formalist perspective such as Szarkowski's, the photograph is its own
meaning. There is no external context that informs and elaborates it. But in
both examples discussed here, the photographs are personalized through the
film's narrative that renders Susan visible and shapes how we understand her
pictures. As *Girlfriends* focuses its attention away from the production of
aesthetic objects and toward Susan's efforts to exhibit them within a marketplace, its reconciliation of the professional and the personal shifts from the

formal questions considered earlier in this chapter to the practical challenges of occupational advancement. It also suggests a movement away from discourses that minimize the artist to guarantee the autonomy of the art (Szarkowski) and toward those that emphasize her to secure the autonomy of the artist (auteurism). Andrew Sarris, whose "Notes on the Auteur Theory" elaborated ideas of authorship developed by the French New Wave, sought to recenter the artist—or auteur—in Classical Hollywood Cinema, whose modes of production obscured an individuated authorial presence. Where Szarkowski is suspicious of any "exaggerated concern for the autographic nature of a personal style," Sarris prioritizes precisely that authorial mark.[23] Asserting that "the distinguishable personality of the director" is "a criterion of value," Sarris argues that "certain recurrent characteristics of style, which serve as [the director's] signature," distinguish the great director from merely the good and are a consequence of the American industrial context, in which "a director is forced to express his personality through the visual treatment of the material."[24] Of course, auteur theory too draws from modernist formal discourses—note, for example, Sarris's use of the Eliotic term "personality." The differences between Szarkowski's and Sarris's approaches arguably stem from the industrial circumstances of the Classical Hollywood Cinema, in which redeeming art from capitalist modes of production proved more urgent than rescuing it from the personal self-expression of the artist. Unsurprisingly, Sarris's theorization of auteurism proved irresistible to the emerging and almost exclusively male directors who formed the directorial core of New Hollywood. It legitimated their claims to personal vision, satisfied their sense of directorial importance, and perpetuated "the fiction that the contest for preeminence is fundamentally one between individuals and institutions."[25] The swaggering, masculinist figure of the auteur—cultivated in press coverage of figures such as Francis Ford Coppola, Robert Altman, and Roman Polanski—became central to New Hollywood mythology.

The primacy Sarris grants to an authorial signature underscores the importance of a personal vision, deliberately disguised in Szarkowski's formalism, to New Hollywood aesthetics, but that importance is as much about professional autonomy as self-expression. As Sarris explains, "The auteur theory values the personality of a director precisely because of the barriers to its expression. It is as if a few brave spirits have managed to overcome the gravitational pull of the mass of movies. The fascination of Hollywood movies lies in their performance under pressure."[26] This observation raises important questions: Does the authorial signature matter as a central part of a formal whole? Or is it the fact that such a signature exists *at all* that matters, given that it emerges within a system assumed to minimize such individuating marks? As *Girlfriends* shifts to consider not the production of the photograph but rather its exhibition, the film attends less to the aesthetic object in and of itself and more to the unsystematic process that brings it to the marketplace. Unlike classical professions with established routes to progress and promotion, creative advancement in *Girlfriends* appears largely a matter of solicitation and networking. The audience watches as Susan approaches editors and gallerists with her portfolio and confronts a lack of concrete paths to a successful career. After a thwarted effort to meet with a photo editor, Susan runs into Julie (Gina Rogak), a fellow photographer a few years further along, who illustrates both the tenacity required to get one's photographs seen and the biases that influence those making the decisions. "You've got to stay on top of these people," Julie tells her. "They love it when they feel like they're being pursued by hundreds of young, energetic women. Get it?" By this account, a magazine assignment or gallery show might depend as much on the charm and aesthetics of the photographer as on those of her photographs.

Girlfriends suggests that the solution to a lack of clear routes to occupational success is the creation of networks of predominantly female support. Julie, Beatrice, and even Anne are central to the ways that Susan's personal becomes professionalized over the course of the film. Yet these networks also suggest a common critique of women's liberation as it moved into its second decade: Is the movement working for the liberation of all women or for the advancement of a few? In an article in *Ms.* from 1982, Gloria Steinem discusses the importance of such networks, noting that if you "travel around this country, you can't miss it: networking is becoming to this decade what consciousness-raising was to the last."[27] Yet this analogy exposes a central problem. Consciousness-raising, the primary means through which the personal is made political, was adopted from "a Chinese revolutionary practice of 'speaking bitterness'" and is based around the notion that "women's oppression is hidden far from consciousness." As Juliet Mitchell explains, "It is this acceptance of a situation as 'natural,' or a misery as 'personal' that has first to be overcome."[28] But that original obstacle must be understood as part of a larger political project. The goal is not individual but rather systemic change. Mitchell observes, "Some of the Women's Liberation 'consciousness-raising' groups have suffered the fate of the whirlpool. Individual—small group—individual.... Never moving out of the small circle, the fervour of the Chinese peasant has become the fashion of the middle class American."[29] If the personal in consciousness-raising is never analyzed, abstracted, and transformed into action for systemic reform—if it is never politicized—it neither changes the status quo nor increases liberation for anyone beyond the white, cisgender, PMC women whose participation advanced individual goals. Steinem acknowledges this danger, explaining that "unlike the old consciousness-raising groups, the new networks are often seen as imitative of Establishment tactics."[30] Noting "real and functional differences between incumbent networks who try to guard power, and insurgent networks who try to disperse it," Steinem defends a practice that might easily appear less about shared liberation than about individual promotion. She argues that "women tend to define power differently"—they distribute rather than horde it—and insists that women's networks help women "go beyond our secondary role in the family and in the workplace—to leave the tyranny of society's expectations behind."[31] But despite Steinem's insistence to the contrary, the question of whether networking exists to transform gender-discriminatory structures or strategize routes to their highest floors is unresolved. Those questions persist as perhaps the most trenchant critique of women's liberation from numerous intersectional feminisms dissatisfied with the limits of the second wave.

Steinem identifies confidence as one of the central goals of women's networks. "Without this source of confirmation and mutual support," she argues, "women may not have the confidence to use the rights they already have, much less the strength to demand more."[32] Ehrenreich and Ehrenreich characterize the PMC's primary aspiration as autonomy. "The roles the PMC was entering and carving out for itself," they explain, "required a high degree of autonomy, if only for the sake of legitimization. Claims to 'objectivity' cannot be made from an objective position of servility."[33] *Girlfriends* reveals these concepts as fundamentally connected: both confidence and autonomy are crucial to Susan's feminist professionalization. In a representative example, Susan returns to the editor who purchased the dawn photo of Anne to show him new material. Surrounded by large-scale, close-up photographs of women, she tolerates his unsolicited advice—"You've got to work closer, Susan. That's a problem.... Take that lens and get right in their face"—and then discovers that he cropped her photograph. "I felt that the blond in the bed needed reframing," he explains. "See what I mean? That little bit makes all the difference." For Susan, that cropping means that the photograph is "changed." As she explains to Rabbi Gold: "It was cropped. It's not mine anymore." When he demands, "So what did you do about that?" she admits, "Nothing. I'm too chicken-shit." In Sarris's terms, her "brave spirit" failed its "performance under pressure."

Yet the nature of this failure is important. Susan did not disagree with the editor's evaluation and end up overridden; she did not say anything at all. The former would constitute a failure of autonomy, suggesting that Susan lacks authority to enforce her own aesthetic judgments. Such a lack presumably would stem from a power imbalance between a middle-aged, white, male editor and a young, white, female photographer at the beginning of her career. But Susan's failure is one of confidence. She is unwilling to risk censure by offering an aesthetic judgment different from the editor's own. By presenting this issue as a problem of self-assurance, *Girlfriends* imagines the solution as individual rather than systemic. A systemic solution might require reimagining a system in which editors have more power than photographers and men have more power than women to allow for a greater diversity of perspectives. In contrast, an individual solution requires developing Susan's self-confidence so that she can express opinions about her own photographs that differ from the editor's.

I draw attention to the distinction between a lack of confidence in one's judgments and a lack of power to enforce them for reasons that will become clear later. For now, I observe that *Girlfriends* is more invested in the development of confidence than in the systemic inequalities between female photographers who are beginning their careers and the (almost entirely) male editors and gallerists who are gatekeepers to advancement. In a film that avoids "the famous 'linearity' of classical construction," in which "characters act towards their goals" through "cause-effect developments," one of the few clear narrative arcs involves Susan's growing self-assurance.[34] Though Susan initially appears highly confident in her judgments, she wrestles with moments of insecurity, both professionally and personally. She fails to confront the editor (mentioned earlier), she cannot decide whether to move in with Eric, and perhaps most important, she fails to assert herself when planning her exhibition with Beatrice—a failure that leads to the sharp chastisement with which this analysis began. Yet with Julie's help, Susan develops confidence in her abilities. After Julie encourages her to be more assertive, Susan immediately asks if she needs an assistant and she responds, "Yes, I might. See, you're catching on!" Julie's support is not limited to a career in photography; as they become friends, she praises Susan's work, counsels her on the advantages of living alone, and listens to her anxieties surrounding Eric and Anne. She becomes both mentor and friend and evokes Steinem's observation that "very few of us grew up with mothers who were allowed to be powerful in the world . . . [and] in the freedom and support of groups run by women, we are becoming our own mothers."[35] Steinem's metaphor suggests the collapse of professional and personal boundaries for which *Girlfriends* advocates.

The success of Julie's mentorship is enacted in a key moment when Susan attempts to meet with the gallerist Simon Carpel and is thwarted by his

FIGURE 8.3 Carpel's pelvis print (*Girlfriends*, 1978)

assistant. Susan pauses in retreat, and the audience likely recalls Julie's advice about young, energetic women in pursuit, then Susan claims a referral that she does not have and talks her way into Carpel's office. A large-scale print of a woman's pelvis in lingerie dominates the mise-en-scène and returns the viewer to the aesthetic questions that dominate *Girlfriends*'s early scenes (figure 8.3). The photograph suggests the woman as an anonymous object of desire subjected to the controlling gaze of the camera. When Carpel asks where Susan has shown before, she speaks frankly of the challenges of professionalization, noting, "You know the story. I mean, you can't have a show until you've. . . ." The sentence trails off: the absence of a clear trajectory has confounded Susan from the beginning of the film. As the gallery owner flips through her portfolio, he pauses over a different shot of a pelvis (figure 8.4). Given the angle of the camera, it is most likely Susan's own: the image is a version of a self-portrait in which natural pubic hair and commonplace setting contrast sharply with the prissy, objectifying eroticism of the gallery owner's print. Here, the personal elements are structured within the formal elements of the photograph itself, suggesting the imbrication of the formal and the personal, of the art object and the artist who created it. This self-portrait unites the formal and the personal through explicit reference to gender and suggests the lived particularity of women's lives that was central to women's liberation strategies. The presence of the American flag on the television set likewise constitutes a feminist engagement with the explicitly political: formal components reinscribe the artist into the artwork and

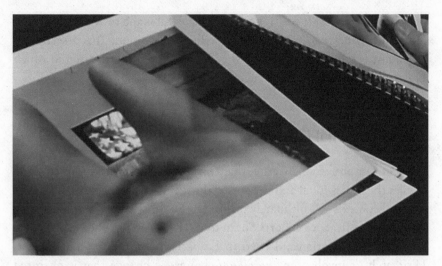

FIGURE 8.4 Susan's pelvis photograph (*Girlfriends*, 1978)

reassert her place in an ongoing American story. As important, both Susan's confidence and autonomy are on display in this moment. Though Carpel explains that her photographs "are not for [him]," he admires her persistence, describes her work as "good" and "funny," and sends her to meet with Beatrice—the gallerist who sponsors her first gallery show.

There is another way to analyze the quotation that began this analysis: Beatrice's comment that Susan must not be patronized because she is "a professional, now." In this moment, the audience can see the unification of the feminist goal of confidence (the ability to assert oneself both professionally and personally) and the professional-managerial goal of autonomy (the capacity to have one's judgment and values legitimated within the marketplace). A closer analysis of Susan's behavior suggests the important role that both qualities play in their conflict. When Susan insists that *Bar Mitzvah Boy* needs to be hung, she demonstrates her confidence in her own judgments: her right to assert the value of her photographs and her ownership of the work as a whole. The editor's cropping of the photo of Anne meant it was not Susan's anymore, but here Susan fights for her own authorship of her exhibition, insisting, "Beatrice, it's my show. Can't we put it up?" Beatrice's retort is arguably as much an interpellation as a rebuke; she indicates to Susan the occupational standards to which she now is expected to conform, but she also calls Susan to the status that she has sought throughout the film. Though Beatrice does not acquiesce to Susan's request—"It's too late," she snaps, "people are already coming"—it is easy to imagine that Beatrice calls Susan a professional both to chide her for forgetting to check her exhibit and to acknowledge her judgment that *Bar Mitzvah Boy* is worthy of exhibition. That assertion of autonomy is the first step toward the independent authority around which professional discourse is constructed.

The Professional Is Political

The feminist professionalization that *Girlfriends* documents—one that reconciles the professional and the personal within aesthetic objects and occupational contexts—is ultimately realized by Susan's growing confidence. To "grow up," as Beatrice exhorts Susan to do, is to develop one's capacity for autonomous evaluation and assert that capacity in the creative marketplace. Ultimately, it involves an *individual* change—a change that is nurtured through networks of personal connection and support but that happens on the personal rather than the systemic level. Yet the limits of such individual change can be seen not in *Girlfriends* in and of itself but rather in the story of Claudia Weill's own professionalization. Weill's career suggests the opportunities available to highly talented, hardworking, and well-networked white cisgender women educated at Radcliffe College in the late 1960s.[36] Though she may have suffered from a lack of confidence, that lack is not readily apparent in her work bringing *Girlfriends* to audiences. *Girlfriends* began as a short film funded with an American Film Institute grant; further support from the National Endowment for the Arts, the New York State Council for the Arts, the Creative Artist Public Service program, and private donors allowed Weill to expand it to feature length.[37] It was screened at the Directors' Fortnight at the Cannes Film Festival, won the People's Choice award at the Toronto International Film Festival, was purchased for distribution by Warner Bros., and received highly favorable reviews.[38] Weill then directed *It's My Turn* (1980), starring Jill Clayburgh and Michael Douglas, for Ray Stark's production company Rastar Films, and then cultivated a successful career directing theater and television, shooting episodes of *Cagney and Lacey*, *ThirtySomething*, *My So-Called Life*, and, most recently, *Girls*.[39]

Yet Weill's press promoting first *Girlfriends* and then *It's My Turn* suggests that New Hollywood's institutional and cultural realities provided regular challenges to that confidence and autonomy—as well as the limitations of solutions that advocate purely individual change. Two central topics emerge within these interviews: first, whether or not her films are "personal" to Weill, operating as a mode of subjective self-expression rather than as a disinterested aesthetic object; and second, how being female influences her direction, her experiences on set, and the films ultimately that result. Not surprisingly, these topics are fundamentally linked. Presumably familiar with auteurist discourses prioritizing "the distinguishable personality of the director," interviewers ask Weill if *Girlfriends* is a personal film and then document her efforts to assert a professional detachment from the material. In a representative instance, Marsha Kinder observes that though *Girlfriends*'s "characters and situations are so firmly rooted in specific details that the story feels like autobiography . . . Weill claims that the film 'is autobiographical only in the sense that I know the material—the milieu, not the events. I feel that I've been Susan. I've been Anne. But it's not my story.'"[40] Two years later, when Brooks Riley asks the same question, Weill argues: "Film is always personal. It's almost not possible for it not to be personal." But she explains, "If you're asking if it's autobiographical—no. It's personal in that it expresses things I believe."[41] These comments suggest the careful negotiation of the boundary between the expressive and the disinterested dictated by professional ideologies.

Yet Weill's efforts to disavow a personal component to *Girlfriends* and maintain her professional detachment are undercut by questions that intentionally or not draw attention to the novelty—if not outright incongruity—of a professional director in the New Hollywood era who happens to be female. In a 1980 interview with Roger Ebert, she says that her status as a woman director "used to be the first question" she was asked. "Now," she observes, "it's been downgraded to an afterthought: 'Oh, yeah, uh . . . how's it being a woman movie director?'"[42] Yet in her discussion with Riley, she admits she "look[s] forward to the day when nobody'll ask me that question any more" and implies all the frustration and weariness that accompanies early admittance to previously restricted communities and organizations.[43] But she is quick to assert that being a woman neither interests nor obligates her professionally. Ebert writes, "Weill said she doesn't even particularly care whether she makes movies about 'woman's themes.'"[44] It is unclear whether Ebert intends this comment skeptically—he immediately notes that "her first two films belong in that category"—but one can easily imagine the opportunity costs that would accompany an expressed investment in so-called women's themes. As she observes with Carey Winfrey, "I think it's dangerous to put yourself in a kind of ghetto, doing nice little films about how women live and what they're all about. It's much more effective and interesting to become a really good director—hopefully, eventually—who happens to be a woman. And to make really good films."[45] The dismissal of the subjective and personal ("who happens to be a woman") in favor of the expert and detached ("make really good films") expresses the central discourses of professional and modernist ideologies.

Yet in the same discussion with Ebert, she tells what she probably intends to be a humanizing story about a new director just starting out, which instead evokes a powerful image of the challenges of those discourses for women and other individuals historically excluded from their use—and, more important, from the occupational stratum that deployed them. Asked the familiar question about being a female director working with a predominantly male crew, Weill responds: "Everybody's professional. What makes me so mad is when I forget I'm professional. The other day I was on Kup's Show. With John Huston? And John Huston has such a presence . . . he's so legendary and fascinating that instead of sitting there like a movie director, I sat there like a little girl. A girl! I've got to get over that."[46] The humorous opposition Weill establishes between a "movie director" and "girl"—conveyed in a charming, self-deprecating anecdote designed to put her audience at ease at her own expense—cannot just be attributed to the fact that the girl is still a child ("little"). The implication is that directing a movie and being female are incompatible states of being, an assumption that was a connotation of the concept of the professional from its beginning. And while it is easy to understand how a female director in New Hollywood might imagine that the solution is to "get over" a momentary lack of confidence and claim professional autonomy, a closer look suggests that confidence alone was not going to provide it. Of course, that autonomy might have been more rhetorical than actual, given the realities of studio filmmaking. Describing the working conditions at Rastar, Weill comments, "The truth of working in the system is that it's not my money; finally, I don't own the film. It's not *my* film." One could imagine any director on their first studio film expressing the same frustration. Yet she continues: "I think that people still aren't used to giving $7 million to a girl. That's what it's coming down to. 'What's she going to do with it?'"[47] The autonomy that might have been granted to a male director in New Hollywood is unavailable for a female one.

In more recent discussions, Weill has been up-front about the harassment she experienced and makes clear that individual solutions—developing one's confidence, asserting one's autonomy, "get[ing] over that"—would not work. The past decade has seen a resurgence of interest in *Girlfriends*. Allison Anders (*Gas Food Lodging*), Lena Dunham (*Girls*), and Greta Gerwig (*Ladybird*) have underscored its importance to a new generation of female filmmakers;[48] the Melbourne International Film Festival, UCLA Film and Television

Archive, and BAMcinématek have included it in recent series on women directors; the Criterion Collection released a restored edition in 2020; and Weill has discussed its production and impact in recent articles and conversations about her career. Weill appears more at ease in these later interviews, acknowledging that *Girlfriends* "was loosely based off of my own experience, which was that literally everybody I knew was getting married. . . . It was also loosely based on my experience of trying to find myself as an artist in New York." This description sounds significantly more personal than those of the earlier interviews. Weill also acknowledges that not everyone on the set was as professional as she maintained in the press surrounding *It's My Turn*. "Making a film in Hollywood, particularly in the early 80s, was a very #MeToo kind of experience," she explains. "The idea of a young woman, particularly one who was, at the time, attractive, being the boss of all these guys on the set—because the director is really 'the boss' on the set—was very challenging for people. Consciously or unconsciously, there were many efforts to undermine my authority."[49] In a different interview, she remembers that Ray Stark would run his hand up her back on set and say, "'Claudia, you're not wearing a bra today.'" She notes, "If I was to say, 'Fuck you, get your hand off my back' in front of an entire cast and crew, most of them middle-aged men, what would it have served me? I would have become 'that bitch.'"[50] Maya Montañez Smukler documents rumors about Stark's treatment of Weill that circulated throughout Hollywood, including stories that he undermined her with cast and crew and ultimately reedited the film before release—a fundamental denigration of directorial autonomy.[51] Were these rumors to be true, Weill's assertion "It's not *my* film" takes on a much more literal aspect. Her experience is appalling but not surprising—another story in what appears to be an endless number of stories about the systematic harassment of women and deprecation of their labor in New Hollywood. But it also underscores the fundamental limitations of *Girlfriends*'s own emphasis on individual solutions to the challenges of women's professionalization. The personal cannot become professional without first becoming political.

Notes

1 Barbara Ehrenreich and John Ehrenreich, "The Professional-Managerial Class," in *Between Labor and Capital*, ed. Pat Walker (Boston, MA: South End Press, 1979), 9.
2 See, for example, Lucy Fischer, *Shot/Countershot: Film Tradition and Women's Cinema* (1989; Princeton, NJ: Princeton University Press, 2014); Karen Hollinger, *In the Company of Women: Contemporary Female Friendship Films* (Minneapolis:

University of Minnesota Press, 1998); Annette Kuhn, *Women's Pictures: Feminism and Cinema*, 2nd ed. (London: Verso, 1994); and Barbara Koenig Quart, *Women Directors: The Emergence of a New Cinema* (New York: Praeger, 1988).

3   John Szarkowski, "August Sander: The Portrait as Prototype," *Infinity* 12, no. 6 (June 1963): 23.

4   Gloria Steinem, "Sisterhood" (1972), in *Outrageous Acts and Everyday Rebellions* (New York: Holt, Rinehart and Winston, 1983), 115.

5   For scholarship considering New Hollywood and the emergence of the PMC, see Jerome Christensen, *America's Corporate Art: Studio Authorship of Hollywood Motion Pictures* (Stanford, CA: Stanford University Press, 2011); J. D. Connor *The Studios after the Studios: Neoclassical Hollywood* (Stanford, CA: Stanford University Press, 2015); Jeff Menne, *Post-Fordist Cinema: Hollywood Auteurs and the Corporate Counterculture* (New York: Columbia University Press, 2019); Derek Nystrom, *Hard Hats, Rednecks, and Macho Men: Class in 1970s American Cinema* (New York: Oxford University Press, 2009).

6   Derek Nystrom, "Hard Hats and Movie Brats: Auteurism and the Class Politics of the New Hollywood," *Cinema Journal* 43, no. 3 (2004): 18. Whether auteurism constitutes an actual shift in Hollywood industrial practices is debatable. Geoff King argues that auteurism represents less a newfound directorial autonomy than a marketing strategy designed to capitalize on recognizable directors. See Geoff King, *New Hollywood Cinema: An Introduction* (New York: Columbia University Press, 2002), 91.

7   Roger Ebert, "Interview with Claudia Weill," *RogerEbert.com*, October 20, 1980. https://www.rogerebert.com/interviews/interview-with-claudia-weill.

8   Weill says she turned to feature filmmaking because she was "'sick of following people around with a camera forever and ever and waiting for them to say what I wanted them to say and then spending months in the editing room manipulating what they had said,'" which suggests the methodologies of Direct Cinema and fits well the overall style of *Girlfriends*. Carey Winfrey, "Claudia Weill: It's Her Turn, Now," *New York Times*, December 7, 1980, 210, 224.

9   T. S. Eliot, "Tradition and the Individual Talent," in *Selected Prose of T. S. Eliot*, ed. Frank Kermode (New York: Harcourt and Farrar, Straus and Giroux, 1975), 40.

10 Eliot, "Tradition and the Individual Talent," 42.

11 Joel Eisinger, *Trace and Transformation: American Criticism of Photography in the Modernist Period* (Albuquerque: University of New Mexico Press, 1995), 12, 210.

12 John Szarkowski, *Mirrors and Windows: American Photography Since 1960* (New York: The Museum of Modern Art, 1978), 15.

13 Szarkowski, *Mirrors and Windows*, 11.

14 Jonathan Green, *American Photography: A Critical History 1945 to the Present* (New York: Harry M. Abrams, Inc., 1984), 97.

15 Winfrey, "Claudia Weill," 224

16 Eisinger, *Trace and Transformation*, 172.

17 John Szarkowski, introduction to *Walker Evans*, by Walker Evans (New York: The Museum of Modern Art, 1971), 10, 11.

18 Talcott Parsons, "The Professions and Social Structure," in *Essays in Sociological Theory*, rev. ed. (New York: The Free Press, 1964), 35.

19 Szarkowski, *Mirrors and Windows*, 21.

20 Margali Sarfatti Larson, *The Rise of the Professions: A Sociological Analysis* (Berkeley: University of California Press, 1977), 40

21 Eisinger, *Trace and Transformation*, 224.

22 Szarkowski, "August Sander," 23.

23 Szarkowski, *Walker Evans*, 10.

24 Andrew Sarris, "Notes on the Auteur Theory in 1962," in *Film Theory and Criticism: Introductory Readings*, ed. Leo Braudy and Marshall Cohen (New York: Oxford University Press, 2004), 516.

25 Connor, *The Studios after the Studios,* 99.

26 Andrew Sarris, "Towards a Theory of Film History," quoted in King, *New Hollywood Cinema*, 88.

27 Gloria Steinem, "Networking" (1982), in *Outrageous Acts and Everyday Rebellions* (New York: Holt, Rinehart and Winston, 1983), 197. Originally published as "Create Psychic Turf—How to Survive Burn-Out, Reagan, and Daily Life," *Ms.*, February 1982, 95.

28 Juliet Mitchell, *Women's Estate* (1971; London: Verso, 2015), 62.

29 Mitchell, *Women's Estate*, 63.

30 Steinem, "Networking," 197.

31 Steinem, 200, 204.

32 Steinem, 205.

33 Ehrenreich and Ehrenreich, "The Professional-Managerial Class," 22.

34 David Bordwell, *Narration in the Fiction Film* (London: Routledge, 1985), 158.

35 Steinem, "Networking," 205.

36 Her fellowship with Walker Evans at Yale University led to a summer job on Jack O'Connell's documentary film *Revolution* (1968). Weill then took a semester off to apprentice with the editor, Carl Lerner. Dayna Wilkinson, "Alumni Profiles: Claudia Weill '69," *Harvardwood*, June 2, 2015, https://www.harvardwood.org/mp201506. On graduation, she made short documentaries for public television and codirected *Joyce at 34* (1972) with filmmaker Joyce Chopra. The film caught the attention of Shirley MacLaine, with whom Weill then codirected the Academy Award–nominated documentary *The Other Half of the Sky* (1975). See Winfrey, "Claudia Weill," 24.

37 "Claudia Weill," *Gaysweek* 83 (September 25, 1978): 12.

38 "Girlfriends (1978)," AFI Catalog of Feature Films, http://catalog.afi.com/Film /56340-GIRLFRIENDS?sid=822c2a9e-beda-4a65-985e-e55b6cda2847&sr=0 .8563489&cp=1&pos=2#3.

39 "Claudia Weill," *IMDb*, https://www.imdb.com/name/nm0918041/?ref_=nv_sr _srsg_0.

40 Marsha Kinder, "Girlfriends" *Film Quarterly* 32, no. 1 (Fall 1978): 50.

41 Brooks Riley, "A Woman's Turn," *Film Comment* 16, no. 6 (November 1980): 36.

42 Ebert, "Interview with Claudia Weill."

43 Riley, "A Woman's Turn," 37.

44 Ebert, "Interview with Claudia Weill."

45 Winfrey, "Claudia Weill," 225.

46 Ebert, "Interview with Claudia Weill."

47 Riley, "A Woman's Turn," 36.

48 Ryan Gilbey, "How Claudia Weill's Girlfriends Influenced a Generation of Filmmakers," *New Statesman*, July 21, 2021, https://www.newstatesman.com /claudia-weill-girlfriends-re-release-review.

49 Victoria Myers, "Claudia Weill on Directing Theatre, Film, and Television," *The Interval*, May 30, 2018, https://www.theintervalny.com/interviews/2018/05/claudia -weill-on-directing-theatre-film-and-television/.

50 Alex Godfrey, "Claudia Weill on 1970s Hollywood Sleaze: 'They'd Never Seen a Woman Direct,'" *The Guardian*, July 20, 2021, https://www.theguardian.com/film /2021/jul/20/claudia-weill-1970s-hollywood-sleaze-woman-direct-lena-dunham -quentin-tarantino.

51 Maya Montañez Smukler, *Liberating Hollywood: Women Directors and the Feminist Reform of 1970s Cinema* (New Brunswick, NJ: Rutgers University Press, 2018), 200–203.

9

A Different Image

Studies in Contrasts by
Women Filmmakers of
the L.A. Rebellion

VIRGINIA BONNER

The L.A. Rebellion filmmakers studying at UCLA in the 1970s, once relatively obscure in film history, are now renowned for their collective defiance
of Hollywood's limited representations of Blackness, particularly those in its
Blaxploitation films of the early 1970s but also its long prior history of racist
and sexist stereotypes, assimilationist fantasies, and elisions. Contemporaneous Blaxploitation films did feature Black narratives, casts, and heroes, but
at the cost of hypermasculinist violence, sexism, and caricature as well as
romanticized poverty and crime in the ghetto.[1] Instead, this UCLA student
group used their filmmaking as a revolutionary tool in the service of a radically different image—one that portrays vivid and multivalent representations
of Blackness. Formally and politically influenced by the Black Power movement, Third Cinema, and multiple New Waves around the world in the 1960s,

their films interrogate issues of gender, race, class, and sexuality—always intersectional and complex.

By 2009, most L.A. Rebellion films had been unavailable for decades, and scholarship on them was passionate but scant. But in that year, the UCLA Film and Television Archive began to preserve these films, in 2015 publishing an anthology, *L.A. Rebellion: Creating a New Black Cinema*, and releasing a three-disc DVD set of twenty-five short films.[2] These resources now make access to these important films all the more possible and exciting—their long-silenced voices, anti-racist themes, and defiance of Hollywood conservatism still incredibly current.

To convey these bold themes, the films evince remarkably expressive editing but also methodical framing, nuanced sound design, and symbolic mise-en-scène. The archive's anthology surveys the films well, yet the precision of these formal choices demands a closer scrutiny than they have received to date; the remainder of this chapter will explore several of these short films closely, in order to best illuminate their radical style. Film scholarship usually reserves this deepest level of analysis for films by Great (White Male) Masters of Cinema, who profit from and perpetuate the "white supremacist capitalist patriarchy," to borrow bell hooks' phrasing.[3] And select male filmmakers of the L.A. Rebellion's first wave have received some close attention; yet films by the female filmmakers of the L.A. Rebellion's second wave equally merit readings at this closest level. They crafted and loaded every shot to tell a very different story than the tales told in the language of Hollywood. Indeed, these films yield their richest meanings when we attend to their subtly inflected cinematic language: their formal choices, symbolic meanings, and embodied affect.

Each of these women's short films is unique, and yet they share formal and thematic elements. This is not surprising, given their UCLA cohort's commitment to radical consciousness-raising, Third Cinema, and Black feminist thought (even among many of their male colleagues) in the era of New Hollywood—an era often regarded as "maverick" in mainstream Hollywood studies, even as its strides failed Black women nonetheless. So, these women's films defy capitalist, racist, imperialist, and sexist oppressions by defying the Hollywood style that so strongly espouses them all. Their nonlinear, creative editing and symbolic imagery challenge the gloss of the 1970s Hollywood blockbuster, as does the short film format on black-and-white 16mm. And despite their short running times, each film essays extensively on social justice themes so vital to Black women's experiences, yet largely ignored by Hollywood—even New Hollywood. As critic Clyde Taylor asserts, "Their particular contributions came in presenting self-defining black women on the screen. . . . What is remarkably fresh about the films of Julie Dash, Alile Sharon Larkin, and Barbara McCullough is their portrayal for nearly the first time of black women with an existence for themselves."[4] In short, these films challenged the fantasy images, myths, elisions, and stereotypes of white supremacy and Black inferiority that Hollywood perpetuates.

Alile Sharon Larkin names such practices "cinematic genocide,"[5] particularly in Hollywood's omission of narratives of Black family and love, so her short films of the 1970s emphasize family and children. Barbara McCullough agrees: "We have an obligation to show truth—to show Black people as they *are* as opposed to who somebody else thinks we are."[6] All the women filmmakers of the L.A. Rebellion expose America's racist, sexist, classist history for which Hollywood (and America) "is unable to stand accountable."[7]

These themes are also central to the work of Julie Dash, who has received the most acclaim of the L.A. Rebellion women, but mostly after the 1991 release of her spectacular feature film *Daughters of the Dust*, for which she began preproduction as early as 1975. *Daughters* captured Black women on-screen like no feature film before it, and in a necessarily non-Hollywood style.[8] Its emphasis on Black women's diversity, beauty, pain, grace, and spirit has influenced many filmmakers since, and its twenty-fifth-anniversary restoration and rerelease in 2016 secured its influence on new generations of filmmakers and films, Beyoncé's video album *Lemonade* (2016) among them. The success of *Daughters* inspired subsequent attention to Dash's earlier *Illusions* (1982), her thirty-four-minute thesis film that exposes how the Hollywood industry thrives on its racist, sexist, and heterosexist practices. Set in a 1940s Hollywood film studio, the story centers on the dynamic between Mignon—a light-skinned executive who is passing as white so she can make films about the ignored stories of nonwhites—and Esther, a darker-skinned woman the studio hires to post-dub a musical number, so that the song appears to be sung by the white actress on-screen (though it is actually an Ella Fitzgerald recording that both actresses are lip-syncing). On many levels, *Illusions* interrogates the structural racism of Hollywood, its appropriation and elision of Black culture, and the roles of Black women in perpetuating or defying it; scholars have written at length on the race, gender, sexuality, and industry "illusions" that circulate in *Illusions*.[9]

Unfortunately, other L.A. Rebellion women filmmakers have not enjoyed the acclaim extended to Dash. This chapter focuses on two lesser-known but no less accomplished filmmakers and their short films from the 1970s: Alile Sharon Larkin's *The Kitchen* (1975, 6:30 minutes) and *Your Children Come*

Back to You (1979, 29:43 minutes), and Barbara McCullough's *Water Ritual #1: An Urban Rite of Purification* (1979, 5:00 minutes).

These films embody studies in contrasts, frequently turning upon choices posed to the characters and viewers alike. Political consciousness is raised or suppressed, and children are sometimes cast to symbolize or to inspire adult coming to consciousness. Purification rituals expose and cleanse exploitative practices. Women's quotidian routines and roles are lovingly rendered, while the masculinist narratives of Hollywood heroism are eschewed. And European beauty standards are critiqued while Black women's skills and bodies are celebrated—sometimes with nudity, but not the gratuitously sexualized and racialized nudity as in Blaxploitation or Bond films of the era. Instead, this nudity strategically recalibrates Black women's selfhood and embodiment. Black people—especially Black women—are fully the *subjects* of these films in a radical new way that embodies "a different image," anathema to Hollywood.[10]

*

Larkin's Project One film at UCLA, *The Kitchen*, foregrounds how self-destructive the internalization of European beauty standards can be to Black women. The extant film does not include credits or even its soundtrack.[11] Yet the images are so powerful and their editing so expressive that the film's anti-assimilationist message resonates clearly. Its nonlinear image track depicts the same Black woman in three settings: as a mother at home with her daughter, as a domestic worker in a white woman's house, and as a patient in a psychiatric institution.

The black-and-white film begins in long shot as the straitjacketed woman is escorted by two white-clad hospital employees, a white woman and a Black man, down a long white corridor toward the camera. A close-up emphasizes the woman's forlorn facial expression and her wig of straightened short curls in a glamorous pixie style. Her black skin and hair are engulfed in a sea of whiteness, foreshadowing the cause of her mental breakdown. In a flashback to the woman in medium close-up looking into a mirror, again in white clothing against white walls, she rubs and scowls at her short natural Afro; she then pulls on the wig and smiles approvingly. Significantly, Larkin's camera here frames just the woman's reflection, not the actual woman herself. We only realize that it is a reflection when her arm blocks the camera while placing the wig, creating a disorienting doubling between the reality of her actual body just off-screen and the reflected image of that body that she strives to change with the wig.

The next shot returns to the psychiatric institution; the woman's white straitjacket is removed, and she sits on a bed, her dark skin and wig prominent against her white dress, bed sheets, and wall. As she reaches up to touch

FIGURE 9.1 Behind the bars of a window (*The Kitchen*, UCLA, 1975)

her wig, a graphic match of the same gesture cuts to another flashback, now in medium close-up behind bars—a metaphor for her imprisonment to white beauty standards of straight hair. With downcast eyes, she touches her wig with one hand as she clutches at the bars with the other before another angle reveals that the bars encase the window of the home in which she works as a domestic—yet another mode of her imprisonment (figure. 9.1). She again wears all white as she places a laundry basket full of white clothing on her head, passing a white woman in black clothing seated against a white wall, who eyes the Black woman warily over her white coffee cup. Returning to the hospital, the time jumps backward to the pensive woman being escorted down the hall before abruptly cutting forward to the white nurse attempting to remove the wig; a cut-in intensifies the woman's anguish as she grasps at her wig, now rocking in agony, setting up for another flashback.

A low-angle medium-close-up now ominously frames the woman, again in white clothing against white walls but her dark hair is natural here in her home. Alone in a one-shot, she looks down at something off-screen, her facial expression annoyed as she repeatedly lifts a brush. A close-up then shows a young girl wincing and rolling her eyes; she is seated in a kitchen in front of the woman, who is brushing her hair roughly. Her mother's face remains off-screen until the end of this shot, when the camera tilts up to exclude the daughter's face and frames only her mass of untamed hair that the mother scowls at angrily. These two shots introduce the important character of the daughter, yet their editing and framing distance the mother from her; she remains literally and figuratively blocked behind the barrier of her daughter's natural hair.

After a quick return to the hospital, where the woman stumbles in anguish at this memory, the flashback continues. The woman and her daughter walk away from the camera in long shot on a sidewalk, the daughter's hair now brushed into a high, sleek ponytail. The woman pauses to smooth her daughter's hair into place, lest it reflect poorly on her mothering and self-worth. The woman again wears light clothing, and her hair is now doubly covered by the wig and a white scarf, but the less indoctrinated daughter wears a dark jacket over a T-shirt and pants and no hair covering.

Larkin then contrasts this hair-brushing flashback with another. This time, the white woman employer brushes her own daughter's hair, both of them smiling, talking, and laughing animatedly in the foreground of their two-shot, indicating their closeness. Both wear their long, straight hair parted in the middle, a style favored by white women in the 1970s. The Black woman is relegated to their background, ironing their white laundry, wearing all white, standing in front of white window drapes with bright white sunlight backlighting her so that she once again almost disappears into whiteness. A cut to a medium shot shows the Black woman standing still, her iron abandoned face-down as she stares dejectedly at the white women's hair in the foreground. After a cut back out to the white women, the daughter wrinkles her nose and asks, "What's that smell?" Their long hair fans around as they spin to investigate, the white woman rushing to the background; her blocking completely eclipses the body of the Black woman in another strong metaphor for white power. In a medium close-up two-shot, the white woman angrily shakes the Black woman by the shoulders and thrusts the burned white clothing at her accusatorily, but the Black woman's expression does not register the complaint. Instead, her furrowed brow shows only confusion, before she then lifts the white woman's long hair in her hand, relaxes her face, and smiles appreciatively as the hair sifts smoothly through her fingers.

Larkin then segues back, via a quick shot of the woman in the hospital again, to a continuation of the previous flashback. The woman on the sidewalk, still wearing her wig and white clothing, removes her white headscarf. Her point of view (POV) sees her daughter happily running toward her, smiling and waving in direct address to the camera—positioning the viewer as the mother. In the reverse shot, the mother is smiling broadly at her daughter—also in direct address, now suturing the viewer into the daughter's position. But the mother's ensuing POV shot shows her daughter still in direct address to the camera not as she was dressed but a fantasized version of her twirling girlishly in a more feminine dress with her hair arranged in an elaborate straightened updo—the way the mother *wants* to see her daughter and, of course, conforming to the white supremacist beauty standards imposed on her. A match-on-action jump cut snaps back to reality as her daughter continues to twirl in the same motion but now dressed as she actually is—in the high ponytail, pants, and T-shirt. From off-screen, the mother's white-sleeved arm reaches into the frame to grab her daughter's hair in a clawlike grip, jerking her head sideways—a foreshadow of the violence to come.

An abrupt cut returns to the kitchen, the mother angrily hot-combing her daughter's hair to straighten it. The camera lingers on her daughter's face as she sighs and winces. When the mother reheats the comb, it becomes so hot that it is smoking; the woman stares at it, holding it before the camera for a full ten seconds. She then forcibly presses it against the back of her daughter's head, scorching her so much that her daughter hunches over in pain and grasps her head frantically. Several quick cuts witness their struggle: a fierce yet pained expression on the mother's face, but the daughter's face remains bent low and once again completely obscured by her natural hair.

It is only then that *The Kitchen* cuts back to the hospital, where the woman sobs and clasps her head in agony at the memory before she is strapped to the bed by the two hospital employees. Having been driven to insanity and abuse of her own child by her internalized racism and assimilationist self-hatred, she lies on the bed in medium close-up and stops struggling, her wig still intact on her head.

*

Your Children Come Back to You begins with African drums over black leader and simple credits. This Blackness and music signal the film's solidarity with Pan-African liberation struggles, well before the plot manifests a choice to be made between assimilation or consciousness. Larkin subtly introduces this choice in the very first shot (figure 9.2): a black-and-white long shot reveals two pieces of fabric pinned to a clothesline, blowing in the breeze. The fabric hanging closer to the camera features black African print patterns on a white ground. The fabric in the middle ground is a panel of white European-style lace; a corner of its whiteness challenges the African print, overlapping it as

FIGURE 9.2 Contrasting fabrics (*Your Children Come Back to You*, UCLA, 1979)

the wind blows both fabrics, but the African fabric remains dominant in the foreground as the breeze lifts it high. The African percussion from the credits continues, emphasizing that dominance.

Glimpsed just behind and between these two fabrics—and the heritage each represents—a young Black girl kneels on the ground, digging playfully with a stick; her head and shoulders are clearly visible between the two fabrics, and she faces screen left, toward the African print fabric. Yet her body is largely obscured behind the translucent white lace. A young Black woman unpinning laundry from the clothesline smiles at the girl. Both are bathed in warm, dappled sunlight, dressed casually and with natural hair.

As the percussive music fades, the girl, now foregrounded in medium close-up, daydreams aloud in a forthright voice about a wonderful country in which everyone is Black. Inserts show the woman smiling as the girl describes "Black people on the signs, and TV, and radio, and magazines, and shows, and circus—everybody would be Black. It would be *our* country." And yet she concludes, "But then, I thought, it'd be real dirty." The camera lingers on her hands in the dirt before tilting back up to her face. The woman pauses at the clothesline in low angle and looks down at the girl, concerned and unnerved. An abrupt close-up then shows the girl's hands under a faucet;

white soapy lather covers her dark skin, continuing the contrasts of black and white, dirty and clean, degraded and prized. The woman, now folding the laundry behind the girl and clearly agitated, asks, "Tovi, why do you think your country would be dirty?" Tovi answers flatly, "The white people say we dirty." "Tovi, you know better," corrects the woman, and Tovi sighs, "I know," but immediately adds, "Is Chris coming?" This quick addition associates the arriving character of Aunt Chris with "the white people" who revile Black people. The woman, however, folds the same African print cloth from the film's first shot, lifting it high before the camera so that its patterns once again fill the entire frame, as if to reassert African pride in the face of the racist white people and assimilationist Black people like Chris.

Larkin soon strengthens this initial contrast between Tovi's Aunt Chris and the young woman, Lani, who celebrates her heritage with African print fabrics and art, natural hair, and a job teaching at an Afrocentric liberation-ist school. Unlike Lani, Chris is middle-aged, anti-Black, and bourgeois in her wig, clothing, speech, and financial comfort, repeatedly asserting that she has "more than enough." But Lani is struggling financially since her partner, who is Tovi's father, Michael, left to join freedom struggles in Africa. Flash-backs later in the film frame Michael's cause nobly, as when he teaches Tovi about the People's Movement for the Liberation of Angola (MPLA). But a later scene reveals that Lani now needs welfare in order to care for Michael's daughter, and she is pregnant with their baby. Tovi's POV shots document how poor, boarded-up, and littered their neighborhood is as she waits for middle-class Aunt Chris to arrive.

During the next scene when Tovi eats dinner at Aunt Chris's house (fig-ure 9.3), Larkin unequivocally characterizes Chris as Eurocentric and assimi-lationist, particularly symbolized by the white milk that she pours—the camera following her glass in close-up. Chris soon encourages Tovi to drink the milk and heartily drinks a glass herself, literalizing her internalization of whiteness. Condemning her brother Michael's prolonged absence, Chris dis-misses Africa as "the one place I *haven't* been," but she boasts of her travel "all through Europe—often the *only* Negro in the group!" An extreme close-up of Tovi's eyes shows her contemplate this statement as her appraising POV then scans the European dishware displayed throughout the comfortably appointed home. She pointedly asks Chris *why* she needs "more than enough" and delib-erately leaves her own milk undrunk, refusing the symbol of Chris's white-aligned bourgeois luxury and reaffirming her own woke Blackness. She soon refuses Chris's invitation to come live with her so that she could "wear pretty dresses" and "fix" her braided hair; Tovi counters, "I like my hair the way it is!"

FIGURE 9.3 Dinner at Aunt Chris's house (*Your Children Come Back to You*, UCLA, 1979)

Tovi then confidently recounts for Chris (and the viewer) her "favorite story" that she learned at her Afrocentric liberation school, as soft rhythms of African drums and flutes rise to accompany her. The image track shifts to flashbacks of Lani and Michael teaching a group of Black schoolchildren, then to close-ups of each child attentively listening—modeling attentiveness for the viewer too. In voice-over, Tovi tells a tale of slavery in which white strangers "adopted" and enslaved "yellow and brown and red and black children from all over the world." Mother Africa awaits her Black children's return home to her—alluding to the film's title, *Your Children Come Back to You*—but first the stolen children must reclaim the "land, houses, money, selves" and truth stolen from them by the white strangers—charging the film's viewers with the twin tasks of resistance and emancipation.

When she learns of Michael's death in Africa at the end of the film, Tovi rejects Chris's reiterated offer to take care of her, Lani, and the baby too. Defiant in her tone, Tovi declares that Chris is "adopted" and too much "like the white strangers," another metaphor for Chris's wrong path of assimilation and the facile lure of her capitalistic bourgeois comfort. Tovi's choice, as she navigates these two paths embodied by Lani and Chris, clearly represents the film's endorsement of consciousness as well. It is all the more impactful because Larkin presents it as a child's coming to consciousness—a frequent strategy in Third Cinema and censored global cinemas, in which children represent not only "a blank slate" on which to write a "new, revolutionary consciousness" but also investment in the next generation of that raised consciousness.[12]

Immediately after this flashback about slavery, another flashback returns us to the African music and Michael teaching Tovi about the MPLA. In loving father-and-daughter two-shots, their two hands together carve the four letters into the ground with a stick—just as Tovi was using her stick in the soil at the start of the film. The next shot quickly echoes this lesson, now embraced by her younger generation, as she traces and retraces the letters "MPLA" onto a white wall in black charcoal. Larkin echoes here her theme of Blackness surrounded by whiteness, so prominent in *The Kitchen*; far from being driven to insanity and self-negation by oppressive whiteness, though, the young Black female in *Your Children Come Back to You* asserts pride in her Blackness repeatedly and rebelliously, marking her black letters insistently onto the white background, much like the African print fabric from the opening shot. Her revolutionary consciousness is far more developed than her assimilationist aunt's, and at her young age she is already expressing her solidarity with international freedom struggles, thanks to her pro-Black parenting and schooling. Significantly, as Larkin's camera pans in close-up across the MPLA letters that Tovi inscribes, it lingers on the last two: "LA." As Tovi overwrites both letters multiple times, Larkin clearly links the Black liberation struggles in Angola and across Africa with those of Los Angeles, UCLA, and the L.A. Rebellion itself.

*

Barbara McCullough's *Water Ritual #1: An Urban Rite of Purification* has been proclaimed "one of the very greatest of the Rebellion short films."[13] It is more experimental and abstract than Dash's and Larkin's narratives, yet equally symbolic in its formal techniques, reveling in its textural qualities and contrasts, and equally incisive in its Black feminist politics.

The plot of *Water Ritual* is deceptively simple: a Black woman moves through a deserted urban landscape and performs a sacred purification ritual.[14] As in Larkin's and Dash's films, though, it is the subtle details more than the plot that really tell the story—perhaps all the more because of its experimental style. McCullough explains the need for this creative ambiguity: "I was understanding who I was as a female person, as a creative person, even . . . as a mother, even as a lover. And also understanding my body. . . . So [*Water Ritual*] had meaning in a sociopolitical way, in terms of okay, fine, I'm a part of a culture that I don't have—that I'm mentally informed about. So I'm gravitating toward something that I can't totally verbalize."[15] So McCullough necessarily wields her cinematic language obliquely, to better verbalize cultural exploitation and exclusion, but also autonomous selfhood, as they all affect the Black female self.

The abandoned urban location of the woman's ritual situates McCullough's sociopolitical critique: it is an area of Watts, Los Angeles, that was razed in the 1970s to construct the I-105 Century Freeway. Because many neighborhoods demolished for the freeway were predominantly Black and poor, *Water Ritual* expresses "concern for how conditions of poverty, exploitation and anger render the Los Angeles landscape not as the fabled promised land for Black migrants, but as both causes and emblems of Black mental anguish."[16] McCullough echoes this in her outrage against injustices that target Black communities; her filmmaking strives to "expose what the real United States is about, give people here something to think about, . . . legitimately [show] our anger or our frustration."[17] To voice this outrage in *Water Ritual*, McCullough limits dialogue; the only vocals consist of deep male African chanting that accompanies Los Angeles native Don Cherry's Afro-jazz rhythms, and a closing female voice-over. Yet McCullough's images speak forcefully.

For example, *Water Ritual* begins with dramatic black leader, accompanied by sounds of crickets and then African chanting. A simple title card also features the symbol of woman, but it is slightly elongated, doubling as a religious cross and an ankh, symbolizing life. Three chimes segue into deep male vocals whispering in rhythmic repetition, with slowly building jazz accompaniment that continues throughout the film: first deep bass, then added layers of piano, drums, and finally trumpet. When the male vocals begin, the dark screen transitions to a static black-and-white long shot of a dilapidated, charred shack.[18]

A minute-long take—one-fifth of the film—then frames this shack's exterior wall, giving the viewer time to explore the collage of patterns rendered from shattered white plaster, chicken-wire hexagons, dark interior shadows, and wooden wall studs forming vertical stripes and a huge symbolic X across the back wall. Natural textures of a woven rug, scarf, straw bag, and basket hang along the midline exterior, and a woman is visible through the missing door, seated on the ground and facing away from the camera. She then walks to the doorframe and lingers in its open space, her light clothing contrasting with dark shadows behind. A stark cut to a wider shot centers this tiny dilapidated shack amid an arid, decimated city block baked by bright sunshine, only sand and weeds nearby. Returning to focus on the woman, a low-angle, chiaroscuro close-up of her side-lit face reveals her stately features as she surveys the desolate area, curls of dark hair escaping her patterned headscarf; her smooth, dark skin contrasts with the shadow void to the right and the rough straw bag and chicken-wire textures to the left. Through this rich visual detail, resonant music, and lingering camerawork, we absorb how the woman moves—both physically and emotionally—through this charged space.

The ritual ceremony equally attends to her rhythms and her power amid a plethora of textures and contrasts. The woman sits on the dry ground in front of the shack, spreading her legs wide to face ritual items arranged before her: various found objects and rocks in a semicircle, the woman's outstretched legs completing the circle, but also an African female sculpture positioned opposite the woman—its silhouetted curves of hips, breasts, and hair foreshadowing the finale of both the ritual and the film. The woman gently scatters small white shells, while a superimposition of the same action lags slightly behind in time, supernaturally doubling the pattern. She spreads cornmeal from a calabash mortar in a smaller semicircle between her open legs, then blows more from her hands in a slow-motion close-up. Again this action dissolves in superimposition over a long shot of the woman still sprinkling the powder around her, arms now wide at her sides, echoing both the wide angle of her legs and the shack's powerful X from the first shot. A close-up profile of her sunlit face, now dusted with the windblown powder, emphasizes the textures of her scarf, hair, and luminous skin against the dark void of shadow. McCullough's quicker pacing during this ritual moment—shimmering with multiple dissolves, superimpositions, slow motion, and close-ups—elevates the woman's mystical intensity.

The film's most daring image is its climactic purifying act, when the woman, now fully nude, makes the ritual water herself by urinating on the debris of a burned shell of a house. As the crickets grow louder and the music rises, McCullough's framing of the house again emphasizes this environment's textures and damage—both physical and, by extension, emotional (figure 9.4). The composition divides into three textured triangles: the wreckage of a wall spills into the center foreground, the light dry grasses the woman lithely walks on illuminate the right side of the frame, and the dark burned interior fills the left side, pierced by pockets of light from the structure's missing window and door. The handheld camera pans left to follow the woman as she walks behind the house. A female voice-over whispers, "She moves towards the water. It offers peace. Then the purging and purification began."

The woman steps through the doorway in long shot, her bare feet impervious to the detritus of the burned house, and squats in the center foreground.

FIGURE 9.4 Framing emphasizes destruction and purification (*Water Ritual #1: An Urban Right of Purification*, UCLA, 1979)

Her smooth, sunlit skin again contrasts the rough, charred textures that surround her. In a handheld close-up of her face, chin resting on her hand in pensive judgment, she surveys the scorched remains, her brow slightly furrowed. As the woman looks down at her squatting body, still entirely nude except for a simple necklace and ring, the camera follows her gaze, tilting down her body past her breasts and abdomen to rest at her legs and pubic area, clearly visible due to her spread knees. After a few moments of pause, like a goddess, she makes her own water, letting a stream of urine flow onto the wreckage under her. *Water Ritual* ends with a quick close-up of the woman's face, chin again resting on her hand and lips slightly parted as if to sigh or speak, gazing at the camera in direct address. As the music ends, only the crickets remain, fading to white, then to black and credits.

This culminating urination often surprises and shocks viewers; my students often express initial confusion and disgust, repeatedly questioning *"Why? Why?!"* We then discuss how purification heals after contact with polluting or evil forces, and water cleanses, as do wind, sun, heat, and fire—all elements prominent in the film. And urination purges the body's toxins too. For McCullough, it symbolizes "removal of the putrefaction of society" from the body.[19] Indeed, her entire mise-en-scène conjures a rebellious, cathartic expression of personal and political freedom struggles, both international and local in America and Los Angeles: "The woman was intended to symbolize all displaced people from developing countries who are forced to live according to the values of other cultures. Her act of defiance in a strange land asserts her freedom over her own body."[20]

Some describe this moment of urination as celebrating the Black woman's body as "a force of nature."[21] Others see it as wielding agency and vitality—a replenishing watering of the earth, and a physiological extension of the boundaries and "lived experience of the Black gendered body."[22] There is certainly agency in the woman's forthright urination, as "the woman reclaims her environment, her body, and her soul,"[23] and even the camera must pause to wait for *her* bodily rhythms.[24]

Yet, we must also read this agential moment as trenchant condemnation by the woman: she is cleansing this exploited environment, its structural impoverishment and subsequent razing of Black people's homes and lives by their own government. The woman and McCullough both are quite literally pissing on the capitalistic destruction of this Watts neighborhood. Here McCullough (like Dash, Larkin, and all of her L.A. Rebellion sistren) demands that we respect the detritus—both the neighborhood and the people—ignored by white bourgeois Hollywood and larger America. These L.A. Rebellion women visualized a different image, one that powerfully refracted the limiting images of Blackness that came before them (and that persist today). Their films continue to model the transgressive possibilities of nuanced, justice-oriented filmmaking by and about Black women.

Notes

1   Ed Guerrero, *Framing Blackness: The African American Image in Film* (Philadelphia: Temple University Press, 1993). See also Jan-Christopher Horak, "Tough Enough: Blaxploitation and the L.A. Rebellion," in *L.A. Rebellion: Creating a New Black Cinema*, ed. Allyson Nadia Field, Jan-Christopher Horak, and Jacqueline Najuma Stewart (Oakland: University of California Press, 2015), 119–155. Hereafter, this anthology is cited as *L.A. Rebellion*.
2   Unfortunately, the DVD is not commercially available, though it is free to libraries, archives, and educators. However, a selection of these and other short L.A. Rebellion films can be found streaming free via the UCLA Archive's website at https://www.cinema.ucla.edu/la-rebellion/project-one-films. See also the *liquid blackness* website (www.liquidblackness.com) for its collaboration with the UCLA Archive on researching these films and filmmakers.
3   bell hooks, *Black Looks: Race and Representation* (Boston: South End Press, 1992).

4 Clyde Taylor, "L.A. Rebellion: New Spirit in American Film," *Black Film Review* 2, no. 2 (1986): 29.

5 Alile Sharon Larkin, "Cinematic Genocide," *Black Camera* 18, no. 1 (Spring–Summer 2003), 3–4, 15.

6 Barbara McCullough, "Barbara McCullough, Independent Filmmaker 'Know How to Do Something Different,'" interview by Elizabeth Jackson, *Jump Cut* 36 (May 1991): 94–97.

7 Alile Sharon Larkin, "Black Women Filmmakers Defining Ourselves: Feminism in Our Own Voice," in *Female Spectators: Looking at Film and Television*, ed. E. Deidre Pribram (London: Verso, 1988), 161.

8 For more on *Daughters of the Dust*, begin with Julie Dash, Toni Cade Bambara, and bell hooks, *Daughters of the Dust: The Making of an African American Woman's Film* (New York: New Press, 1992).

9 See, for example, Nick Davis, "The Face Is a Politics: A Close-Up View of Julie Dash's *Illusions*," *Camera Obscura* 29, no. 2 (86) (2014), 149–183; S. V. Hartman and Jasmine Griffin, "Are You as Colored as That Negro? The Politics of Being Seen in Julie Dash's *Illusions*," in *Black American Literature Forum* 25, no. 2 (Summer 1991), 361–373; bell hooks, *Reel to Real: Race, Class and Sex at the Movies* (New York: Routledge, 1996); Patricia Mellencamp, "Making History: Julie Dash," in *Redirecting the Gaze: Gender Theory and Cinema in the Third World*, ed. Diana Robin ad Ira Jaffe (Albany: State University of New York Press, 1999).

10 This chapter's title quotes Larkin's third film, *A Different Image*, which could equally be included in this chapter, but its 1982 date lands it outside the 1970s scope of this collection. For more on this film, see Larkin, "Black Women Filmmakers Defining Ourselves." Likewise, several other women filmmakers of the L.A. Rebellion could have been included in this chapter if space permitted, like Carol Parrott Blue and Melvonna Ballenger, although most, like Shirikiana Aina and Zeinabu irene Davis, participated during the 1980s and thus fall outside the bounds of this collection. See the far more inclusive scope of the *L.A. Rebellion* anthology, cited in note 1, for more on their work.

11 Field documents that the sound originally consisted of a Black woman's voice-over wishing for her white employer's long, straight hair ("Rebellious Unlearning: UCLA Project One Films 1967–1978," in *L.A. Rebellion*, 105).

12 Field, Horak, and Stewart, in *L.A. Rebellion*, 25–26.

13 David E. James, "Anticipations of the Rebellion: Black Music and Politics in Some Earlier Cinemas," in *L.A. Rebellion*, 162.

14 The credits identify the woman as Milanda (played by performer Yolanda Vidato), though she remains unnamed in the film.

15 McCullough, interview in "Oral Histories," in *L.A. Rebellion*, 337.

16 Jacqueline Stewart, "Water Ritual #1: An Urban Rite of Purification," UCLA Film & Television Archive website, n.d., https://www.cinema.ucla.edu/la-rebellion/films/water-ritual-1-urban-rite-purification.

17 McCullough, interview, *Jump Cut*.

18 McCullough later modified the original black-and-white film to add a dynamic layer of colorized posterization. However, since the UCLA Archives opted to include the original 1979 black-and-white version on its DVD, that is the version I have analyzed here.

19 McCullough, video interview on "The View," UCLA student cable channel, 1979.

20 Claudia Springer, "Black Women Filmmakers," *Jump Cut* 29 (February 1984): 34–37.

21 Jacqueline Bobo, *Black Women Film and Video Artists* (New York: Routledge, 1998), 35.

22 Ayanna Dozier, "Affect and the 'Fluidity' of the Black Gendered Body in *Water Ritual #1: An Urban Rite of Purification* and *Cycles*," *liquid blackness* 2, no. 5 (September 2015): 60–63.

23 Gwendolyn Audrey Foster, *Women Film Directors: An International Bio-critical Dictionary* (Westport, CT: Greenwood Press, 1995), 248.

24 Alessandra Raengo, "Encountering the Rebellion: *liquid blackness* Reflects on the Expansive Possibilities of the L.A. Rebellion Films," in *L.A. Rebellion*, 300.

Barbara Loden's
Wanda (1970)

A Radically Negative
Feminist Aesthetic

ANNA BACKMAN ROGERS

Barbara Loden's *Wanda* is unrelentingly and determinedly fixated on the poetics and aesthetics of failure. It does not just center on characters who are refused, rejected, and treated as detritus: it *is* a film that at its very core, as Elena Gorfinkel, Sue Thornham, and Kate Zambreno have argued astutely, is formed by a politics of negativity, refusal, and rejection.[1] The ethical import of *Wanda* lies in this aesthetics of denial, of the margin, its exploration of the underside, its use of slowness, its persistent use of counterimages and in-between-images, and its invocation of crisis.[2] *Wanda* does not brook the comforts of positivity, of aspiration, or even the luxury of selfhood. It is, I contend, so radical in its feminist, anti-capitalist politics of refusal that we are still struggling to keep up with it. It delineates precisely how the personal is

167

political and why this matters now more than ever. *Wanda*, this film about a woman who refuses to be saved or to save herself; who lacks the means and energy to alter anything in her life; who lives in a permanent state of blockage, impasse, and failure is, I suggest, in its use of a feminist negative aesthetic the film of our contemporary moment.

Loden's inspiration for her film came from a newspaper article about a woman, named Alma Malone, who had acted as sentinel and accomplice to a small-time bank robber. Upon being sentenced, she thanked the judge for sending her away for twenty years. The emotional complexity of a woman who would regard incarceration as a welcome reprieve from her daily life touched Loden as a working-class woman and intrigued her as an artist. The resulting film, which was in gestation for the best part of a decade, is set against a backdrop of an industrial and working-class environment that defines the people who live within its limits. In particular, the camera tracks the peripatetic and aimless movement of Wanda, an unemployed, working-class woman who has left her husband and two children, but who lacks the perspicacity, means, and energy to alter her life. The film's ethical core, in fact, is concerned with the possibility of change and upward mobility. Eventually, Wanda stumbles into a relationship with Mr. Dennis, an abusive man, whom we sense is full of self-loathing and whose criminal aspirations (which he hopelessly believes will alter his own course in life) prove to be destructive for both characters. At once both a road movie and a heist film, *Wanda* is also neither of these things in any "major" sense. Rather, Loden uses genre subversively to indict specific American values through a woman's perspective. As a viewing experience, it is emotionally eviscerating and cannot be forgotten.

Writing in 1971, Estelle Changas identified *Wanda*'s "problem of feminism," for which, as we shall see, it was readily criticized and dismissed by contemporary critics. Changas states: "Wanda is so burdened with the horror of belonging to the abject, outcast race of impoverished Americans that she hasn't the luxury to lament her role as a female. Loden is concerned with a more basic, universal question than sexual politics—the stark deprivation of the abandoned poor. The film seems almost anachronistic because it evokes the depression thirties;[3] the ravaged faces of its Appalachian coal field inhabitants resemble those of dust-bowl dwellers."[4] Here, Changas not only addresses the specific forms of "feminism" that the film implicitly critiques but also intimates the radical nature of Loden's images: precisely, that she attends to that which is overlooked, forgotten, and rejected from the grand (and generic) narrative of Hollywood's vision of America. As such, Changas sets up Loden's radical feminism as a form of negation in contradistinction to contemporary narratives (into which the film simply could not fit). The revelation is that *Wanda* is, in fact, not anachronistic in any sense. Loden's subject, as she revealed in an interview, is the ongoing toil of millions of forgotten Americans who are struggling to attain "dignity," but who can never escape the place and class into which they are born.[5] Social mobility is the cruelest lie America may have peddled to its citizens, she suggests.

Having won the International Critics' Prize for Best Film at the Venice Film Festival in 1970, *Wanda* went on to play at the London and San Francisco festivals of film and then was screened at Cannes in 1971. However, the film failed to gain traction and was poorly distributed; it played at only a single film theater in New York (Cinema II) and again only at a single cinema in Los Angeles (the Plaza at Westwood)—and both screenings had a limited run (the spring of 1971). Thereafter, *Wanda* fell into obscurity since it received no international distribution. It was not until 1995, due to the staunch efforts of Bérénice Reynaud, and subsequently of Isabelle Huppert, that the film gained renewed attention and deserved appreciation. Within its contemporary context, *Wanda* was characterized as "depressing" and "nihilistic" and met with consternation from second-wave feminists in particular;[6] Pauline Kael denounced Wanda as being too much of an "ignorant slut" to be worthy of the viewer's time, empathy, or interest and the film itself as so minor and muted that it is impossible to gain any purchase on the film's "message."[7] Conversely, Marion Meade labored suspiciously hard to redeem Wanda as a character who has "the guts to hit the road with only the clothes on her back" out of a vehement need to find a "life of her own" only then to chastise Loden for not providing any ready prophylactic to lessen the spread of the depressive condition she loosens in the film.[8] Where does a woman go once she has rejected the roles laid out for her by society? What can she do with her life once she has turned her back on everything she has known? Meade suggests that Loden's pill is one that is altogether too bitter to swallow. In other words, *Wanda* does not leave the viewer with any sense of comfort or relief. The film refuses to attenuate the pain of this woman's existence. The suggestion that lives are daily lived up against the impossible, that to live inside oneself can be a most vicious form of hell was, and is, not a message that many people are willing to countenance (invested as we all may be in a dominant cultural narrative of happiness).

Embedded or implied in the tenor of much of the critical discourse devoted to *Wanda* is the assumption that the role of art in society is a redemptive one (a benchmark against which this film is deemed as a failure). Leo Bersani has written at length about the alacrity with which writers, artists, scholars, and thinkers alike work to salvage their arguments from their most radical implications.[9] Radical because in following through on the inferences of their arguments, they arrive at propositions that are wholly counter to the way in which society functions, our place within it, and our most basic and comforting assumptions about our own psyches. He argues that this work partakes in a "culture of redemption," the cardinal conjecture of which is "that a certain type of repetition of experience in art repairs inherently damaged or valueless experience."[10] Moreover, he opines that an implicit hierarchy exists therein by which it is postulated that "the work of art has the authority to master the presumed raw material of experience in a manner that uniquely gives value to, perhaps even redeems, that material."[11] The role of art is a compensatory one, then. It appropriates the crude, visceral, and brutal stuff of life and shapes it into an experience that works to crystallize and elevate in order to deliver perspicacity, nuance, and insight. As Bersani puts it: "The catastrophes of history matter much less if they are somehow compensated for in art."[12] For Bersani, taking his cue from Friedrich Nietzsche, this redemptive form of aesthetics is predicated on the negation of life, which, in turn, results in the negation of art.[13]

It is my contention then, extending Bersani, that *Wanda* is a film that proffers an art artform of negation, of detritus, of refusal, of rejection, and in this sense it has much in common with Nikolaj Lübecker's conception of "feel-bad" cinema that eschews any possibility of catharsis for its viewer.[14] *Wanda* dares to suggest that, for many, the life into which one is born is inherently damaged and damaging and that not all experience is equally valuable. It is a film that rejects radically the entire enterprise of liberal humanism as a positivist form of teleology. It refuses the notion that a human life adds up to something; that we are all going somewhere; that to live a life, to be a person, is to accumulate experience in the name of becoming a unified, integrated, and consistent self (the phallic self).[15] And in the place of that *something* and *somebody*, Wanda gives the viewer *nothing* and *nobody*. In place of an accumulative model, it gives us a woman who abandons the roles that might define her *as a good woman* and who then goes on to lose the few possessions she has (many of them literally ejected out of a car's window). In place of forward momentum, it gives us a woman who can only stare out of the rear window of a stolen car, watching her past recede while literally being unable to turn around to face a future that will simply be another, paler iteration of what has already come to pass (in *Wanda*, to accumulate experience is to reiterate failure, tedium, boredom, impossibility ad infinitum). Wanda ends up precisely where she started, utterly alone and reliant on the dubious kindness of strangers, but her slate is never blank. There are no fresh starts in life for Wanda, and there is no prospect of failing better.[16]

Loden's film does not partake in a so-called pathos of failure—that specifically priapic form of post-1960s cinema that arose around political stasis, impotence, and disillusionment expressed through a form of white masculine crisis on the cusp of erupting into violence.[17] Her film stages a far more intricate, subtle, and somatic form of crisis that is both distinctively feminine and working-class. At the center of *Wanda* is a crisis of movement that problematizes definitively who gets to take up space both bodily and geographically (Wanda is not the lone American outlaw of myth). Loden performs her feminist politics as a question of the body and its symptoms. We can see this in her performance of Wanda as a woman who is continually on the threshold, unable to claim that most elusive and exclusive of feminist tenets: a space and room of one's own. *Wanda* presents a diegetic space in which the protagonists are profoundly out of step with the environment that surrounds them to the extent that it subsumes and overwhelms them; Wanda is neither merely a "floater" nor a figure who simply "drops out" of American society. The film, in its aesthetic construction, renders clear that this is a world in which there never was any room for her in the first place. She assumes the form of ghost flesh, a figure who lives out her life permanently in spaces that are designed specifically for the transitory, fleeting, and liminal moments of life (motels, roadside cafés, shopping malls). She is fundamentally a woman who cannot gain purchase on any space of her own: she physically subsists and stands on the threshold (of the poverty line, of rooms she cannot enter and, notably, the film frame itself) (figure 10.1). As a woman who is incapable of occupying the center of the image, Wanda emerges from the margins of the frame as a decentered, displaced, and nebulous adumbration of a person.

Loden is not concerned with anything as simplistic and naïve as "positive" representation, then. *Wanda* is affectively alien and cannot be read alongside superficially comparable, contemporary films (many of which are documentaries) such as *Growing Up Female* (1971), *Janie's Janie* (1971), *The Woman's Film* (1971), *Anything You Want to Be* (1971), *Three Lives* (1971), and *Joyce at 34* (1972).[18] Ivone Marguiles has noted of these kinds of film that they were "engendered directly by the [second-wave] feminist movement" and thus "partake of the idea of transparency that is endemic in socially corrective realist cinema: the belief in the cinematographic record as an automatic guarantee of cinema's inclusiveness."[19] In making a holy alliance of anti-illusionism and identity politics, a certain core of 1970s feminist cinema posited that by adopting a cinema verité style and by attending to the shared and common

FIGURE 10.1 Wanda at the threshold (*Wanda*, 1970)

everyday, political unity could be forged. *Wanda* is a film that, despite frequently being described as cinema verité, effects a far more complex transformation of reality as elusive and complex and suggests that reality is, in fact, always necessarily what recedes from the frame of representation and our most vehemently held ideals about its constitution.[20] Indeed, Thornham notes that the film, especially in relation to space, has a "doubled quality, at once observed with documentary precision and having the distanced quality of a surreal fantasy."[21] It should be clear that this is not, in any sense, a naive or jejune conception of realism. In positing a character who does not even have the luxury of knowing her own self at the heart of this story, Loden reveals, perhaps inadvertently, the fundamental flaw of any politics that is predicated on our ability to identify and organize collectively (while Loden supported women's liberation, she professed vehemently that this was not a subject that interested her artistically). After all, how can we identify with a woman who cannot even identify herself as a person? Indeed, with a woman who goes so far as to say that she is *not* a person? Dirk Lauwaert notes: "*Wanda* is no official film. Wanda represents no collectivity.... *Wanda* does not stand for mothers, or for modern women, or for victims. There is no representation. *Wanda* always comes up absent."[22] The implication of this radical gesture of absence on the part of Loden is also, by extension, the (gendered) subject of this chapter: because the call of feminism demands that women self-define, self-identify, and self-represent while functioning as a collective.

Yet Loden's rejection of Hollywood's slick and glossy veneer that, in her own words, renders everything like "Formica, including the people," is not a mere aesthetic or economical choice because, for her, Hollywood is a sovereign part of a capitalist system that keeps people "stupid" and "ignorant" of their own condition and that works assiduously to turn them into good consumers in order to perpetuate that cruelest form of oblivion.[23] That they cannot afford the "dream" (a mirage of the "good life") toward which they are so relentlessly propelled is a central part of the mechanism that keeps the entire aspirational system operational. As Loden remarks: "They work in the factories to make all those ugly cars that don't last so they can get paid to buy a few of those ugly cars and to buy the things that others are making in other factories—to own a color television. It's a whole aspect of America."[24] Loden cannot work within a system in which she does not believe—a system that she felt was only fit for abrogation. To choose to film the everyday, then, is, for her, to render the personal as political: to examine a system that functions through cycles of consumption and disposal by attending carefully to what and who is discarded (notably, Wanda is discarded from working in a garment factory because she is too slow for its operations). Loden is only concerned with what is rejected from the production line, the casualties of capitalist society and the American Dream; she has no interest in either the much feted, yet notably scarce, stories of success or the captains of industry.

Set between two stages of capitalism (postwar and late/finance), *Wanda* is positioned on the cusp of an era that ushered in post-Fordist capitalism and neoliberalism on a global scale: a combination that has only intensified with the advent of an all-pervasive technology. Yet it is also a film that reveals the lie at the heart of the postwar American Dream of upward mobility and prosperity as evinced through highly specific forms of consumerism. As Franco Berardi argues, this postwar ideology centered on "notions of ever progressing development . . . the bourgeois mythology of a linear development of welfare and democracy; the technocratic mythology of the all-encompassing power of scientific knowledge; and so on."[25] Notably for Berardi, this is not only a cultural but also a psychological perspective: it is hard labor to work against the grain of an ideology into which one is born and inculcated (we cannot simply shrug it off). What this so-called progressive modernity implies for Berardi is a form of slow death or "cancellation of the future" by which forms of exhaustion, impossibility, and impasse increasingly come to define us culturally and politically. *Wanda* explores precisely this notion of a slow

FIGURE 10.2 Wanda in the coalfields (*Wanda*, 1970)

slide into death: it examines what it means to live within that cultural impasse in which nothing is possible (in which the future is canceled). The film can be defined as a work of hauntology—that is, following Jacques Derrida, as an ontology of absence—by which the images are defined through what does not happen, what does not come to pass, the promises that cannot be fulfilled, and the frustration and impotence that result in a stillborn life.[26] It is no accident that Wanda speaks of herself as already being dead. She is frequently cast as a friable, white specter on the periphery of the frame, as a ghost that tears a small hole in the fabric of the film. Thornham describes her as "a tiny sharp white figure in the vast grey industrial landscape."[27] Wanda is imaged and understood as a void. One shot of just under two minutes that details Wanda's slow progress on foot out of the coalfields that have come to define her existence has been remarked upon by many scholars and critics in this respect (figure 10.2). Crucially, she is decentered and displaced by the landscape she traverses. It dominates her frame and absorbs her into its grainy textures and muted chromatic scheme so that she appears, at strategic moments, to be on the verge of disintegration. In some sense, then, the landscape defines her.

Wanda as a character is a woman who has forsaken a specific image of "happiness" for life. Her quest (since *Wanda* is a road movie) is one defined not by a horizon of expectations (the horizon is notably absent) but rather by what she does *not* want (which is not the same thing as knowing what she does want). Reynaud has noted that "the film is constructed without a vanishing point. . . . its reverse-angle shots [do] not follow the rules of classical narrative filmmaking."[28] If Renaissance perspective, the representative trope of "a window of enlightenment" onto the world, is missing in *Wanda*—if the horizon does not appear and the human form is diminished and displaced within the diegetic frame—it is because *Wanda* is not a film that partakes in the notion of progression toward a better future and the place of the sovereign individual within it. Contemporary critics were, then, too keen to impress a radical feminist agenda upon the film by noting that it is the nuclear family model and its adumbration of a "woman's role" therein from which Wanda is in flight. This is not entirely erroneous as a reading, but rather overdetermined. The film's politics is, in fact, far more iconoclastic than this relatively contained rejection of societal norms might suggest. Within forty minutes, the American flag features prominently in the film frame in three key scenes (the opening scene, the courtroom scene, and the motel scene in which Wanda begins to sense what kind of a man Mr. Dennis might be). And since *Wanda* is not a film, in my view, that is determined by an arbitrary and random aesthetic selection, but rather is a film that is the result of rigorous and deliberate thought on the part of Loden, this inclusion is of cardinal importance if we are to grasp the political meaning of the film's aesthetics. That is, the model of "happiness" that Loden is contesting is not merely the nuclear family but rather the aspirational model of the American "good" life of which the nuclear family is but one imperative, operative vessel.

The scene set within the courthouse is especially important in this respect. Wanda's former husband is intent on delivering an excoriating portrait of Wanda to the judge in a stream of monologue. He says: "She doesn't care about anything. She's a lousy wife. She's always bumming around. Always drinking. Never took care of us. Never took care of the kids. I used to get up for work and make my own breakfast. Change the kids. Come home from work and she is lying around on the couch and the kids are dirty and there are diapers on the floor. Sometimes the kids are outside running around with nobody watching them." As his speech draws to a close, Wanda appears tentatively at the back of the courtroom. The judge calls her—by using her full name Wanda Goronski—to the front of the court. She approaches but is holding a cigarette in her hand and is immediately reprimanded for it by the judge. She still has a set of rollers in her hair and is not formally dressed. The camera frames the former couple in medium shot. Wanda, notably, does not look at her children as she passes them and issues only a momentary glance to her former husband. In response to the judge's assessment of her as a woman, she responds that she has "nothing" to say. With no visible emotional difficulties, she grants a divorce to her husband along with full custody of their children. She meets neither the eyes of the judge (there is, in fact, a marked refusal of countershot so the judge's perspective appears as a disembodied voice, an apt metaphor for patriarchal law) nor the condemning gaze of her former husband; and so she affirms that she thinks the children would be better off without her presence as a mother figure. While he is keen to portray himself as a decent man (we are kept from knowing the reality of how he may have treated Wanda during their marriage, since it is only his perspective that is impressed upon the judge), she is someone of extremely limited resources (we cannot know the internal bargains she must make emotionally in order to hand over custody of her children). Within the opening ten minutes of the film, she has been forced to leave what we presume to be, in some sense, a family home because she is considered a nuisance, she has had to ask for a meager amount of money from a man who clearly has little to get by on himself (a potential father figure), and she has been denigrated and condemned both in a personal capacity by her former husband and in an official capacity by an anonymous agent of patriarchal law. This is a woman who must beg favors from and suffer the limited and pious judgments of men who are sanctioned to arbitrate over her life. It is no wonder she thinks her children would be better off with somebody else. She does not speak her case because she knows it was written long before she arrived in this particular court of law (which is simply a manifestation of the wider constraints placed on women socially, politically, economically, and spiritually). As a woman, in the specific roles of wife and mother, she has been deemed a failure. Why should she bother to make the effort of removing those hair rollers?

Failure is important here, since Wanda's rejection of and seeming inability to follow this path of happiness ("I'm just no good"), of acceding to the "good" life (which, by extension, demands she be a "good" woman), is vehemently political. Writing forty years after the making of *Wanda*, Sara Ahmed has argued that "the demand for happiness is increasingly articulated as a demand to return to social ideals, as if what explains the crisis of happiness is not the failure of these ideals but our own failure to follow them."[29] The crisis Ahmed writes of is firmly rooted in the current exhaustion of late capitalism, but *Wanda* is, in some sense, a film from the future since its politics is so prescient of the endgame currently being played out politically, economically, and ethically on a global scale. That failure is personalized, so that blame lies not with the body politic and corporations but with the individual who has proved unable to concede to and maintain the strict mores of the capitalist model (made evident as the practice of being a "good" citizen) is precisely what Loden sets out to critique in her film.

Thirty-eight years after *Wanda* was made, Kelly Reichardt (Loden's cinematic inheritor and successor) made *Wendy and Lucy* (2008). Reichardt's film provides another vital future intertext for viewers of Loden's work; with devastating clarity, Reichardt reiterates Loden's critique of America: "You can't get an address without an address, you can't get a job without a job. It's all fixed." *Wanda* and *Wendy and Lucy*, two films made nearly forty years apart from one another and that center on women who fall between the cracks, tell us how very little a so-called progressive form of politics has wrought for the average, everyday citizen of America. Wendy may as well be Wanda's daughter (and perhaps we should read her as such). Both women show us that it is impossible to "bootstrap" one's way out of economic deprivation within a system that has pulled away the safety net.[30] To suggest otherwise is not only ridiculous and cruel but also irresponsibly dangerous. This pursuit of happiness can be thought of as a disciplinary technology that works to orient us toward a life lived within highly specific hermetic boundaries and to turn away from those who cannot be made to fit within that model. *Wanda* is about a woman who has no access to any space of her "own" (that most utopian room of feminist thought), who lives out her life within transitory, provisional, and liminal spaces. Wanda is a figure of the threshold and the margin. She cannot step into and thus claim a space and identity of her own. By attending to failure, to impossibility, to the impasse, we can attain a greater understanding of the ways in which happiness, as a disciplinary ideology, comes to shape our understanding of what it means to be a person in the world: that is, our sense of self and our relationships with other people. It determines who gets to occupy space and thus can be extended and interpolated into the body politic. The loser, the reject, the outsider are important character motifs in art for this very reason: if failure is a refusal to be assimilated, the view from the margin, the canted perspective (that which is askew and awry) may render visible that which is kept from dominant forms of narrative (this is why *Wanda* does not trade in clichéd images even though it adopts a generic framework—that of the heist film and road movie).

Happiness as a disciplinary notion orientates people toward the promise of a future through a horizon of expectations, which is, more often than not, understood collectively as a set of images and ideas that play directly into notions of a good and happy life. Indeed, Lauren Berlant has remarked of this aspirational perspective: "Fantasy is the means by which people hoard idealizing theories and tableaux about how they and the world *add up to something*."[31] It is the promise of the good life, made manifest through generic, easily assimilated images, that is at the root of the American Dream—images that coalesce around certain institutions and gendered roles (the husband as breadwinner, the wife as homemaker). The very concept of the future keeps us on a path that constrains movement: to be invested in happiness is to stick to the path that promises (but never ensures) you a return on your investment. To err from or to stray off that path is to risk a landslide of sadness, depression, disillusionment, and anger. It is to "leave happiness for life" and to recognize that "loss can mean to be willing to experience an intensification of the sadness that hopefulness postpones."[32] Wanda is a woman who refuses to stay on the path set out for her; as such, contemporary critics were right to understand that particular choice as being at the heart of Loden's burgeoning feminist politics. But *Wanda*'s refusal goes beyond binary gender roles and their coterminous emotional burdens: it has to do with the eschewal of a whole value system that is so intrinsically tied to the notion of "good American" citizenship. In this sense, the film's feminism is wholly radical. This is presumably what made Wanda such a seemingly unsympathetic figure for contemporary critics, since she not only abandons her husband and children, an act that is controversial but nothing new, but also refuses to place value in the very *things* and ideals that define the society in which she lives.

Wanda, a depressed woman, does not have it within her to effect or feign happiness in a society that remains defiantly unresponsive and intransigent to the needs of ordinary people (it is not a society worth participating in and lying for). Wanda does not have the luxury of being invested in the future and its promise of happiness. The idea that one must keep to a path that ushers all human experience into what Shulamith Firestone has referred to as that "narrow, difficult to find alleyway" is to lead a life fundamentally outside of oneself in which one's path is predicated on a set of predetermined and limiting choices (indeed, the very notion of having a choice within this context would be an illusion).[33] In this light, Wanda's passivity can be seen as a radical indictment of the multitudinous and infinitesimal ways that women every day are forced to subjugate and deny their personhood—that for many women, an existence as a sovereign individual not defined by men or patriarchal law is an impossible myth. Wanda cannot survive without appeal to the callous indifference of men who treat her as an object to be discarded. Thornham notes astutely that Wanda is a character caught up in a "fantasy scenario" in which men play the part of "writer and director but also star"—a performance to which Wanda remains but a supporting actress and audience.[34] Wanda's sense of the future, even once she has left her domestic setting and its concomitant identity and role, remains precarious and fractious because her choice, regardless of its intent, cannot change her material and social circumstances. That horizon of expectations that shores up a grand narrative of the good life betrayed her long ago.

Wanda examines the attrition of this fantasy of the good life. It centers on the affective bargains a working-class woman must make to survive in a world in which she has no hope of attaining the material comforts and upward mobility that American society promises to its citizens within a capitalist system that admits of no alternative. It reveals that narrative always to have been a lie and as a form of what Berlant has termed "cruel optimism." It examines the "affective rhythms of survival" that erupt in the wake of abandoning the narrative that has been sold to an entire nation—a nation that has been taught to think that there is only space in life for the winners.[35] This is precisely why meticulous attendance to every aspect of the film's aesthetics is so vital. Leaving behind that narrative is hard labor and results often in breakdown, impasse, and unbearable forms of depression in a world that seemingly offers few alternatives. As Berlant notes: "Even though its presence threatens their well-being, because whatever the *content* of the attachment is, the continuity of its form provides something of the continuity of the subject's sense of what it means to keep on living on and to look forward to being in the world."[36] Rejection of that hopeful narrative, false and pernicious as it may be, vitiates the capacity to have faith in that highly specific image of the future. This is precisely the affective territory *Wanda* palpates. The film, through the figures of both Wanda herself and Mr. Dennis, offers a dual portrait of this "cruel" attachment to such a promise of happiness. Wanda's melancholy and despair—as a woman who has precisely abandoned happiness for life—is politicized through Loden's performance and the film's aesthetics, while Mr. Dennis offers the counterpoint of a man who refuses to abandon his "stupid optimism" and chastises Wanda for her lack of investment in the American vision of happiness.

Notes

Portions of this chapter appear in Anna Backman Rogers, *Still Life: Notes on Barbara Loden's* Wanda *(1970)* (Santa Barbara, CA: Punctum, 2021).

1   See Elena Gorfinkel, "Wanda's Slowness," in *On Women's Films: Across Worlds and Generations*, ed. Ivone Marguiles and Jeremi Szaniawski (London: Bloomsbury,

2019), 27–48; Sue Thornham *What If I Had Been the Hero* (London: Palgrave Macmillan, 2012); Kate Zambreno, *Screen Tests* (London: HarperCollins, 2019).

2 Conversely, Raymond Carney, in his analysis of the film, has suggested that *Wanda* is edited to effect "extreme rush and haste." See Ray Carney, *American Dreaming: The Films of John Cassavetes and the American Experience* (Berkeley: University of California Press, 1985). For intricate analysis of the negative politics and slowness of *Wanda*, see especially Gorfinkel, "Wanda's Slowness"; Adrian Martin and Cristina Álvarez López, *Wanda* http://www.filmcritic.com.au/reviews/w/wanda.html (2016(2019); and Zambreno, *Screen Tests*, 222–276.

3 Gorfinkel also points out that these images resemble the Depression era portraits of Robert Franks and the photographs of Walker Evans. Gorfinkel, "Wanda's Slowness," 34; Estelle Changas, "Wanda," *Film Quarterly* 25, no.1 (Autumn 1971): 34–39.

4 Gorfinkel, "Wanda's Slowness," 50; Changas, "Wanda."

5 See Ruby Melton, "Barbara Loden on *Wanda*: An Environment That Is Overwhelmingly Ugly and Destructive," *Film Journal* 1, no. 2 (Summer 1971): 11–15.

6 Chuck Kleinhans, "Seeing Through Cinema Verité in *Wanda* and *Marilyn Times Five*," *Jump Cut* 1 (1974): 14–15.

7 Quoted in Kate McCourt, "Who Was Barbara Loden: *Wanda* and the Life of an Actual Woman," *Propeller Magazine*, 2012, accessed October 2022. Kael's review is available to read in full at https://achives.newyorker.com/newyorker/1971-03-20 /flipbook/136t.

8 Marion Meade, "Movies," *New York Times*, April 25, 1971, 11, https://www.nytimes .com/1971/04/25/archives/lights-camera-women.html.

9 Leo Bersani, *The Culture of Redemption* (Cambridge, MA: Harvard University Press, 1990).

10 See Bersani, *Culture of Redemption* 1.

11 Bersani, 1.

12 Bersani, 1.

13 Bersani, 2.

14 Nikolaj Lübecker, *The Feel-Bad Film* (Edinburgh: Edinburgh University Press, 2015).

15 Toril Moi, *Sexual/Textual Politics* (London: Routledge, 1985), 1–18.

16 Samuel Beckett, "Worstward Ho," in *Nowhow On* (London: Calder, 1984), 7–8.

17 See Thomas Elsaesser, "The Pathos of Failure: American Films in the 70s," in *The Last Great American Picture Show: New Hollywood Cinema in the 1970s*, ed. Thomas Elsaesser, Alexander Horwath, and Noel King (Amsterdam: Amsterdam University Press, 2004).

18 See Sara Ahmed, *The Cultural Politics of Emotion* (Edinburgh: Edinburgh University Press, 2004); Ivone Marguiles, *Nothing Happens: Chantal Akerman's Hyperrealist Everyday* (Durham, NC: Duke University Press, 1996).

19 Marguiles, *Nothing Happens*.

20 In this sense, *Wanda* has far more in common with Dudley Andrew's concept of a Bazinian aesthetics and politics of the image that it does with so-called cinema verité. See Dudley Andrew *What Cinema Is!* (London: Wiley-Blackwell).

21 Thornham, *What If I Had Been the Hero*, 73.

22 Dirk Lauwaert, "Wanda . . . ," *Sabzian*, originally printed in *A Prior 15* (2007), https://www.sabzian.be/article/wanda.

23 Lauwaert, "Wanda . . ."

24 Lauwaert.

25 Quoted in Mark Fisher, *Ghosts of My Life: Writings on Depression, Hauntology and Lost Futures* (Winchester: Zero Books, 2014), 6–7.

26 Jacques Derrida, *Spectres of Marx* (London: Routledge, 1994); Fisher, *Ghosts of My Life*.

27 Thornham, *What If I Had Been the Hero*, 70.

28 Bérénice Reynaud, "For *Wanda*," *Senses of Cinema*, no. 22 (October 2002), http://sensesofcinema.com/2002/feature-articles/wanda/.

29 Sara Ahmed, *The Promise of Happiness* (Durham, NC: Duke University Press, 2010), 7.

30 See "The American Con of Bootstrap Optimism," *Austin Chronicle*, February 20, 2009, https://www.austinchronicle.com/screens/2009-02-20/744096/.

31 Lauren Berlant, *Cruel Optimism* (Durham, NC: Duke University Press, 2011), 2 (emphasis added).

32 Ahmed, *Promise of Happiness*, 75.

33 Shulamith Firestone, *The Dialectic of Sex: The Case for Feminist Revolution* (New York: William Morrow, 1970), 155.

34 Thornham, *What If I Had Been the Hero*, 72.

35 Berlant, *Cruel Optimism*, 11.

36 Berlant, *Cruel Optimism*, 24.

Part 3

Theory and Criticism

Genealogies of
a Decade

Classifying and
Historicizing Women of
the New Hollywood

AMELIE HASTIE

French writer Nathalie Léger opens her 2012 book *Suite for Barbara Loden* with a depiction of a scene from Loden's 1970 film *Wanda*. As she describes it, we see, from above and beyond, "an ethereal figure as it makes it way intently along the forbidden horizon."[1] This "blurry smudge, now almost transparent, like a backlit hole in the picture" is "a blind spot on the decimated landscape. Yes, it is a woman." She describes, too, the process of researching, talking about, and writing an encyclopedia entry on the film that becomes, of course, her little book. After exhaustive research—on the U.S. coal-mining industry, the invention of hair curlers, and the New York theater scene, among other things—she writes: "I felt like I was managing a huge building site, from which I was going to excavate a miniature model of modernity, reduced to its simplest, most complex form: a woman telling her own story through another woman."[2] *The simplest most complex form*. I am haunted by this phrase as I think through not just *Wanda* but also the roles of women in the New Hollywood more broadly.

Certainly, this phrase makes sense, as well, in relation to the common narratives told of the era. In essence, U.S. film production and reception of the "New Hollywood" has been widely understood as an era of "independence": liberation in ideas and aesthetics, as well as "freedom" from the Hollywood studio system. Consistently heralded in these narratives of the era are those male maverick directors who are understood as forces behind these changes. But given that this period of liberation coincides with both the civil rights movement and the women's movement, the time was ripe for changes to that system and our conception of it, not only in terms of rebellious men but also in terms of women's contributions to productions on both sides of the camera. But, of course, both in academic scholarship and in popular histories of the period, until recently, women's contributions to narrative fictional film of the period have been rarely documented or understood. By thinking through various cases of women's work and images, I hope to offer alternatives to those stories we have been told.[3]

As I will discuss, the story of the origins of feminist film theory in the 1970s can, too, be reduced to its "simplest, most complex form." The same can be said for women's film productions of the time, and for popular and academic feminist film criticism. But like film narratives, these stories (or genealogies or trajectories) do not follow a straight line. In structuring this chapter, I have battled these lines, as it is not easy to set up a path of history and of theory that is at once simple and complex, at once straight or parallel and intersecting. As I have battled these lineages, I keep coming back to a series of images from the films that have informed my thinking: images of women moving in straight or diagonal lines, women moving off course, women stopping short in order to redirect themselves. I think of the eponymous character of *Alice Doesn't Live Here Anymore* (1974) suddenly careening off a highway onto an exit ramp. I see the hapless botanist, played by writer-director Elaine May, in *A New Leaf* (1971) as she is carried by a current toward a waterfall— her head and hands going under and then bobbing back up again. I think of another titular character, Claudine (Diahann Carroll) (1974), as she navigates work and family and friendships in New York City: she is on the bus amid other women going to work as the film begins and is hitching a ride on the back of a police paddy wagon with her children and new husband as the film ends. I envision another ending as well, when Erica (Jill Clayburgh), in

An Unmarried Woman (1978), lugs a giant painting that was offered as a "gift" from her boyfriend before they separate for the summer months. This "gift" has become an albatross as Erica navigates the streets of New York: stopping and starting and turning around as she attempts to maintain balance and direction, Erica carries this physical burden as she makes her way to her newly independent home. And then of course there is Wanda, whether a smudge on a blurry horizon, abandoned at a burger stand, waking up in a movie theater only to realize she has been robbed, or alone amid a group of other drinkers at a bar upon the film's end. Like so many other women in the New Hollywood, she leaves and is left.

At a moment when we are collectively refiguring U.S. feature film production in the 1970s, I am therefore telling a series of "simple-complex" stories both about the constitution of the New Hollywood and about the contemporaneous work of film scholarship that has run alongside it. Primarily drawing on three films as models and metonyms, I want to think through those categories that we ascribe to women's work in this era—whether creative labor in film production or the labor of film theory and criticism. The three films—*A New Leaf, Wanda*, and *Alice Doesn't Live Here Anymore*—are quite different from one another in narrative, tone, circumstances of production and reception, and in their critical appraisal. *A New Leaf* is at once a dark and sentimental comedy about a man, Henry Graham (Walter Matthau), who seeks to maintain his economic status (and luxurious lifestyle) by marrying, and potentially murdering, a very wealthy woman. He lands on Henrietta Lowell (Elaine May), who is successful in her work as a botanist and scholar but is socially clumsy and domestically disorganized—all features that demonstrate her utter guilelessness and therefore make her a perfect target for Henry's machinations. *Wanda* is a drama focused on the eponymous character, who leaves her husband and children for a seemingly aimless itinerant experience, during which she ultimately partners with a man who plans a bank robbery with Wanda as his getaway driver. *Alice Doesn't Live Here Anymore* follows recently widowed Alice (Ellen Burstyn) and her son, Tommy, as they head west in order for Alice to pursue a singing career in California. Stalled in Arizona, she takes a job as a waitress, where she develops friendships with the other women at the diner and then becomes romantically entangled with a rancher named David (Kris Kristofferson).

Each of these films creatively originated with a woman. Elaine May adapted Jack Ritchie's short story "The Green Heart" into the screenplay *A New Leaf*; in order to get it made—and to have authority in its making—she also took on the job of director and star, but at the fraction of the salary that her costar was paid.[4] Retrospectively, in a 2006 conversation with collaborator Mike Nichols, Elaine May described the effect of complications of the Hollywood system on her films—notably, the changing of studio heads in the middle of her productions, which meant that films such as her *Mikey and Nicky* (1976) were simply misunderstood by those holding the purse strings.[5] Barbara Loden wrote, directed, and starred in *Wanda* as well—less to placate a studio head and more to realize the project on a budget. As she said, she sought to relieve herself of the "Hollywood albatross"; in an interview with the *New York Times*, she declared, "I tried not to explain things too much in the film, not to be too explicit, not to be too verbal."[6] Ellen Burstyn brought her project to Warner Brothers herself and then chose the director, Martin Scorsese, for the job; she did not receive a producing credit. The approaches by these various women were at once humble and resilient. So, while their circumstances were different from one another, in many ways these three works tell the same simple-complex story of women trying to make feature films in an era on the cusp of liberation.

And here is why I like the word "genealogy." On the one hand, as with the word "trajectory" (another favorite of mine, as it also suggests acts of tracing), it may be defined as a "line." But we also often associate the term "genealogy" with a family tree, all terms that in turn become misnomers or misdirections as I think through these films. Yet, I also want to stick with them. For, while I am indeed interested in the trajectories these figures and their films took in both popular culture and film studies, those terms actually get me to trees themselves. A tree, after all, grows both upward and outward; branches beget other branches; and this natural form changes over time with seasons and with passing years. Like stories we tell, the tree is at once a simple-complex form—a bountiful living thing that demonstrates possibilities for a feminist historiographical approach to this era through both the possibility of new growth and the connections to other branches, other histories.

*

But let me start with a humbler genus. In *A New Leaf*, Henrietta Lowell's specialty is the fern. As she tells the scurrilous and potentially murderous Henry Graham when they spend the night together in his broken-down car awaiting a tow, Henrietta hopes "to discover a new variety of fern that has never been described or classified." Henry asks what such a discovery would lead to, and Henrietta reveals that she would be listed as its discoverer in all the atlases, "and the entire species is named after you." Responds Henry, "It's a kind of immortality, isn't it?" The marriage of a fern and immortality is a neat subtle joke. A ubiquitous garden filler (some species are in fact "invasive"),

FIGURE 11.1   Henrietta and fern (*A New Leaf*, 1971)

the fern was also the iconic houseplant of the 1970s, often hung by macramé and filling living rooms, bedrooms, even bathrooms. This potted plant also ventured out of the house, as "fern bars" popped up in the United States with the goal of creating a friendlier environment to cater to women customers. The potential lowbrow quality of the fern remains unspoken in May's film, but as it peppers the decor of Henrietta's own home, it is impossible not to be reminded of its own humbling, if tenacious, qualities (figure 11.1).

In a kind of irony befitting May, her own "classification" and "naming" over the decades has not had the clarity of such an aspirational discovery. Frequently derided in the annals of the Hollywood studio system at the time and largely unrecognized in academic film studies for over four decades, she has been left out of most "atlases" of film history. Over the past two decades, much of the focus on May's work has been to decry this loss. As Ryan Gilbney wrote in *Sight and Sound* in 2012, "Regrettable as it is that the movies she directed are either out of circulation (*A New Leaf*), little seen (*The Heartbreak Kid*, *Mikey and Nicky*) or unfairly eclipsed by financial failure and dim-bulb consensus (*Ishtar*), there is something fitting about May winding up in the lost property box."[7] Other early retrievals concerning May demonstrate this phenomenon in their very titles, whether Chuck Stephens's "Chronicle of a Disappearance" (2006) in *Film Comment* or Jonathan Rosenbaum's "Hiding in Plain Sight: The Mysterious Elaine May" (1997). Sean Rogers even titles a short piece published on the occasion of May's PBS documentary on Mike Nichols as simply "Elaine-less" (2016).[8] Stephens notes that

May is "overlooked in virtually every New Hollywood hagiography," and he goes on to speculate that it was her actual expansiveness as an artist (writer, performer, director in theater and film) that leads to difficulty in "introducing May anew." Only recently has she experienced a renaissance through art house retrospectives, newly accessible DVDs and digital access to her directed work, and critical attention in and out of the academy. Of course, such has been the fate of many, if not most, women who directed, produced, and/or wrote fictional features in the New Hollywood era, women whose work or roles appeared to defy classification for the industry and its champions and for feminist critics and scholars. My point here is neither to repeat claims of loss nor to merely cast May and other women through an act of rediscovery. Rather, guided by *A New Leaf* itself, it is the very story of "classifications" that I am interested in here.

Released a year after Loden's *Wanda*, May's film begins with the near death of Henry Graham's beautiful red Ferrari and then with the imminent demise of his wealth. Upon learning he is broke—"I wish there were some other way to say it. How could I put it? . . . You have no money," his lawyer tells him—Henry drives through the city in his beloved car, clad in his crash helmet, repeatedly mumbling, "I'm poor." This is an uneasy sequence, to be sure; traversing the streets of New York and therefore traveling across class and racial structures embedded in the neighborhoods of the city, Henry is petulant and pitiful, ignoring the relative circumstances of his plight in relation to other city dwellers, whether waiters or doormen or children playing in the streets. Returning to his apartment—itself clad in original art and other accessories of the rich—he confides his circumstances in his butler, who hatches the means for Henry to wrest himself of his predicament: he must get married. "To a woman?" Harry incredulously asks. Surviving on a loan from his rich and delightfully odious uncle (like a king who sits before a glorious buffet, he cuts bites of an unpeeled banana with a knife while he berates his nephew), Henry goes in search of a potential bride—and potential victim, as part two of his plan is to murder her and survive on the inheritance.[9] The search leads him to the socially hapless Henrietta, whom he marries in record time. Upon their return from their honeymoon, as Henrietta lugs a giant fern that will become the realization of her long-hoped-for discovery, Henry cleans her house of ne'er-do-wells while he also continues to plot her mortal demise. He also absent-mindedly grows increasingly affectionate toward her, wiping off her breakfast crumbs and cutting off tags from her clothing before she heads off to the university in the mornings. As Gilbney notes, "The movie hinges on Matthau's ability to convince us that Henry is oblivious to his own fondness for Henrietta. As long as that self-awareness is buried, we can never be entirely sure that his Bluebeard fantasy won't come to fruition, which lends the film a tingle of danger beneath its daftness."[10]

And then comes the day when Henrietta rushes home to share the news of her discovery. While Henry and his butler pack for the couple's impending camping trip (Henry makes sure to include a gun among his things), Henrietta calls to him from outside. He quickly joins her, and the two share a bench on the grounds of her estate while she near-breathlessly tells him about the fern she brought home from their honeymoon: "When I couldn't classify it, I thought it might be a true species." As she announces that she has indeed "discovered a true species," the film cuts to Henry for a reaction shot, and here the grumpy would-be murderer softens. "Now you'll be able to name a whole species," he says as she beams back at him, and they share a private joke that refers back to the conversation of their first night together. When she tells him that she has named the fern *Esophala Grahami*, however, he chides her for using her married name "after doing all your work as Lowell." She explains, in turn, that she has named the species for him and that it is he who will be cross-indexed in all the atlases and appear also as a footnote.

Henrietta's enthusiasm is infectious, and her guilelessness reaches a kind of apex as she awaits Henry's response to this gift of botanical immortality. For the first time in the film, Henry appears actually content. "Are you pleased, Henry?" asks Henrietta. "Yes, it was very thoughtful of you, Henrietta," he responds. "I believe I am pleased." She bequeaths him a frond that she has set in a plastic token attached to a silver chain, "so that you could wear it always, if you want to" (figure 11.2). As she places it over his head, he nervously wonders again if she is certain she should name it for him: "I feel as though you've given me your place in the atlases." (Granted, one could argue that drawing on their nearly shared first names—another fascinating conceit of the film—might have solved the problem, allowing them to share the cross-indexing and footnotes.) But she assures him of her decision, saying that he has helped to make her a "very confident botanist."

Though rather imperfectly edited—including, for example, a discontinuous inset shot of the fern's frond—this is, I think, a perfect scene. Its perfection is not just in the sweetness between the two, or in the climax of the botanist's discovery, or in the demonstration of Henrietta's professional achievements. I find a degree of perfection also in the way the scene offers a kind of model for thinking about May herself and for thinking, too, about other women filmmakers of the era. Not exactly "a woman telling her own story through another woman," as Léger describes *Wanda*, but perhaps a case

FIGURE 11.2 The frond (*A New Leaf*, 1971)

of a woman forecasting her future story and that of others like her through a very confident if clumsy botanist. After all, not unlike Henrietta, who gives over the name of the newly discovered fern to her husband, Elaine May notoriously often removed her name from projects, and she in fact attempted to remove her name from *A New Leaf* after the studio wrested control of the final edit from her (eliminating two murders Henry committed in her original version). As I have noted, until quite recently, her name hardly has appeared in histories of the era or in feminist film studies more broadly. I would argue that this lack of attention is in part due to a difficulty of classification, something akin to a lack of discovery of this species of filmmaker.

Part of the problem, it seems, is that May has never been neatly legible as a feminist. Often aligned with men, such as her comedy partner Mike Nichols (whose own name crops up doubly in the title of her third film, *Mikey and Nicky*) or the male stars who occupy her films, May seemed neither to champion women nor be championed by many other women in her day. Burgeoning feminist film scholars of the 1970s simply did not pay attention to her, nor, until quite recently, have others in the ensuing decades. Only recently has May herself has been the subject of a more nuanced understanding, such as in Alexandra Heller-Nicholas and Dean Brandum's collection *The Films of Elaine May*. In the editors' introduction, they declare, "Her films resist any easy pigeonholing into discourse around what are recognizably understood as 'feminist' filmmaking traditions"; they further note that "self-identifying feminist women critics and academics have historically at least, not all been

May's allies."[11] While they particularly target the work of Barbara Koenig-Quart's "disdain for lowbrow and popular films in favor of highbrow, low-budget art and independent cinema," elsewhere Maya Montañez Smukler cites a series of 1970s feminist critics who were particularly aghast at May's second film, *The Heartbreak Kid*, such as Joan Mellon, Molly Haskell, and Marjorie Rosen.[12] As Montañez Smukler writes, "These critics, who would emerge as some of the most ardent watchdogs of Hollywood sexism, were especially tough on female artists who, because there were so few of them, automatically carried the burden of representing all women directors."[13] Hence, I would argue that May's fate in film history and scholarship has not been unlike that of Ida Lupino, who was less lauded for starring in and directing her own film *The Bigamist* (1953) and more frequently known through a work nearly peopled only with men (*The Hitchhiker* [1953]).[14] For May, her greatest notoriety similarly has come from *Mikey and Nicky*, starring John Cassavetes and Peter Falk, or, later, the much-maligned buddy film *Ishtar* (1987), starring Warren Beatty and Dustin Hoffman. And she is known, too, for ongoing collaborations with men like Beatty or, of course, Nichols. But then my goal is neither to retrieve May from these associations nor to simply reclaim works like hers as part of a feminist output. Instead, I would offer simpler and more complex terms: exploring women's cinematic work through a feminist lens, I want to both understand and reimagine their historical fates. My hope, therefore, is to undo the binaristic question applied at times to film-makers like Dorothy Arzner and Ida Lupino or Elaine May and Barbara Loden: "But was she a feminist?" Rather, I would like to pursue what feminist historiographical practices reveal about disciplinary foundations and allow for their subsequent reconfigurations.

*

If May's film offers a model for thinking through these very issues of classification and women's creative output in feature fictional films of the New Hollywood, Loden's *Wanda* tells an encapsulated story of women's films of the period—both in its fictional narrative and in the story of its production, exhibition and reception, as well as in its recent revival as a cause célèbre in feminist and cinephilic circles. The film begins with the titular character leaving her husband and children and taking off on her own from rural Pennsylvania. Wanda, as her name suggests, is an aimless wanderer (though, notably, it was the name of an actual woman on whom Loden in part based the film). Thus, in 1970, at a near peak of the second-wave feminist movement, this image and the wanderer it depicts do not easily represent this period of action and transformation. And perhaps that fact is in part accountable for the absence of the film in theaters, in feminist film criticism, and, until recently, in historical accounts of the period. Only in the past decade and a half, in great part due to film critic Bérénice Reynaud's labor and the subsequent restoration of the film by UCLA, has Loden's work seen a renaissance—apparent in Léger's book, in a series of public screenings, and then, of course, at recent academic gatherings and a collection like this one for which I am writing now.

Given the focus of this collection, I want to attend briefly to the dearth of reception of films like *Wanda* in the 1970s, during the emergence of both film theory writ large and feminist film theory more specifically. What accounts for this lack of attention? Why did women who were developing a theoretical framework for understanding women and film not consider such directors at length? I would offer a three-pronged explanation.[15] First, the dominant models for feminist film theory at this time grew out of psychoanalytic, semiotic, and ideological approaches to film. With an emphasis on the spectator who is designed by film's formal (and ideological) systems, much of the work of this period was immersed in what I think of as a kind of struggle with the image—a struggle for control. In fact, what many feminist film theorists considered during this period (and since) is that women in film were objects under control: the control of the look of the camera and of the look of the male characters who dominated them. Those looks—of the camera, of the dominant male characters—transferred also to the film spectator. Thus, second, much of feminist film scholarship followed a two-pronged approach, which is neatly laid out in essays like Laura Mulvey's signature "Visual Pleasure and Narrative Cinema" and Claire Johnston's "Women's Cinema as Counter-cinema." That is, most feminist film theoretical scholarship either focused on Hollywood film of the classical period (1930–1960) or on contemporary feminist experimental work. (For instance, those figures who dominated feminist film/media journal *Camera Obscura*'s early days in particular were Alfred Hitchcock, Chantal Akerman, and Yvonne Rainer.) In effect, these approaches were complementary: both the criticism of classical Hollywood cinema and experimental work of this period sought alternative models of visual construction and address. Third, drawing on other theoretical frameworks, much film theory of this period was increasingly suspicious of "the author"; rather than, for instance, considering the conscious "intent" of the director, such film scholarship focused instead on the film text (and therefore the unconscious desires or beliefs that arose through what is understood as a "symptomatic reading").

Hence, though 1970–1971 was in the middle of feminism's second wave, *Wanda* preceded the launch of the mainstream feminist publication *Ms.*

FIGURE 11.3 Wanda at the movies (*Wanda*, 1970)

magazine and scholarly journals *Women and Film* and *Camera Obscura*. Starting in 1972, *Ms.* regularly reviewed films by women (whether directors, writers, or producer-stars), and occasionally it offered information on distribution, booking, and rentals (one such piece included information on *Wanda*). Loden herself noted that her film was picked up for screenings at universities, and after winning the top prize at the Venice Film Festival, it was expected it would take another tour in theaters, particularly given that its initial run was only briefly in one theater in New York City and another in Los Angeles. But neither those screenings nor the eventual reference in *Ms.* seems to have directed contemporaneous feminist scholars toward writing about the work for decades. Moreover, since feminist academic journals helped fuel future scholarly and pedagogical attention to the films that were featured in their pages at the time, *Wanda*, like the hapless main character—which Loden's self-effacing performance (as well as her writing and direction) so compellingly crafted—had no such luck (figure 11.3).

Of course, the film was not entirely ignored by critics in its day, though it was also not easily championed. In *From Reverence to Rape*, Molly Haskell mentions *Wanda* briefly in the first edition, referring to Loden's portrayal as "less compliant zombiism."[16] She also includes Loden in a list of women filmmakers in the penultimate paragraph of the first edition, before ultimately decrying, "Where, oh where, is the camaraderie, the much-vaunted mutual support among women?"[17] Where indeed. Montañez Smukler begins her discussion of *Wanda* in *Liberating Hollywood* with a mention first of a *New York Times* article by Marion Meade on both *Wanda* and *A New Leaf* (followed by a reference to the obituary in the *Los Angeles Times* appearing under the title "'Dumb Blonde' Made One Brilliant Film").[18] Pauline Kael similarly set Loden's and May's films in a review together (along with Eric Rohmer's *Claire's Knee*).[19] In the section on *Wanda*, Kael begins by noting, "There is much to praise in Barbara Loden's film 'Wanda,'" but she immediately shifts to refer to the main character as "dumb" and "unhappy"—"a real stringy-haired ragmop"—and shortly thereafter as "a sad ignorant slut." And while she ultimately proclaims that Loden has "a true gift for character" and "imagery" (with "eloquent touches"), she defines the film as "very touching, but its truths . . . are too minor and muted for a full-length film." She ends by declaring, "It's an exploratory first film, and one respects the director's strength."[20]

Chuck Kleinhans reviewed the film in the very first issue of *Jump Cut*, offering a similarly muted respect for Loden's work amid a critical appraisal of the social work of the film. His focus, therefore, is as follows: "While the film seems simply to record Wanda's life, giving no solution and no perspective to show 'why' as well as 'how,' WANDA has a message: Wanda is a victim."[21] Yet he takes the film quite seriously, even while he decries its lack of a social context for Wanda's "victimhood." Referring to *Wanda* as "one of the most depressing and nihilistic films" he has ever seen, he notes that his experience made him angry precisely for its limitations (and for its demonstration, in Kleinhans's view, of the problems with realism in American cinema at the time). Declaring that "the filmmaker hides her analysis behind the structuring of the film," Kleinhans gets to the heart of what *Jump Cut* as a journal also demanded of the films it considered in its early years especially, as I will discuss in the following section. To put it simply, Kleinhans joins Haskell and Kael in a sense of disappointment over the film. The main character is a terrible model of either feminism or even woman, suggest Haskell and Kael, and the film is a poor model of socially conscious realism, asserts Kleinhans.

Three decades after these reviews, Bérénice Reynaud shifted the perspective on the film, perhaps as only a retrospective analysis could. Writes Reynaud, "As Hollywood was changing during the '70s and B-grade movies were virtually disappearing, 'non-virtuosic cinema,' or cinema of imperfection, was somehow pushed to the margins."[22] She shifts, in other words, the expectations for the film, recognizing the complex social world the film depicts for its main character and alluding to the complexity of Loden's work as a director in an era dominated by men. Again, I would compare the reception and the recognition of Loden's work to those of director-star Lupino, whose stories of women in her directed works *Not Wanted* and *Outrage*, especially, were an earlier example of the "cinema of imperfection." And the ambiguity of all these films, in both style and content, made them difficult to contain, even difficult to "read." They were "imperfect" feminist works. However, over a decade after the publication of Reynaud's essay, the imperfections of the film and its reception have made it a cause célèbre. Through the restoration of the work by UCLA and its release on Criterion in 2019, it has found a new audience among cinephiles and scholars alike, drawing, for instance, a retrospective set of essays by writers including Haskell and Amy Taubin, neither of whom championed the work in writing following its original release.[23] Its title, "Reflections on Barbara Loden's Feminist Masterpiece," is an obvious marker of such recent reconsiderations.

*

At the time of its release and as a result, no doubt, of Scorsese's involvement, *Alice Doesn't Live Here Anymore* received more attention in mainstream and scholarly work than either *A New Leaf* or *Wanda*; as such, it tells a different story of women and the New Hollywood. In this case, it allows for an analytic narrative about the intersections across modes of film criticism, particularly between more accessible feminist analyses and emerging scholarly models of analysis. For instance, in *From Reverence to Rape*, Molly Haskell refers to the film several times in the original and revised editions of her iconic study; she even lists it as a "feminist-inspired movie" alongside *Woman under the Influence* and *An Unmarried Woman*.[24] In an era that she characterizes as ambivalent, the author is less ambivalent about this film than many others that she discusses, though she notes that, like others, its "feminist theme" was "of conflict."[25] The film was also featured in *Ms.* magazine. In a 1973 interview with Susan Braudy for *Ms.*, actress Ellen Burstyn describes the origins of *Alice Doesn't Live Here Anymore*. In seeking to develop the film, Burstyn says that she considered inviting Loden to direct it, but that she felt the screenplay needed a little "roughing up." Having recently seen *Mean Streets*, she thought Martin Scorsese was the man for the job. On the one hand, the decision not to work with Loden was surely a lost opportunity—for Loden herself, for Burstyn, and for women's film production and film criticism. On the other, the decision and the understanding of it together enable another opportunity over forty years later—one, through historical retrospection, that allows us to consider the advantages and disadvantages of such collaborations.

Granted, *Wanda* was already pretty rough itself—not solely for the physical abuse that Wanda endures but also in its visual style and in the character herself. Indeed, even in their contemporary reappraisals of the film, critics Amy Taubin and Molly Haskell both note that Wanda is not a "role model." As Taubin avers, she has "internalized society's contempt for her so deeply that it was impossible for her to speak or act for herself."[26] We see its roughness also in what Reynaud calls its "non-virtuosic" style. We see it in the grainy quality of the image, blown up from 16mm to 35mm. We see it in the characterization of Wanda herself. And we see its roughness in its persistent durational quality. In its insistent depiction of time itself—the time of a walk across a coalfield or the time of various car rides—the film roughs up its audience, too, demanding our observational attention even as it stretches us to the tears (if not the tears) of potential boredom.

Alice Doesn't Live Here Anymore has a different kind of nonvirtuoso style, particularly when read against Scorsese's tightly wound *Mean Streets*, which directly preceded *Alice*. In contemporaneous reviews and essays, scholars and critics often read the film's form and Burstyn's performance as confused or overdone (she, too, was not a great role model). In other words, its confused form represents a kind of lack of control. We hear it (quite literally) in Alice's voice (a voluminous nasal whine). We see it in the altercations between Alice and her boyfriend, Ben (played by Scorsese favorite Harvey Keitel), and in the roughhousing between Alice and her son, Tommy. And structurally its wholly artificial opening invites a sense of confusion. Beginning with a girl singing in a faux Technicolor landscape, it appears to represent the Hollywood of old, the Hollywood on which Scorsese was raised, which he both emulates and rails against. This nostalgic setting is confusing in other ways, too: But is the confusion Scorsese's, one might ask, or Alice's? After all, she is a dreamer who imagines becoming a singing sensation in Monterey, but the film is more focused on her being stalled in her plans—stuck in Arizona on her way to California from New Mexico and in a nostalgic idea of her past.

This sense of roughness, of a film out of control, was recognized in the response to the film in a 1975 issue of *Jump Cut*, which included three review essays about the film. A film journal whose inaugural issue appeared in the spring of 1974 and born through relative collective efforts between its three founders, *Jump Cut* had an editorial practice that was not unlike that of the by-then-defunct *Women and Film* and, subsequently, *Camera Obscura*, which will appear on the scene two years later. In the first issue, the editors described both their subject of interest and their methodologies, particularly their indebtedness to Marxism: "We want to develop a political film criticism; that is, a film criticism which does not accept as binding the bourgeois idea that art is somehow separate and detached from the social life of women and men. Films often entertain, but, more importantly, they manipulate our image of people, of our society, of our world. We feel that it is important to reveal this manipulation in our most popular and successful films. We stand for a political film criticism because understanding film has meaning only when we are also trying to change the world."[27] Whereas popular criticism was primarily a tangent to the work of 1970s feminist film theory, *Jump Cut* poses a kind of third term here, as it overlaps with each. In its project to analyze contemporary film, *Jump Cut* often explicitly engaged with popular criticism, even if it sometimes distanced itself from this criticism. And while it shared this sense of "difference" from the mainstream with more theoretically inclined journals, it also bore critiques of emerging models of feminist film theory, such as in its reviews of the work of Claire Johnston and Pam Cook (its complaints included a lack of "accessibility").[28] In other words, even while we might see *Jump Cut* as branching between the parallel tracks of popular and theoretical work, it also attempted to create a trajectory of its own.

In the publication's seventh issue (May–July 1975), contributors applied elements of these approaches to three essays on *Alice Doesn't Live Here Anymore*. These three pieces are pretty fascinating in and of themselves, but here I want to point to some of their overlapping claims in order to offer a sense of how *Jump Cut* often attended to the context of film production and issues of representation as part of its "political" method.[29] First, these pieces were pointedly critical, focusing, for instance, on the "improbable" representation and performance of working-class identity in Alice's character and Burstyn's role, as well as on the complications of the authorship of the film—from Burstyn to Scorsese to Warner Brothers studio. Writer Russell Davis saw the "confusion" in the story line of *Alice* as resulting from the confused structure of authorship and authority. He claims, "Scorsese's previous work shows clearly that he has rare talent which can be controlled by a creative, personal force"; he goes on to conclude: "Several critics have accused the director of selling out to Hollywood. It is more likely that he was forced to agree with several whom he had expected to control. The result is a flawed picture, more interesting for its possibilities than its finished form."[30] As Davis earlier implied, I would wager that one of the primary figures Scorsese had hoped to control was Burstyn herself.

In their coauthored essay, Teena Webb and Betsy Martens also critique the implausibility of plot and character (which they saw as not sufficiently working-class). They set *Alice Doesn't Live Here Anymore* suggestively within a series of films that grapple with class and gender, including Loden's *Wanda* and John Cassavetes's *A Woman under the Influence*, to initiate a debate about the political potential of film. They further contextualize these films in terms of audience—not the theorized spectator but the "real people" who see them. Their approach is more consciously feminist in their critique than Davis's, as they claim:

> Women's films generally receive more critical attention than, say, current Black films, perhaps because of guilt-tripping by liberal reviewers and editors, aided by the fairly well-organized communications network among active women, a network which is as vulnerable to co-optation and profit-grubbing as any other mass form. Thus it is important to keep a critical eye peeled. *Ms.* called ALICE DOESN'T LIVE HERE ANYMORE, "brilliant." Pauline Kael, although focusing generally on Burstyn's acting, points out that it is a film whose content generates discussion: "How could the new marital comedies not be controversial?"
>
> But if we put the *New Yorker* and *Ms.* to the side for a moment, who is seeing these attempted reflections of ordinary life?[31]

Although they go on to discuss the "message" of the film (which they read as quite flawed), I want to focus here on the context they develop between popular and academic criticism (and, in a nonparallel structure, between high and low culture). After all, here is evidence that some scholars who were part of the movement to found a discipline of film and media studies in the 1970s were engaged with popular criticism while other academic journals at the time radically separated themselves from such work. In fact, the third piece on *Alice* focuses on Susan Braudy's *Ms.* magazine essay on the film—the same one in which Burstyn describes her decision to work with Scorsese—as a means of linking the material relations between production and reception.

In that third essay in the *Jump Cut* dossier, Karyn Kay and Gerald Peary begin by noting that "Warner Brothers [the studio that released the film] and the *Ms.* magazine sisters prove kissing corporate cousins."[32] They therefore see Braudy's piece as "a strangely premeditated, pre-release hype review," declaring, "In the name of women everywhere, *Ms.* editor Susan Braudy thanked the beneficent studio for 'our movie . . . a little gift from Hollywood,' the supposed masterwork of self-admitted macho director Martin Scorsese on his feminist trip." They go on to praise those "dissident views" about the film that were raised by Molly Haskell in the *Village Voice* and other publications as well. But like Russell Davis, they also see Scorsese as having lost control over his actress Ellen Burstyn, allowing her to do "anything she wants." As they explain, "Without properly controlled direction (the kind Cukor gave

Hepburn, for example), this woman's intuition often proves completely wrong. Her Alice is strictly a non-character—floating, undefined, inconsistent—veering this way and that, depending on Burstyn's whims in any particular scene."

These pieces are pointedly mean-spirited, and they are also largely attuned to issues of realism or the political commentary the film offers. In terms of the latter, they are ideologically parallel to other more theoretical work but often without a claim about film form beyond "reflection" on, if not of, the world. However, they do still put the film in the context of "the world" through their recognition of its production history and in their attention to other mainstream venues at the time. And while it is true that I find these pieces to lack analytical nuance (granted, nuance really was not the point for *Jump Cut*), I find their engagement with the facts of production and the space of popular reception to be enormously important. However, consciously or not, these authors together eradicate Burstyn's significant role as another author of this film. Relegating her role in the production to an unhinged actress, they also question the veracity of her work as detailed in the *Ms.* interview. Though having the potential to sit beside works with a significant female authorial presence, instead *Alice* becomes a lesser Scorsese film, seemingly not only confirming for the future the general quality of his oeuvre and his historical importance but also consigning *Alice* and Burstyn to both historical and aesthetic margins.

Yet another review of *Alice Doesn't Live Here Anymore*, published in *Film Quarterly*, points to some of the same refrains as in *Jump Cut* from a different vantage point. Here William Johnson declares, "Scorsese spent a long time with Ellen Burstyn and writer Robert Getchell in working out the final details of Alice's character and experiences. In addition to its obvious advantages, this kind of collaboration involves risks—a possible loss of focus, a compromise rather than a reinforcement of creative ideas."[33] Johnson's essay moves back and forth between his own positions, sparked clearly by the "ambivalence" that he recognizes in the film. But he ends his piece by refusing to see the film merely through a set of oppositions, arguing instead for a recognition of a "flexibility or unexpectedness in the matching of form and content (or language and message)." Unlike the "closed world" of *Mean Streets*, *Alice*, Johnson concludes, "opens up and lets you inside."

What story might *Alice* tell us today? What does it enable us to see? For one, I see Burstyn's performance and the character at once—an obvious recognition, surely, of an actress doing her job, separate from but intertwined with the character herself. But that recognition is also based on an understanding of Burstyn's very controlled performance of a woman who may seem a little out of control (indecisive and certain at once, a whirling dervish with a plan). And I see something else when I watch it, which is not divorced from history or from the critical work of its day: I see Burstyn's own authorial control in bringing this film into being. I see the other women involved in its production, too—women who outnumbered Scorsese, including producers Audrey Maas and Sandra Weintraub, editor Marcia Lucas, production designer Toby Carr Rafelson, and of course Burstyn herself. In looking at the film in this way—somewhere between history and imagination, memory and fictional narratives—I see the lost opportunity of the era in much feminist film criticism and theory to attend to contemporaneous commercial narratives.

*

As I have been thinking through the films of this period and the context of their production—alongside critical models of the era and the context of their production—I know that I am guilty of staging a series of parallels myself. But rather than focus on oppositions, my work is driven to recognize intersections between ideas, between texts, between critical practices. And so I return to botanist Henrietta's species of choice. A peculiarity of most species of ferns is that each leaf grows from its roots through a rhizomatic structure rather than sharing outward branches. For Gilles Deleuze and Felix Guattari, a rhizomatic structure is in opposition to the "hierarchical" nature of a tree. I agree that there is much that is appealing about a rhizomatic structure, particularly in its biological interconnectedness. And from a perspective of moving-image media, the concept is particularly full of possibility: "It is composed not of units but of dimensions, or rather directions in motion."[34] Yet, Deleuze and Guattari also write that "the rhizome is an antigenealogy" or "antimemory."[35] On the one hand, this notion is an important caution to those hierarchies held in place or designed through a genealogical structure. Think, for instance, of the ways in which women filmmakers and artists have not always had a place on the "family tree" of film history. But must the tree itself, as a biological structure, be hierarchical? And must the same be said of a genealogy? My intent is not to retread an old ground of complaints about the anti-historical underpinnings of "theory," whether the work of Deleuze and Guattari or of feminist film theorists of the 1970s. Rather, I think I would just like to read trees differently, as organisms that actually share some of the very connective traits of the rhizome not only through their roots but, even more important, through their very display.

FIGURE 11.4 In the library (*A New Leaf*, 1971)

As *A New Leaf* is nearing its end, Henry and Henrietta explore the flora and waters of the North Woods. Their canoe becomes trapped in a series of rapids until it is finally overturned. Henry swims to safety while Henrietta flails in the rushing water, unable to swim. As he rehearses his speech describing her demise, he suddenly catches sight of a fern: "The *Esophala Grahami*! Here in the North Woods!" He absent-mindedly calls out to Henrietta to share his discovery, and he seeks his encased frond, which he realizes has been lost to the water. Henrietta, it appears, has been an excellent teacher: she has taught Henry to recognize a species of a fern, which has led to another form of recognition—the affection and need for another person. And so, Henry turns back to the water, at once irritated and with a sense of urgency, to retrieve Henrietta from her impending doom. After she emerges from the river with him, Henrietta renews an earlier suggestion: that Henry join her at the university to teach history. Their shared pedagogical project—they even imagine grading term papers together at the end of every semester—intertwines not just the two of them as a couple but, even more important, the "dead" (history) and the "living" (botany) (figure 11.4).

The merging of history and a field like botany offer a further reflection not just on May's film but on those with which I have grouped it here. That is, historically, biological sciences have grouped species together, subsequently naming them based on shared physical characteristics. But as DNA testing has become increasingly prevalent, some species originally classified within the same genus or family have been rediscovered as less closely related, and the reverse is also true.[36] Such a period of difficultly in naming is akin to evolutionary time: as a species evolves, it is not quite recognizable within conventional systems of classification. Hence the notion of the "evolutionary tree" demands a reconfiguration to reflect previously unperceived relationships between organisms. Is this approach not unlike the goal of feminist historiographical practices? That is, what if we apply a logic akin to the evolutionary tree to film canon formations? Such formations are necessarily transformed as we add formerly discarded works into the mix. After all, the classifying systems of the era—whether based on auteurism, genre, feminism, the subjective notion of "quality," or even the constitution of the "New Hollywood"—have been arguably inadequate to name films and figures like the works I have discussed here, in part because they are dependent on stasis and the certainty of categories. A feminist historiographical project—one that intertwines history and theory, critical practices alongside fields of material production—can upend classifying systems themselves. What we might ultimately recognize is not a shared narrative of what constitutes feminist work, whether across films or in history, but rather a shared project with multiple practices and varied branches. In this way, as we cultivate new growth within our disciplines, the histories that we tell necessarily expand not through straight lines or even superficial likenesses but through multiple directions, associations, differences, and interconnections at once. Like film itself, the directions we take in critical practice are guided by motion.

Notes

First and foremost, I wish to thank Aaron Hunter and Martha Shearer, first for inviting me to their game-changing conference "Women and the New Hollywood" and then for their generosity and patience as editors of this volume. Their vision for both projects has been central to a rethinking of the era. I would also like to thank Sam Hood for research assistance and Katie Hastie for her science tutorials and both of them for their keen intellectual support. With thanks, too, to Kiera Alventosa and Ted Melillo for additional guidance, and to Patty White for writing camaraderie and editorial guidance. A section of this chapter was previously published in "The Vulnerable Spectator" column: "It Was the Seventies," *Film Quarterly* 72, no. 1 (Fall 2018): 58–63.

1   Nathalie Léger, *Suite for Barbara Loden*, trans. Natasha Lehrer and Cécile Menon (Dorothy, a publishing project, 2016), 7. Originally published in French as *Supplément à la vie de Barbara Loden* in 2012 by Éditions P.O.L., Paris, France.

2   Léger, *Suite for Barbara Loden*, 11.

3 In fact, Maya Montañez Smukler titles her recent book *Liberating Hollywood: Women Directors and the Feminist Reform of 1970s Hollywood* (New Brunswick, NJ: Rutgers University Press, 2019).

4 Montañez Smukler recounts: "May was paid $50,000 for her three roles; in contrast costar Walter Matthau's salary was $375,000, in addition to various participation bonuses, and Elkins and Koch [who pitched the film to Paramount] each received $50,000. After Matthau received his grosses, May shared 35 percent of the film's earnings with Matthau, Elkins, and Koch." Montañez Smukler, *Liberating Hollywood*, 80.

5 May discussed this issue at some length with Nichols. Their 2006 conversation is transcribed in "Elaine May in Conversation with Mike Nichols," *Film Comment* (July–August 2006), https://www.filmcomment.com/article/elaine-may-in-conversation-with-mike-nichols/. As for *A New Leaf*, Paramount executive Peter Bart said that taking over the film in postproduction "was not a course of action we would follow with a respected filmmaker, but none of us respected Elaine May. She had worn out every shred of goodwill." Maya Montañez Smukler, "Hollywood Can't Wait: Elaine May and the Delusions of 1970s American Cinema," in *The Films of Elaine May*, ed. Alexandra Heller-Nicholas and Dean Brandum (Edinburgh: Edinburgh University Press, 2019), 49.

6 McCandlish Phillips, "Barbara Loden Speaks of the World of 'Wanda,'" *New York Times*, March 11, 1971, 32.

7 Ryan Gilbney, "Lost and Found: *A New Leaf*," *Sight and Sound*, July 2012, https://www2.bfi.org.uk/news-opinion/sight-sound-magazine/comment/lost-found-new-leaf.

8 See Chuck Stephens, "Chronicle of a Disappearance," *Film Comment* 42, no. 2 (March/April 2006): 46–48, 50–53; Jonathan Rosenbaum, "Hiding in Plain Sight: The Mysterious Elaine May," in *Essential Cinema: On the Necessity of Film Canons* (Baltimore: Johns Hopkins University Press, 2008) 364–369; and Sean Rogers, "Elaine-less," *Cinema Scope* 66 (March 21, 2016): 37–39.

9 See also Martyn Bamber, "*A New Leaf*," *Senses of Cinema* 91 (July 2019), http://www.sensesofcinema.com/2019/cteq/a-new-leaf-elaine-may-1971/.

10 Gilbney, "Lost and Found."

11 Heller-Nicholas and Brandum, *Films of Elaine May*, 10–11.

12 Heller-Nicholas and Brandum, 12.

13 Montañez Smukler, *Liberating Hollywood*, 86.

14 See Amelie Hastie, *The Bigamist* (London: BFI, 2009).

15 See Amelie Hastie, "The 'Whatness' of *Ms.* Magazine and 1970s Film Criticism," *Feminist Media Histories* 1, no. 3 (2015): 4–37.

16 Molly Haskell, *From Reverence to Rape: The Treatment of Women in the Movies*, 2nd ed. (Chicago: University of Chicago Press, 1987), 18.

17 Haskell, *From Reverence to Rape*, 371.

18 Montañez Smukler, *Liberating Hollywood*, 96.

19 Pauline Kael, "Eric Rohmer's Refinement," *New Yorker* (March 12, 1971, 136–140. Her review of *Wanda* runs from pages 138 to 140.

20 In her review of *A New Leaf* in the same article, Kael delivers a less ambivalent takedown, calling it "implausibly bad . . . yet it isn't offensively bad." Kael, 140.

21 Chuck Kleinhans, "Seeing through Cinema Verité in *Wanda* and *Marilyn Times Five*," *Jump Cut* 1 (1974): 14–15.

22 Bérénice Reynaud, "For *Wanda*," *Senses of Cinema* 22 (October 2002), https://www
    .sensesofcinema.com/2002/feature-articles/wanda/.
23 "*Wanda* Now: Reflections on Barbara Loden's Feminist Masterpiece," *Current*
    (July 20, 2018), https://www.criterion.com/current/posts/5811-wanda-now
    -reflections-on-barbara-loden-s-feminist-masterpiece.
24 Haskell, *From Reverence to Rape*, 375.
25 Haskell, 377. Haskell is also less ambivalent about calling out various male directors
    of the era. As she writes, "And the Young Turks who might have been expected to
    ally themselves with women—Martin Scorsese, Brian De Palma, Francis Ford
    Coppola, Paul Schrader, George Lucas, Steven Spielberg—burrowed into violent
    male-centered melodramas or retreated into a no less fantastic world of eternal
    adolescence" (377).
26 "*Wanda* Now: Reflections on Barbara Loden's Feminist Masterpiece," *Current*
    (July 20, 2018), https://www.criterion.com/current/posts/5811-wanda-now
    -reflections-on-barbara-loden-s-feminist-masterpiece.
27 "The Last Word: Inaugural Issue of *Jump Cut*," by the Editors, *Jump Cut* 1 (1974),
    https://www.ejumpcut.org/archive/onlinessays/JC01folder/Editorial1.html.
28 E. Ann Kaplan, "Aspects of British Feminist Film Theory: A Critical Evaluation of
    Texts by Claire Johnston and Pam Cook," *Jump Cut* 2 (1974): 52–55.
29 *Jump Cut* is currently open access, which is a present-day indication of its critical-
    political practice.
30 Russell E. Davis, "*Alice Doesn't Live Here Anymore*: Under the Comic Frosting,"
    Jump Cut 7 (1975): 3–4.
31 Teena Webb and Betsy Martens, "*Alice Doesn't Live Here Anymore*: A Hollywood
    Liberation," *Jump Cut* 7 (1975): 4–5.
32 Karyn Kay and Gerald Peary, "*Alice Doesn't Live Here Anymore*: Waitressing for
    Warner's," *Jump Cut* 7 (1975): 5–7.
33 William Johnson, "*Alice Doesn't Live Here Anymore*," *Film Quarterly* 28, no. 3
    (Spring 1975): 58.
34 Gilles Deleuze and Felix Guattari, *A Thousand Plateaus: Capitalism and Schizophre-
    nia*, trans. Brian Massumi (Minneapolis: University of Minnesota Press, 1987), 21.
35 Deleuze and Guattari, *A Thousand Plateaus*, 21.
36 See the summary of recent research on bird evolution and DNA testing in Wildlife
    Conservation Society, "DNA testing challenges traditional species classification,"
    ScienceDaily (24 June 2016), www.sciencedaily.com/releases/2016/06/160624110314
    .htm.

"Women's-Movement Anger"

Pauline Kael and New Hollywood

ADRIAN GARVEY

American Graffiti (1973) follows a group of high school graduates over a single night in California in 1962. A generally lighthearted evocation of teenage culture in the rock and roll era, the film has a sobering end title that covers some of the protagonists' later lives: John has become a writer, while Matt has been killed by a drunk driver and Terry is missing in Vietnam. Reviewing the film for the *New Yorker*, Pauline Kael noted how this postscript ignores the futures of the film's female characters: "For women," she argues, "the end of the picture is a cold slap."[1] Kael grounds her argument in relation to acting, a favored focus, contending that "because of the energy of performers, Laurie and Carol stay in the memory more vividly than the boys," but she is also making a broader argument about "the limited male imagination of the picture," which uses women characters "as plot functions" and provides nostalgia "only for white middle-class boys whose memories have turned to pop."[2] She concludes, however, "I raise this not to make a feminist issue of it (though that's implicit) but to make an aesthetic one."[3] Kael's approach here is characteristic; she offers a trenchant critique of the film's treatment of women but is wary of aligning herself with feminism. Throughout her career, she challenged and mocked such examples of gender bias, but, as a contrarian critic, she preferred the perspective of an individualist outsider over any position she would have considered doctrinaire.

This chapter will consider Kael's significant contribution to American film culture, especially during the New Hollywood period, when she was a prominent critic who arguably helped to define the era. I will outline her long career and attempt to define her distinctive critical voice, which was marked by a carefully crafted sense of informality. As an outspoken and unapologetic critic, Kael was, and remains, a controversial figure (the 2018 release of the documentary *What She Said: The Art of Pauline Kael* reignited some of the debates about her work and its influence).[4] Kael's approach to criticism, especially early in her career, was combative and often personal. While she provoked and invited argument, some respondents also clearly resented such forthright opinions from a female critic, and I will consider the gendered nature of much of the criticism that she received.

As evidenced in her response to *American Graffiti*, Kael was alert to the "limited male imagination" of New Hollywood but also frequently unsympathetic to the manifestations of second-wave feminism during the period, and I will detail how this ambiguity was expressed in her responses to such films as *Alice Doesn't Live Here Anymore* (1975) and *The Stepford Wives* (1975). With regard to women working in the industry, I will consider her analysis of the work of two great female stars of the period, Jane Fonda and Barbra Streisand, which demonstrates her acuity on star images and performance, and look finally at her more ambivalent views on some of the few women directors of the period, including Barbara Loden and Elaine May.

Career and Reputation

Pauline Kael was in her midforties when she first began to earn a living as a critic, and she spoke often of the struggle and frustration of her earlier years.

Born in California in 1919, the daughter of Jewish émigrés from Poland, she was a child of the Depression. Her family moved to San Francisco after the loss of their small farm, and she would later recall witnessing violence on breadlines and her mother feeding "hungry men at the back door."[5] After dropping out of college, she worked in numerous temporary jobs. By the 1950s, she was co-running a San Francisco repertory cinema and also began writing for film journals and broadcasting on local radio, getting her first commission, a review of Chaplin's *Limelight* (1952), after the editor of *City Lights* magazine overheard her in a café as she argued with a friend about a film.[6] She achieved wider attention with her 1963 *Film Quarterly* article, "Circles and Squares," a denunciation of the burgeoning English-language auteurist school of criticism and, specifically, of Andrew Sarris's "Notes on the Auteur Theory," which would become, in James Morrison's words, "the most notorious parry in the anti-auteurist counterblast."[7] Kael identified an adolescent male romanticism in the auteurist veneration of Howard Hawks and other figures, accusing its adherents of "narcissistic male fantasies" and being "unable to relinquish their schoolboy notions of human experience."[8] This article, and the ensuing debate in Anglo-American film culture, established her outspoken and combative style. It was included in her first collection of reviews and essays, *I Lost It at the Movies*, which was published in 1966 and became a commercial and critical success, with Richard Schickel in the *New York Times Book Review* hailing Kael as "the critic the movies have deserved and needed for so long."[9] After brief and unhappy experiences as the film critic for *McCall's* and then the *New Republic*, in 1968 Kael was hired by the *New Yorker*, where, except for an unsuccessful sojourn as a creative consultant in Hollywood in 1979, she remained until her retirement in 1991.

Kael was among the most high-profile and widely read film critics of her era, with ten volumes of collected criticism, in addition to other compilations, published in her lifetime. Always wary of high culture, she championed film as a popular art, demonstrated by her preference for the term "movies." She focused on Hollywood cinema as a distinctly American cultural form and sought to provide "a record of the interactions of movies and our national life."[10] According to Jonathan Rosenbaum, who describes her as one of the most accomplished sociological critics, "It is frequently said of Kael that she reviews audiences as much as film; one might add that her moral evaluations of each tend to precede her analyses."[11]

Kael's career paralleled the development of film studies, but she was always dismissive of theoretical analysis. Her reviews have an immediacy that powerfully conveys her response to a film: *McCabe and Mrs. Miller* (1971) is evoked as "a beautiful pipe dream of a movie—a fleeting, almost diaphanous vision of what frontier life might have been,"[12] while *Mean Streets* (1973) "has its own unsettling, episodic rhythm and a high-charged emotional range that is dizzyingly sensual."[13] Such descriptions demonstrate her highly distinctive, and later much imitated, prose style, described by Philip Lopate as "flexible, persuasive, vivid, and dynamic,"[14] which aimed for a demotic, conversational tone. As Kael described it, "I was trying to get at what I had actually responded to at the movies, and I couldn't do it in formal, scholarly language."[15]

Kael was a polarizing figure, accused of abusing her considerable power by fraternizing with favorites such as Sam Peckinpah and Robert Altman and supporting their work uncritically while damaging the careers of others. She was also deemed to have fostered a group of acolytes, derisively termed "Paulettes" by her colleague James Wolcott, young protégés such as David Denby and David Edelstein, who were thought to imitate her writing style and support her critical battles.[16] The most extensive attack on Kael's work came in a scathing review of her collection *When the Lights Go Down* (1981): writing in the *New York Review of Books*, Renata Adler argued that Kael, whose early work had "seemed to approach movies with an energy and good sense that were unmatched at the time in film criticism," had become hyperbolic and hectoring, judging the book "jarringly, piece by piece, line by line, and without interruption, worthless."[17] Describing her own approach, Kael would later acknowledge a lack of restraint: "I wrote at first sight and, when referring to earlier work, from memory. This had an advantage: urgency, excitement. But it also led to my worst flaw as a writer: reckless excess, in both praise and damnation."[18]

Reviewing Kael's anthology *For Keeps*, Margo Jefferson observed that "she may not care all that much for westerns, but she has done wonders with the western myth of the outsider who strides into a prissy, self-conscious civilization to teach it some much-needed lessons about honor, justice and truth."[19] Always a contrarian, Kael had initially written from the perspective of a bohemian West Coast culture, targeting what she considered a narrow New York elite, later claiming, "I razzed the East Coast critics and their cultural domination of the country."[20] The staid *New Yorker*, emblematic of the metropolitan culture she derided, was never Kael's natural home. During her tenure there, she was in constant negotiation with the magazine's editor William Shawn about her vernacular tone and preference for popular culture, and she alienated some of the magazine's traditional readership, noting, "I got angry responses whenever I panned anything that was liberal in intention or virtuous or European."[21] Kael's oppositional approach often obscured her own politics, but she was broadly a left-leaning critic who enjoyed mocking "liberal pieties."[22]

"Fanatical Feminism": Kael's Critics

"Pauline Kael: Zest But No Manners; She Tramples Down Polite Men," declared a 1966 *Variety* headline for a report of a National Society of Film Critics panel. The article acknowledges that Kael "obviously deeply cares" and concedes that "her volatility is a refreshing switch from the sober, earnest, even disdainful ... approach affected by her confreres," but she is also upbraided for "shock tactics" and for showing a lack of respect to her fellow panelists.[23] "Her informed enthusiasm for films," the article cautions, "shouldn't preclude good manners," with Kael's lack of decorum implicitly framed as unladylike.[24] Kael's forcefully expressed opinions, which often mocked male targets, frequently provoked heavily gendered antagonism, as in the *Sight and Sound* review of *I Lost It at the Movies*, which accused her of "destructive emotionality."[25] Her "Circles and Squares" article had prompted a response from the editorial board of the British auteurist journal *Movie*, which accused her of "fanatical feminism,"[26] a charge she accepted in typically qualified terms: "I suppose that any woman who writes is in that act asserting the rights of women, and in that sense, I am happy to be called a feminist."[27] Andrew Sarris, the main target of that piece, would later note Kael's "misguided feminist zeal," invoking her book title to unapologetically contend that Hollywood was more geared to male-oriented material: "It is her misfortune (though not ours) that the American cinema has always been stronger in bang-bang than kiss-kiss. Whereas Miss Kael believes that Barbra Streisand's cavortings in trashy musicals are worth thousands of words of gushingly Kaeleidoscopic prose, I believe that movies like *Point Blank*, *Gunn*, *Madigan* and *Once Upon a Time in the West* are infinitely more interesting than any of Barbra's barbarities."[28] Sarris's sexist premise, which erases the wealth of Hollywood material aimed at women, is highly dubious, and his attempt to belittle Kael's "feminine" preferences shows little understanding of her tastes. Kael herself noted the "condescension and hostility" of her critics: "Whenever one of my books is reviewed, the same terms come up. I am described as bitchy or nervous or shrill or as impressionistic—that's a favorite term. 'Impressionistic' suggests, of course, that a woman doesn't really have a good mind, but that she somehow takes off sense impressions though she can't organize them."[29]

Reeling: Kael and New Hollywood

The international focus of Kael's first criticism in the 1950s and early 1960s reflected the widespread interest in international art cinema in the postwar era: the French New Wave and its British counterpart, and the work of Federico Fellini, Ingmar Bergman, and Satyajit Ray. Though she admired some American work of the time, such as *The Manchurian Candidate* (1962), she considered much of the late studio era output bloated and artificial, later describing "a kind of idiot smile over the culture" during the period.[30] However, and increasingly from the 1970s, Kael became, in Margo Jefferson's words, "an Americanist: a descendant of Gilbert Seldes and Constance Rourke in her obsession with the love-hate ties that bind our high culture and our mass cultures; arty trash and trashy art; tradition and invention; the layers of meaning even the crudest cultural product possesses, and the reverberations it can set off in any and all viewers."[31] Kael's focus on, and expectations for, Hollywood cinema grew considerably in this period; she suggests in her foreword to *Reeling* in 1976 that "[a] few decades hence, these years may appear to be the closest our movies have come to the tangled, bitter flowering of American letters in the early 1850s."[32]

Kael is inextricably linked with New Hollywood cinema. She made one of her earliest appearances in the *New Yorker* in October 1967 with a 7,000-word review of *Bonnie and Clyde* (1967) that had been rejected by the *New Republic*, her employer at the time. The film had been poorly received by critics, most notably by Bosley Crowther, the veteran film critic of the *New York Times* and a longtime nemesis of Kael's. Her review opened by asking, "How do you make a good movie in this country without being jumped on?"[33] For her, the film's ambivalent tone, especially in relation to its antiheroic protagonists, and its explicit depiction of violence powerfully addressed the mood of America in the Vietnam era, bringing "into the almost frighteningly public world of movies things that people have been feeling and saying and writing about."[34] Kael's dynamic intervention into the debate about the film undoubtedly established her as someone in touch with contemporary cinema and its audience, in sharp contrast to Crowther, who was removed as the *Times'* film critic in January 1968.[35] Kael's *New Yorker* career began shortly after this, and she would achieve the peak of her influence during the 1970s and early 1980s, when, according to Sanford Schwartz, she "seemed to be putting into perspective, in the very weeks the movies opened, what the onrush of new directors, new actors, and new themes meant to the large audience responding to them."[36]

On Feminism

Nathan Heller has written of Kael's work during this period that "her key insight" was "seeing American creativity in the context of a culture whose premises were being overturned."[37] However, despite her interest in the way in which contested social change was being represented on-screen, she expressed little sympathy for the counterculture, noting, for example, the "numbing hopelessness" and "cool, romantic defeatism" of *Easy Rider* (1969).[38] And, despite her enduring interest in gender politics, Kael was generally dismissive of second-wave feminism and its manifestations in film. In a characteristic quip, she argued that in *An Unmarried Woman* (1978), director Paul Mazursky "touches so many women's-liberation bases that you begin to feel virtuous, as if you'd been passing out leaflets for McGovern."[39] Craig Seligman has suggested that, rather than being anti-feminist, Kael only took issue with expressions of "shallow and self-serving feminism,"[40] and she clearly found some discourse of the period insubstantial and overly earnest. But her desire to distance herself from the movement supports the recollections of friends quoted by her biographer Brian Kellow, as with Karen Durbin's suggestion, "I thought Pauline was deaf to feminism. . . . Not hostile. It just wasn't something she could hear. If she had been younger, my generation, I'm convinced she would have been a feminist firebrand. But as it was, she fought the fight by herself."[41]

Discussing *Alice Doesn't Live Here Anymore*, the most high-profile feminist-themed film that New Hollywood produced, Kael seizes on both its topicality—"I think people will really fight about it"[42]—and its incoherence, calling it "a bigger movie for what's churning around in it."[43] In a long, ambivalent review she describes it as "the first angry-young-woman movie,"[44] considering Ellen Burstyn's Alice as "very harsh, with sheared-off emotions and abrupt shifts of mood."[45] While understanding this anger in feminist terms, as a release from the pressure to conform to feminine norms, Kael is also critical of what she perceives as an ideological impulse behind Burstyn's performance, suggesting that she "flings women's-movement anger into her work," and so, "instead of seeing Alice we're seeing the collision of Alice with Ellen Burstyn's consciousness of this moment."[46] Kael links this to what she identifies as a general shift in the actor's approach to performance, but her criticism of female assertiveness is jarring, and her unease with the tenets of contemporary feminism itself seems to influence this judgment.

The critic Molly Haskell makes some similar criticisms of the film in her two-part *Village Voice* review, suggesting that while Alice is presented as "the victim of Hollywood brainwashing, men and the American dream . . . [h]er strings are not being pulled by men, but by something called the Raised Consciousness."[47] Haskell similarly holds Burstyn responsible for the character's incoherence, arguing that while *Alice* fits the requirements of "the new woman's film," in execution "the actress has taken over and the woman has refused to come alive."[48]

Haskell's work, like Kael's, often adopts a feminist perspective while seeming uncomfortable with feminism itself; she declares herself "a film critic first and a feminist second."[49] Though a contributor to *Ms.*, which, as Amelie Hastie has shown, provided a crucial forum for diverse feminist film criticism in this period,[50] Haskell has claimed that the magazine refused to publish a section of her book "because of my thesis that women had been better off in movies when the studios ran things."[51]

Kael's argument that "what makes the film seem of this moment is the suggestion that Alice has been a victim" is echoed in her review of *The Stepford Wives*, a dystopian drama in which the men of an idyllic suburban small town are revealed to be replacing their wives with placid robots.[52] She rejects the film's implicit critique of patriarchy (the conspiracy is organized by the "Stepford Men's Association"), arguing that "if women turn into replicas of the women in commercials, they do it to themselves." She contends that "as long as they can blame the barrenness of their lives on men, they don't need to change. They can play at being victims instead, and they can do it under the guise of liberation."[53] Noting that a number of critics accused the film of anti-male bias, Anna Krugovoy Silver argues that Kael "simplifies the power of cultural gender norms, ignoring the ways that women internalize gender expectations," and associates her reluctance to hold men responsible with the liberal feminist position of the time.[54] Kael's distaste for expressions of contemporary feminism is evident throughout her work of the period. Despite her consistent interest in gender politics, she clearly found little empathy for what she characterized as "the new women's rhetoric."[55]

"Two Great Heroines": Fonda and Streisand

Kael has argued that, for audiences, "it's the human material we react to most and remember longest," and her criticism shows an enduring interest in star personae and the detail of film performance.[56] George Toles has described how she "chronicles the ebb and flow of viewer attachment to performance effects in her reviews, and suggests that the intermittent excitement of most movies, good or bad, is more dependent on this slippery, massively subjective investment in acting presence than on anything else."[57] Kael was especially drawn to the work of female stars with transgressive screen personae such as Katharine Hepburn and Bette Davis, whom she once described as "the two great heroines of American talkies, the two who dared to play smart women (who *had* to), the two most specifically modern of women stars—the tough, embattled Davis, and the headstrong, noble Hepburn."[58] The New Hollywood era, with nearly all its key films skewed to male perspectives, and with such emblematic performers as Jack Nicholson, Al Pacino, and Robert De Niro, produced few female stars. While Kael admired the work of some who did emerge at the time, such as Sissy Spacek and Diane Keaton, she noted regretfully that "at the moment there are so few women stars in American movies."[59] During this period, she was especially drawn to the work of Barbra Streisand and Jane Fonda, two actors who had achieved stardom in the 1960s but significantly refashioned their images in the following decade.

Kael had effusively greeted Streisand's first film appearance in *Funny Girl* (1968), describing the climactic rendition of "My Man" as "a gorgeous piece of showing off, that makes one intensely, brilliantly aware of the star as performer and of the star's pride in herself as performer. The pride is justified."[60] Kael applauded Streisand's unconventionality and directness, noting "the audacity of her self-creation" in her review of *Up the Sandbox* (1972),[61] and suggesting that Streisand's role as a political activist in *The Way We Were* (1973) drew on the star's own confrontational manner.[62] However, Kael became disillusioned with the actor's work during the 1970s, even confessing, "I fell out of like with Barbra Streisand" in *Funny Lady* (1975).[63] By the time of Streisand's version of *A Star Is Born* (1977), Kael was dismayed by the emphasis on her character's self-sacrifice and felt that the star, who "acts a virtuous person by not using much energy," was stifling her talent to present herself more sympathetically.[64] Her sense of disappointment in Streisand was palpable, but her faith would be restored in the following decade.

Kael became similarly disenchanted with some of Jane Fonda's later roles and acting choices. While Fonda was initially identified with romantic comedies, such as *Any Wednesday* (1966) and *Barefoot in the Park* (1967), Kael had first expressed admiration for the actor in the science fiction comedy *Barbarella* (1968), finding her "more charming and fresh and bouncy than ever—the American girl triumphing by her innocence over a lewd comic-strip world of the future."[65] Fonda's next two roles however, in *They Shoot Horses Don't They* (1969) and *Klute* (1971), represented a radical break with her previous persona and performance style. In describing the first of these, Kael argued that Fonda, as Gloria, the embittered, cynical marathon dance contestant, "stands a good chance of personifying American tensions and dominating our movies as Bette Davis did in the thirties."[66] As *Klute*'s Bree, the New York prostitute who is threatened by a former client, Kael suggested,

"There isn't another young dramatic actress in American films who can touch her," noting that "she gives herself over to the role, and yet she isn't lost in it—she's fully in control, and her means are extraordinarily economical."[67] Fonda has discussed how her approach to this role was influenced by her nascent feminism.[68] These beliefs became more evident in her subsequent work, when, as Maria Pramagiorre suggests, "after her post-Vietnam 'comeback' in 1977, she was constructed as an emblematic figure for second-wave feminists on the path of self-discovery."[69]

For Kael, however, this ideological impulse hampered Fonda's work. After admiring Fonda's "stubborn strength" in *Julia* (1977), playing Lillian Hellman as "a driven embattled woman," she mourned the actor's lack of energy in *Coming Home* (1978) and *Nine to Five* (1980).[70] In the Vietnam war drama she felt that "Jane Fonda's face seems a little vague and pasty, as if she didn't want to stand out too much; her features seem to have disappeared. She's trying to act without her usual snap,"[71] while noting in the feminist comedy that "it's easy to forget that Jane Fonda is around; this must be the first time that she has ever got lost in the woodwork."[72] As with Burstyn's portrayal of Alice, Kael found Fonda's perceived agenda constricting and limiting in terms of performance (saying of *Nine to Five* that "it's not much fun watching her get politicized all over again")[73] and seems to have especially mourned the absence of Fonda's drive and asperity on-screen.

Women Directors

Although generally very attentive to issues of gender in cinema, Kael wrote little about women as directors, though in part perhaps because of the dearth of examples. Talking in 1972 about the obstacles that have historically faced women in Hollywood, she argued with considerable optimism that "there have always been paths and loopholes that we have been able to find"; acknowledging that "it was almost impossible for women to become directors," she contends that, instead, "they became script girls, and then from that, when talkies came in, they became screenwriters."[74]

Never very sympathetic to the woman's film, she wrote little about the melodramas of Dorothy Arzner, one of the very few women directors of classical Hollywood. In a capsule review of the director's *Dance, Girl, Dance* (1940), a film that was reclaimed by feminist film criticism of the 1970s, she does, however, acknowledge the potential of female authorship in suggesting that "the RKO B-movie plot undermines the attempts of the director,

Dorothy Arzner, and the writers, Tess Slesinger and Frank Davis, to work in modern, liberated-woman attitudes."[75]

Kael unexpectedly evoked Arzner in the context of the independent Western *Billy Jack* (1971), considering a sequence in which Jean, played by the film's co-screenwriter and coproducer Delores Taylor, describes her experience of rape. For Kael, Jean speaks "in terms of a specific feminine anger at the violation of her person," and she argues that "her reactions have some truth to women's feelings and to women's difficulties in articulating these feelings."[76] She links this moment with a sequence from Arzner's *Christopher Strong* (1934), in which the aviator played by Katharine Hepburn is persuaded to give up her career: "It is the intelligent women's primal post-coital scene, and it's on film; probably it got there because the movie was written by a woman Zoe Akins, and directed by a woman, Dorothy Arzner."[77]

Kael's interest in discerning a female point of view is also very evident in her review of Agnès Varda's *Cléo de 5 a 7* (1962), which she describes as "one of the few films directed by a woman in which the viewer can sense a difference," identifying "an unsentimental yet subjective tone that is almost unique in the history of movies."[78] However, Kael was deeply unsympathetic to much of Varda's later work, identifying a "sunshiny, masscult-hip simplicity" in the feminist message of *One Sings, the Other Doesn't* (1977) that she found "laughable."[79]

Kael often seemed grudging in her assessments of the few women directors of the New Hollywood era, as if reluctant to overpraise them. Of *Hester Street* (1975), she wrote that "Joan Silver may not have a very large talent (at least, in this first feature there's no evidence of shattering vitality), but she *is* gifted."[80] Reviewing *Harlan County USA* (1976), she echoes this judgment, suggesting that "Barbara Kopple isn't a great documentarian, but she has a great subject in *Harlan County, U.S.A.*, and she has the taste and sensitivity not to betray it."[81] Kael does, however, acknowledge the significance of the director's gender in this instance: "This is not the sort of film in which one would expect the sex of the director to make much difference, but Barbara Kopple has unusual rapport with the women, and throughout—in groups, at meetings, talking—they're observed in a relaxed, friendly way."[82]

Strikingly, Kael's *New Yorker* column for April 13, 1971, included reviews for two films that credited a woman as director, screenwriter, and star: Barbara Loden's independently financed *Wanda* (1970) and *A New Leaf* (1971), which made Elaine May the first female director hired by Paramount Studios since Dorothy Arzner in 1932.[83] Though she described *Wanda* itself as "an extremely drab and limited piece of realism," Kael also found "much to praise" in the film, the story of a withdrawn, aimless young woman, played by Loden herself, who is brutalized by the men she encounters.[84] Kael is deeply unsympathetic toward the central character, who she variously terms "a bedraggled dummy," "a real stringy-haired ragmop," and "a sad, ignorant slut."[85] But she is admiring of Loden's characterizations, of some of the visual qualities of the film, and especially of the director's integrity in "doing things the hard way rather than falling back on clichés."[86]

Kael is almost entirely dismissive of May's film, though acknowledging that studio interference may have been to blame for its weaknesses, and even her very limited praise is double-edged: "Somehow—and this may be a feminine contribution—there is a sweetness about its absence of style, about its shapeless, limp comic scenes."[87] She was, however, much more enthusiastic about the director's second feature in 1972, "a comedy with a director's style and personality," declaring that "Elaine May finds her comic tone in *The Heartbreak Kid*, and she scores a first besides: No American woman director has ever before directed her daughter in a leading role."[88] Kael commends May for transcending the formulaic screenplay of Neil Simon and for establishing a distinct register: "a special, distracted comic tone . . . uncertainty as a comic attitude."[89]

Kael's greatest praise for the work of a female director came at the end of the New Hollywood period, in her review of Barbra Streisand's *Yentl* (1983). The praise is not unqualified, and some of her criticisms of the film—songs that are "tainted with feminist psychobabble,"[90] and the altered ending in which Yentl leaves for America suggesting "a sisterhood fable about learning to be a free woman"[91]—reflect Kael's perennial resistance to overt women's movement themes. However, despite these caveats, the review as a whole has some of the entranced tone of her responses to Altman and other favorites, declaring that "there is something genuinely heroic in the mixture of delicacy and strength that gives this movie its suppleness."[92] Kael also identifies the contribution of a female point of view, finding in Streisand's work with her costar Amy Irving "a kind of rapport that you don't see in movies directed by men," and crediting the film with "a modulated emotionality that seems distinctively feminine."[93] The review also seeks to vindicate Streisand for her "difficult" reputation, with Kael clearly relishing the achievement and vindication of a performer she has championed.

Conclusion

Pauline Kael was undoubtedly an advocate for women in cinema, as well as an astute critic of men's work in the medium. However, while the height of her career in the 1970s coincided with the rise of second-wave feminism, she was never an ally for the cause, feeling distanced from the movement by age, by class background, and, above all perhaps, by temperament. Kael often presented herself as a hard-bitten, no-nonsense character: as someone who "went to the liquor cabinet and poured a good stiff drink" after reading a patronizing critique of her radio show.[94] She admired Katharine Hepburn and Bette Davis for their strength and independence on-screen, and regretted what she saw as Jane Fonda's and Barbra Streisand's failure to retain these qualities in their roles. She contrasts Hepburn, who "made ordinary heroines seem mushy," with other female stars "who cop out in their roles by getting pregnant, or just by turning emotional—all womanly and ghastly."[95] Elsewhere, she unfavorably compares the "tart, independent women" of "wisecracking comedies" with "the sobbing and suffering ladies" of the "lachrymose, masochistic" woman's film.[96] In the vivid contrasts here between strength and emotionalism, there are echoes of Kael's views on feminism, something she associates with victimhood and special pleading, and of her mocking allusion to "sisterhood." For her arguably, second-wave feminism itself seemed "mushy," an ineffectual and sentimental movement.

Perhaps, as Karen Durbin has suggested, Kael "fought the fight by herself," and her prolific career stands as a testament to her achievements as a writer and an incisive, original critic. Acknowledging Kael's influence, Annette Michelson suggests that "a generation of fairly casual filmgoers were inducted by her into a literate cinephilia, through work infused with energy, courage, enthusiasm, and an informed intimacy with her chosen field."[97] One of this generation, Farran Smith Nehme, has recalled, "I would read her capsules in the front, or her ever-lengthening reviews in the back, and marvel at the syncopated, give-a-damn writing style and her utter faith in her own judgment. The fact that she was a woman mattered to me, too."[98]

Notes

1 Pauline Kael, "Un-People," *New Yorker*, October 29, 1973, 154.
2 Kael, "Un-People," 154–156.
3 Kael, 156.
4 See, for example, "What She Said: The Art of Pauline Kael, Q&A DOC NYC 2018," November 11, 2018, https://www.youtube.com/watch?v=ndaeg_T5u1s.
5 Pauline Kael, quoted in Studs Terkel, *Hard Times: An Illustrated History of the Great Depression* (New York: New Press, 1986), 33.
6 See Brian Kellow, *Pauline Kael: A Life in the Dark* (New York: Viking, 2011), 45.

7   James Morrison, *Auteur Theory and "My Son John"* (New York: Bloomsbury Academic, 2018), 66.

8   Pauline Kael, "Circles and Squares," *Film Quarterly* 16, no. 3 (Spring 1963): 26.

9   Richard Schickel, "A Way of Seeing a Picture," *New York Times Book Review*, March 14, 1965, 6.

10 Pauline Kael, *Deeper Into Movies* (London: Calder and Boyars, 1975), xv.

11 Jonathan Rosenbaum, *Goodbye Cinema, Hello Cinephilia: Film Culture in Transition* (Chicago: University of Chicago Press, 2010), 341.

12 Pauline Kael, "Pipe Dream," *New Yorker*, July 3, 1971, 40.

13 Pauline Kael, "Everyday Inferno," *New Yorker*, October 8, 1973, 157.

14 Phillip Lopate, "Pauline Kael," *American Movie Critics: An Anthology from the Silents until Now*, ed. Phillip Lopate (New York: The Library of America, 2006), 330.

15 Pauline Kael, quoted in Sam Staggs, "Did She Lose It at the Movies?," in *Conversations with Pauline Kael*, ed. Will Brantley (Jackson: University Press of Mississippi, 1996), 95 (hereafter cited as *Conversations with Pauline Kael*).

16 See James Wolcott, "Waiting for Godard," *Vanity Fair*, April 1997, 124–132.

17 Renata Adler, "The Perils of Pauline," *New York Review of Books*, August 14, 1980.

18 Pauline Kael, *For Keeps* (New York: Dutton, 1994), xxii.

19 Margo Jefferson, "Pauline Kael: Loving and Loathing," *New York Times*, December 28, 1994, C19.

20 Kael, *For Keeps*, xix.

21 Marc Smirnoff, "Pauline Kael: The Critic Wore Cowboy Boots," in *Conversations with Pauline Kael*, 156.

22 Pauline Kael, "Bonnie and Clyde," *New Yorker*, October 21, 1967, 170.

23 "Beau," "Pauline Kael: Zest But No Manners," *Variety*, December 13, 1967, 1, 54.

24 "Beau," 54.

25 Geoffrey Nowell-Smith, "I Lost It at The Movies," *Sight and Sound* 34, no. 3 (Summer 1965): 154.

26 Ian A. Cameron, Mark Shivas, Paul Mayersberg, V.F. Perkins, "Correspondence and Controversy: 'Movie' vs. Kael," *Film Quarterly* 17, no. 1 (Autumn 1963): 61.

27 Pauline Kael, "Criticism and Kids Games," *Film Quarterly* 17, no. 1 (Autumn 1963): 62.

28 Andrew Sarris, "Notes on the Auteur Theory in 1970," *Film Comment* 6, no. 3 (Fall 1970): 7.

29 Leo Lerman, "Pauline Kael Talks about Violence, Sex, Eroticism and Women and Men in the Movies," in *Conversations with Pauline Kael*, 40.

30 Michael Sragow, "Passion of a Critic: Kael on Mediocrity, Risk and American Movies," in *Conversations with Pauline Kael*, 103.

31 Jefferson, "Pauline Kael," C19.

32 Kael, *Reeling*, xiv.

33 Kael, "Bonnie and Clyde," 147.

34 Kael, 147.

35 "Crowther Named Critic Emeritus," *New York Times*, November 20, 1967, 60.

36 Sanford Schwartz, "Visionary, Romantic, Down-to-Earth Pauline Kael," in *Talking about Pauline Kael: Critics, Filmmakers and Scholars Remember an Icon*, ed. Wayne Stengel (Lanham, MD: Rowman and Littlefield, 2015), 106–107.

37 Nathan Heller, "What She Said: The Doings and Undoings of Pauline Kael," *New Yorker*, October 24, 2011, 76.

38 Pauline Kael, "Americana," *New Yorker*, December 27, 1969, 48.

39 Pauline Kael, "Empathy, and Its Limits," *New Yorker*, March 6, 1978, 99.

40 Craig Seligman, *Sontag & Kael: Opposites Attract Me* (New York: Counterpoint, 2004), 161–162.

41 Kellow, *Pauline Kael*, 174.

42 Pauline Kael, "Woman on the Road," *New Yorker*, January 13, 1975, 74.

43 Kael, "Woman on the Road," 77.

44 Kael, 77.

45 Kael, 75.

46 Kael, 76.

47 Molly Haskell, "Will Odysseus Stay Home and Do Needlepoint While Penelope Wanders Off in Search of Herself and Maybe Gets a Job Singing?," *Village Voice*, February 17, 1975, 67.

48 Molly Haskell, "Alice in Actor's Studio Land," *Village Voice*, January 6, 1975, 2.

49 Molly Haskell, *From Reverence to Rape: The Treatment of Women in the Movies* (Harmondsworth: Penguin, 1974), 38.

50 See Amelie Hastie, "The 'Whatness' of *Ms.* Magazine and 1970s Feminist Film Criticism," *Feminist Media Histories* 1, no. 3 (Summer 2015): 4–37.

51 Matt Zoller Seitz, "Molly Haskell on Feminism, Censorship, Screwball Comedy, and Life after Andrew Sarris," *RogerEbert.com*, January 2, 2017, https://www.rogerebert.com/mzs/molly-haskell-on-feminism-censorship-screwball-comedy-and-life-after-andrew-sarris.

52 Kael, "Woman on the Road," 77.

53 Pauline Kael, "Male Revenge," *New Yorker*, February 24, 1975, 112.

54 Anna Krugovoy Silver, "The Cyborg Mystique: 'The Stepford Wives' and Second Wave Feminism," *Women's Studies Quarterly* 30, no. 1/2 (Spring–Summer 2002): 61.

55 Kael, "Empathy and Its Limits," 101.

56 Pauline Kael, "Trash, Art, and the Movies," *Harper's Magazine*, February 1, 1969, 74.

57 George Toles, "Writing about Performance: The Film Critic as Actor," in *The Language and Style of Film Criticism*, ed. Alex Clayton and Andrew Klevan (Abingdon: Routledge, 2011), 96.

58 Pauline Kael, "The Lioness in Winter," *New Yorker*, November 9, 1968, 190–191.

59 Pauline Kael, "Three," *New Yorker*, October 15, 1973, 160.

60 Pauline Kael, "Bravo," *New Yorker*, September 28, 1968, 137.

61 Pauline Kael, "Star Mutations," *New Yorker*, December 30, 1972, 48.

62 Kael, "Three," 177–178.

63 Pauline Kael, "Talent Isn't Enough," *New Yorker*, March 17, 1975, 118.

64 Pauline Kael, "Contempt for the Audience," *New Yorker*, January 10, 1977, 90.

65 Pauline Kael, "A Fresh Start," *New Yorker*, November 2, 1968, 182.

66 Pauline Kael, "Gloria, the Girl without Hope," *New Yorker*, December 20, 1969, 67.

67 Kael, "Pipe Dream," 42.

68 See Jane Fonda, *My Life So Far* (London: Ebury Press, 2006), 247–254.

69 Maria Pramaggiore, "Jane Fonda: From Graylist to A-List," in *Hollywood Reborn: Movie Stars of the 1970s*, ed. James Morrison (New Brunswick, NJ: Rutgers University Press, 2010), 19.

70 Pauline Kael, "A Woman for All Seasons?," *New Yorker*, October 10, 1977, 99.

71 Pauline Kael, "Mythologizing the Sixties," *New Yorker*, February 20, 1978, 119–120.

72 Pauline Kael, "Tramont's Mirror/Women à la Mode," *New Yorker*, March 9, 1981, 111.

73 Kael, 111.

74 Lerman, "Pauline Kael Talks about Violence," 40.

75 Pauline Kael, *5001 Nights at the Movies: Shorter Reviews from the Silents to the '90s* (New York: Marion Boyars, 1993), 169.

76 Pauline Kael, "Winging It," *New Yorker*, November 27, 1971, 148.

77 Kael, "Winging It," 148.

78 Kael, *5001 Nights at the Movies*, 140.

79 Pauline Kael, "Scrambled Eggs," *New Yorker*, November 14, 1977, 75–76.

80 Pauline Kael, "Becoming an American," *New Yorker*, November 24, 1975, 167.

81 Pauline Kael, "Harlan County," *New Yorker*, January 24, 1977, 84.

82 Kael, "Harlan County," 84.

83 Maya Montañez Smukler, *Liberating Hollywood: Women Directors and the Feminist Reform of 1970s American Cinema* (New Brunswick, NJ: Rutgers University Press, 2019), 80.

84 Pauline Kael, "Eric Rohmer's Refinement," *New Yorker*, March 20, 1971, 138.

85 Kael, "Eric Rohmer's Refinement," 138. In her feminist chronology of Hollywood cinema, Marjorie Rosen also admired the film but similarly characterized Wanda as a "pathetic simpleton." See Marjorie Rosen, *Popcorn Venus: Women, Movies and the American Dream* (New York: Avon Books, 1974), 385.

86 Kael, "Eric Rohmer's Refinement," 140.

87 Kael, 140.

88 Pauline Kael, "New Thresholds, New Anatomies," *New Yorker*, December 16, 1972, 126.

89 Kael, "New Thresholds, New Anatomies," 128.

90 Pauline Kael, "The Perfectionist," *New Yorker*, November 28, 1983, 170.

91 Kael, "The Perfectionist," 174.

92 Kael, 176.

93 Kael, 176.

94 Pauline Kael, "Replying to Listeners," in *I Lost It at the Movies: Film Writings 1954–1965* (New York: Marion Boyars, 1994), 233.

95 Kael, "The Lioness in Winter," 191.

96 Kael, "Winging It," 152.

97 Annette Michelson, "Eco and Narcissus," *Artforum*, March 2002, 165.

98 "Self-Styled Siren" (Farran Smith Nehme), "Lucking Out and Pauline Kael: A Life in the llDark," October 25, 2011, http://selfstyledsiren.blogspot.com/2011/10/lucking-out-and-pauline-kael-life-in.html.

13

Feminism,
Auteurism, and the
1970s, in Theory

MARIA PRAMAGGIORE

All culture implies knowledge of a past, a past we begin learning as soon as we enter school.

ANDRÉ BAZIN, "Let's Rediscover Cinema"

The 1970s enjoy a privileged place within Anglo-American film studies as the decade of theory, an "intellectual constellation" that reconsidered "the fundamental terms through which cinema was experienced and understood in classical film theory and in standard modes of film criticism and analysis."[1] At a time when unprecedented changes were sweeping through the U.S. film industry—led by the decline of the studio system and the advent of the

New Hollywood filmmakers known as the first film school generation—the academic study of film was also experiencing a profound transformation.[2] The earliest sites where film production programs were established included Columbia University (1910), the Moscow Film School (1919), and the University of Southern California (1929), whereas film studies programs typically trailed or "piggybacked" on production programs, emerging throughout the midcentury.[3] By 1960, according to E. Ann Kaplan, the "disciplining of cinema" had begun, inaugurated by the publication of books commissioned by the BFI's Education Department that "prepared for film's entry into the academy."[4]

During the 1960s, film was increasingly viewed not only as an art form but also as the "art of the youth generation," becoming the "fastest growing area of arts study in American universities."[5] Michael Zyrd considers 1970 a turning point distinguishing the decade that followed from a prior era in which films were screened and debated in museums, libraries, films clubs, and film societies. In the early seventies, however, film studies achieved academic institutionalization and recognition through the acquisition of department status and the dissemination of research by university presses.[6] Amid the rapid growth in courses, programs, students, and instructors, academic film studies departed from film industry practice on at least one important dimension. Unlike Hollywood—where macho antiheroes raged on-screen, male wunderkind-auteurs reigned behind the scenes, and women creators and craftspeople generally remained unsung collaborators—academic film studies gave voice to feminist approaches.[7] More specifically, film theory became heavily indebted to, and, in the view of some scholars, nearly synonymous with, a single text of feminist criticism: Laura Mulvey's *Screen* essay "Visual Pleasure and Narrative Cinema" (1975).

Mulvey's complex, hybrid methodology, drawn from Marx and Althusser as well as Freudian and Lacanian psychoanalysis, combined with her self-professed cinephilia to lend a specialized intellectual rigor and timely social awareness to Anglo-American film theory. The article's political call to action enhanced its salience in a period marked by activism around Black civil rights as well as feminist, gay, and disability rights. Zyrd argues Mulvey's widely anthologized essay was key to the academic recognition of the field, helping "the fledgling discipline of film studies to raise its academic profile in the 1970s and 1980s and approach the status of literary, art, and critical studies."[8] Other scholars contend that the auteur theory, adapted from the writing of the *Cahiers du Cinéma* critics by Andrew Sarris, had already performed this work during the 1960s.[9]

Like other film theorists in the 1970s, Mulvey draws upon French post-structuralist theory, crediting the film apparatus with the capacity to impose ways of seeing (notably, the male gaze) while also organizing her argument around the predilections of two well-known Hollywood auteurs: Josef von Sternberg and Alfred Hitchcock. This confluence of approaches suggests the overlapping interests, intersections, and tensions that inform the relationship between feminist and auteurist approaches: the former primarily interested in challenging the gendered and hierarchical politics of representation (a full engagement with film production cultures would come later), and the latter, particularly the version of the auteur theory *la politique des auteurs* engendered in the United States, engaged in reifying male directors who, it was argued, had successfully navigated the constraints of the Hollywood studio system to produce distinctive work.

There are several ironies at work here: first, that film studies, an emerging discipline aspiring to legitimacy within a canon-dependent university milieu that it also sought to resist, successfully leveraged an oppositional feminist work to establish its authority. Second, the poststructuralist theory subtending debates around the *politique des auteurs* and auteur theory was also a key element within Mulvey's argument. Bazin's 1957 statement in *Cahiers du Cinéma* that "there can be no definitive criticism of genius or talent which does not first take into consideration the social determinism, the historical combination of circumstances and the technical background which to a large extent determine it" does not overtly name the poststructuralist crisis of the speaking subject but nevertheless argues forcefully for the importance of contextualizing individual agency within systems of culture, history, and technology.[10] Mulvey's essay manages Bazin's delicate balance by situating her case studies of Sternberg's fetishism and Hitchcock's sadistic scopophilia within a broader analysis of gendered ways of seeing that "traces cinema's complicity with patriarchy."[11]

Finally—though these observations by no means exhaust the complex relationship between feminism and auteurism—one should be wary of attempts to cast "Visual Pleasure" as an origin story for second-wave feminist academics, an intellectual counterpart to Helen Reddy's pop anthem, "I Am Woman" (1972). Recalling that, at the time of the essay's publication she was emerging from writer's block and in danger of missing her deadline, Mulvey writes that *Screen* editor Ben Brewster titled the article, usurping a critical function generally assigned to the author.[12] Mulvey's "germinal essay"—"cited and reprinted . . . more often than any other [in] film theory," has been treated as the founding document of feminist film theory, though there were feminist film publications prior to its appearance.[13] Moreover, it became synonymous with film theory itself across humanities and social science disciplines for decades, primarily because of the conceptual power of gaze theory.[14]

This chapter revisits Mulvey's essay as a uniquely influential academic intervention and explores its relationship to auteurism, a sibling theoretical construct associated with film theory and filmmaking during the 1960s and 1970s. Despite repeated "disdainful dismissal[s]," especially of the crudest form of auteurism—the celebration of individual male genius—the auteur approach continues to "open up avenues for exploring key questions in film theory."[15] For example, James Morrison finds Peter Wollen's view of the central argument of auteur theory compelling: "Any film, certainly a Hollywood film, is a network of different statements, crossing and contradicting each other, elaborated into a final 'coherent' version."[16] In his discussion of film production in the 1970s, Aaron Hunter goes further, identifying an alternative to the single-author model in the notion of multiple authorship, which addresses Wollen's polyphony by recognizing "distinct authorial contributions."[17] Hunter argues that the concept of the single author "played a significant role in the branding of the [New Hollywood] era as one of a director's cinema," an observation that artfully embraces both filmmaking and academic film studies.[18]

I would like to propose that the concept of the single author played a similar role in branding academic auteurs, with Mulvey among the most prominent. As Corinn Columpar observed twenty-five years after the essay's publication, many feminist film critics "still feel the need to preface our own remarks" with at least a gloss on "Visual Pleasure": a "near compulsive return to a hypothetical theoretical origin" that "laid the foundation for an entire field of critical inquiry."[19] The opening epigraph from Bazin sketches my relationship to Mulvey's essay: "Visual Pleasure" formed a significant part of the knowledge of the feminist film studies "past" I imbibed as a doctoral student in the 1990s and remains a significant element within the culture of academic feminism well into the 2020s.

My return to "Visual Pleasure" is not motivated by mere historical coincidence or a fondness for 1970s nerd kitsch; rather, I believe it offers an opportunity to consider the way concepts of authorship, authority, and creativity infuse academic scholarship. In this chapter, I read Mulvey's essay and its reception in relation to auteur theory, then explore some implications for a broader notion of the gaze and auteur, moving beyond film studies research to examine practices of authorship in academic research. Collaborative pedagogy is a well-established field with strong ties to feminist praxis and draws upon the work of W.E.B. Du Bois and Paolo Freire to argue that academics and students can be cocreators of knowledge.[20] With a few exceptions, however, a culture around collaborative research remains elusive in film and media studies. Coedited books and journal issues are far more common than coauthored work, for example. The groundbreaking *Camera Obscura* feminist editorial collective, founded in the 1970s, remains an anomaly in the field.

What might a consideration of Mulvey's "Visual Pleasure" as an example of scholarly auteurism, one whose reception seems to contradict feminist principles of collaboration, bring to a discussion of academic practices around research? And what insights might this inquiry yield regarding the academy's increasing co-optation of creative labor and intellectual property, enabled by digital technologies and the increasing emphasis on making as well as critiquing media objects, for example, in videographic criticism?

My examination of Mulvey's essay does not seek to relitigate its arguments, concepts, or methods. Instead, I am interested in understanding how the essay shaped the decade of theory, helping to write the history of academic film studies. Analyzing "Visual Pleasure" in relation to the concept of the single author, I argue that Mulvey's notion of the authorizing male gaze, which holds within it far more radical possibilities for practices of looking at and, indeed, multiply authoring media texts, was embraced within academic film studies through an auteurist and anti-feminist paradigm linked to the rise of the academic star system. I conclude by considering possibilities for multiple authorship (using Hunter's term), including posthuman collaborations, in film and media studies research.

The Subjects of "Visual Pleasure"

Describing "Visual Pleasure" as both pioneering and polemical, Shohini Chaudhuri speculates that it "has generated such a huge response that it must surely rank amongst the most provocative academic essays ever written."[21] According to Google Scholar, in late 2022, twenty versions of "Visual Pleasure" had garnered 20,373 citations. (To offer a comparison, *The Foucault Effect: Studies in Governmentality* [1991] had a similar number of citations.) This metric refers to the version of the essay reprinted in Mulvey's 1989 collection, *Visual and Other Pleasures*, a book associated with 4,572 citations. The number of "hits" associated with the widely circulated (and often photocopied) original *Screen* article remains conjecture. Statistics aside, "Visual Pleasure" catapulted Laura Mulvey to the forefront of film studies as a "founder of discursivity," a phrase Michel Foucault reserved for Marx and Freud, towering figures in critical theory whose ideas, read through Louis Althusser and Jacques Lacan, underpin Mulvey's essay.[22] Founders do more than establish disciplines; they also enable the "endless possibility of discourse" such that "the science or the discursivity"—in this case, feminist film theory—"refers back to their work as primary coordinates."[23]

One strategy for institutional legitimation of the nascent field of film studies was to renounce its roots in amateur cinema appreciation societies and literary-minded English departments by embracing Continental theory, in solidarity with humanities disciplines across the United States and the United Kingdom.[24] Thus, the figure Mulvey may be most closely associated with is another "founder of discursivity," Jacques Lacan, the French psychiatrist whose postwar rereading of Freudian psychoanalysis was inflected by French existentialism and Saussurean linguistics. Lacan's reframing of the split subject using the visual metaphor of the mirror stage became an animating principle for Anglo-American feminist theory. If, as Judith Feher-Gurewich argues, "feminist theory brought Lacan to the academic scene" during the "the golden age of academic feminism," then one important reason for that was "Visual Pleasure."[25]

By the mid-1980s, feminist film theory had "almost become the orthodoxy of film theory, such was its influence in the field."[26] Ultimately, Mulvey the author (as distinct from the person) became a disciplinary figure both literally and metaphorically, one used to "[mark] the manner in which we fear the proliferation of meaning."[27] Ironically, as film studies embraced feminist film theory, it also circumscribed its development through the reification of a single essay and a single author, thwarting the proliferation of meaning.

Moreover, some of the meaning(s) that may have been constrained by the ascension of Mulvey as a theory auteur were ideas generated within the thriving body of feminist film criticism that existed before 1974, appearing in academic monographs and professional journals. The proliferation of this work was a manifestation of both the growth of film studies and of theory's dominance within the field. *Cinema Journal*, now *JCMS*, was founded in 1961, and *Screen* spun out of *Screen Education* in 1969, marking a shift away from its earlier pedagogical focus.[28] Especially relevant to feminist film theory was the emergence of *Camera Obscura* (1972), *Women and Film* (1972–1975), *Jump Cut* (1974), and *Signs: Journal of Women in Culture and Society* (1975). A number of feminist film monographs were published prior to "Visual Pleasure," including Claire Johnston's *Notes on Women's Cinema* (1973), Marjorie Rosen's *Popcorn Venus* (1973), Joan Mellen's *Women and Their Sexuality in the New Film* (1973), and *Village Voice* critic Molly Haskell's *From Reverence to Rape* (1974). Johnston published books in 1974 (with Pam Cook) and 1975 examining the "place of women in the films of Raoul Walsh" and the films of Dorothy Arzner, which indicate some interest in using the auteur concept within feminist film studies. Taken together, these books pioneered the methodological approach of Anglo-American film studies: interpreting the ideological content of male-authored stereotyped screen images and searching for examples of women's authorship. An important exception was Johnston's *Notes on Women's Cinema*. A member of a feminist filmmaking collective in London, Johnston focused on production rather than spectatorship. Her "cinefeminist" intervention urged women filmmakers to produce a feminist countercinema outside the conventions of Hollywood.[29] Johnston's focus on women as image makers has been used to champion women's avant-garde and independent filmmaking, as well as women Hollywood directors.[30]

By contrast, Mulvey's essay focuses primarily on representation and spectatorship, despite her association with avant-garde filmmaking and especially *Riddles of the Sphinx* (1977, with Peter Wollen), which enhanced her credibility as a filmmaker-theorist, a status similar to that of many of the *Cahiers* critics. Mulvey may not have been the first feminist theorist, but she became the movement's brand identity, its catchphrase becoming "the male gaze." David Sorfa notes that the phrase "male gaze" occurs only twice in "Visual Pleasure" but has become the "shorthand for describing the main point of the essay (undergraduates particularly seem to like referring to 'the male gaze theory')."[31]

"Visual Pleasure" diagnoses the male-centered narrative formulas of Hollywood auteurs Sternberg and Hitchcock using a Freudian terminology of scopophilia, narcissism, and fetishism, informed by Lacan's split subject and Althusser's view that ideology permeates culture, interpellating individuals by "hailing" them as subjects of a particular economic, political, and social order. Mulvey weds the idea that ideology calls upon us as subjects who maintain an unequal social order with the pleasure of Hollywood narrative to produce gaze theory. She posits the existence of a "masculine perspective," defined as "in-built patterns of pleasure and identification that impose masculinity as 'point of view'" that render women spectacles: passive objects of male fantasy, defined by their "to be looked at ness."[32] In the wake of "Visual Pleasure," questions regarding spectatorial agency would animate feminist film theory, and film theory more generally, for decades.

The central proposition that a powerful male gaze defines, circumscribes, and controls women on-screen—and in off-screen contexts as well—was embraced by feminist, women's and gender studies, and visual culture scholars. From the vantage point of the late twentieth century, the male gaze, and its implications for spectators who attempt to resist its power of interpellation, offered massive explanatory power. The gendered gaze has been developed, challenged, and extended through explorations of the ways fiction and documentary cinemas interpellate subjects, and how people resist interpellation, from discussions around the colonial gaze; heteronormative, queer, and transgender gazes; and the ableist gaze.[33]

The most radical implication of Mulvey's gendered gaze, however, is that "the gaze" never seems to remain the possession or province of "the" auteur or "the" spectator, a fact that undermines the singularity and agency of both positions. Gazes are powerful tools, yet they seem not to remain under anyone's control, even when employed oppressively within aesthetic works. Extending this logic, this implies that when humans make or consume visual media forms, they are never singular authors of meaning; instead, gazes are social, contextual, collaborative, and multiauthored, developing from embodied experiences and the multiple communities in which people learn to see and be seen.

Although hinting at the radical possibilities for gazes that resist discipline, "Visual Pleasure" appears on its surface to be an auteur-driven essay affirming the power of the single author. Its ostensible subjects were the films of Sternberg and Hitchcock. Yet by situating the authorial gazes of these directors within a Freudian-Lacanian-Althusserian context, I would argue, Mulvey undermines the power of any author. The fetishism of Sternberg and the sadistic scopophilia of Hitchcock were framed as unconscious, ideological, psychocultural practices, not merely authorial signatures: they invite shared pleasures and interpellate Hollywood audiences precisely because they resonate with broader, gendered practices of looking.

Mulvey has published numerous essays on authors and authorship, including *Morocco* (1930), *Citizen Kane* (1941), *Viaggio in Italia* (1954), *Imitation of Life* (1959), *Psycho* (1960), *Angst essen Seele auf* (1974), *Xala* (1975), and *Blue Velvet* (1986).[34] Throughout these works, she both subtly and overtly challenges the notion of the author. In her book *Citizen Kane* (2012), she embraces a posthuman definition by identifying the competing author "personalities" associated with the project as Orson Welles, William Randolph Hearst, and the film itself: "Over the last few years, *Citizen Kane* criticism has become less polemical and more rigorous and is now beginning to liberate the film from its own reputation so that it can begin to speak, as it were, for itself."[35] Moreover, Mulvey's thoughts about authorship (like mine) have sometimes strayed from film direction to feminist critical practice. She writes about moments when the feminist critic "feels like an investigator, and psychoanalytic theory like a code-book key which can at least begin to crack the cipher."[36] Code breaking can be understood as an act of multiple authorship, where, using Hunter's definition, the film director and the feminist critic's contributions can each be clearly identified.

By no means a methodology embraced by every feminist scholar, Mulvey's psychoanalytic approach encountered friendly and hostile challenges, including from Judith Butler, Gayatri Spivak, and Hortense Spillers. Still, most serious feminist film criticism during the 1970s, 1980s, and 1990s had to take account of, even if to ultimately reject, Mulvey's work. In the mid-1990s, the "historical turn" presaged by Thomas Elsaesser in "The 'New' Film History" (1986) displaced theory as the central tendency of academic film studies.[37]

The historical turn raised new questions related to auteurism, however. Within feminist film studies, empirical and archival approaches had to confront the "male bias of auteur theory, which promulgated film criticism in the 'great man' or 'male genius' tradition with no reference to women's images or women's position in films—a tendency they were keen to remedy. They also set about bringing to light works from women directors of the past."[38] But the existential challenge auteur theory's single-author model poses for feminism extends beyond its historical use as a tool to celebrate male genius, and simply elevating women auteurs cannot address this problem. As Linda Nochlin writes in another important work of 1970s feminist theory, "Why Have There Been No Great Women Artists?," rather than "attempt to answer the question as it is put: i.e., to dig up examples of worthy or insufficiently appreciated women artists throughout history," the scholar must first critically examine the political and historical contexts both for the question and for the evidence on which it is based, then perform an intersectional analysis. Further, the analysis must acknowledge the challenges associated with evaluating contributions by individuals never deemed to be members of the category (e.g., "great women artists"; "women film auteurs"): "As we all know, things as they are and as they have been, in the arts as in a hundred other areas, are stultifying, oppressive and discouraging to all those, women among them, who did not have the good fortune to be born white, preferably middle class and, above all, male."[39]

Feminist film historian Jane Gaines performs Nochlin's dual analysis when she situates the project of reclaiming the multifarious work of silent era women filmmakers in relation to feminist theory. She points to a contradiction between the empirical research—which suggests the existence of many women working at every level—and the "'loss' narrative" of 1970s feminist theory, which promulgated "the feminist principle of women's symbolic exclusion."[40] This project, coming from a different direction than Mulvey's work, also has the potential to challenge the traditional understanding of film authorship by including the diverse ways women worked in the early industry, many of which depart from the *Cahiers* and Sarris models of the singular genius.

(Academic) Stardom and "Visual Pleasure"

The proposition that screen narratives and viewing practices are indelibly marked by gender and power was inextricable from Mulvey's status as the iconic signifier of feminist/film theory. The essay became a canonical text and its author an academic "star." Mulvey introduced revolutionary ideas about gender difference that circulated within an academic context that, despite (and because of) its regard for the work of Roland Barthes and Foucault, Jacques Rivette, François Truffaut, and Sarris, continued to privilege the single-author model in writing, filmmaking, and academic research.

Mulvey was among the first supernovas in the pantheon of the academic star system, a "new form of intellectual authority and professional status" that David Shumway links to the rise of theory in the 1970s, the growth of the conference circuit, and broader trends in media celebrity in the United States.[41] Shumway also credits the academic star system with changing assumptions about authorship. "Theory not only gave its most influential practitioners a broad professional audience," he writes, "but also cast them as a new sort of author. Theorists asserted an authority more personal than that of literary historians or even critics," noting a fundamental incongruity between theory's dependence on poststructuralism and the "name of the theorist": "Theory has undermined the authority of the text and of the author and replaced it with the authority of systems, as in the demystifying readings of Marxism or psychoanalysis. . . . And yet these claims are belied by the actual functioning of the name of the theorist. It is that name, rather than anonymous systems or the anarchic play of signifiers to which most theoretical practice appeals."[42] As Columpar and Sue Thornham, among others (along with my own anecdotal observations) have attested, for decades, "Visual Pleasure" enjoyed a version of authority based on the "name of the theorist."

The A-list stars Shumway examines include Jacques Derrida, Stanley Fish, Jane Tompkins, Cathy Davidson, Frank Lentricchia, Marianna Torgovnick, and Eve Kosofsky Sedgwick. Many became objects of gossip, he writes, when they published autobiographical material; others, like Judith Butler, had zines written about them.[43] In terms of name recognition and field-defining leadership as "founders of discursivity," Mulvey might appropriately be compared to Butler (*Gender Trouble*, 1990) and Sedgwick (*Epistemology of the Closet*, 1990). Yet the "autobiographical" content of Mulvey's work is subtle, embedded in her insistence on a connection between feminist theory and cinephilia and her collaboration and partnership with Peter Wollen. Mulvey herself has acknowledged the autobiographical aspects of "Visual Pleasure": "The essay is really autobiographical ... because it was based on my own patterns of spectatorship—before encountering feminism and after. Along with a changed viewing strategy, I discovered the potential for emerging critique and analysis, and my desire to see a new kind of counter or avant-garde cinema was born."[44] This version of intellectual autobiography, while demure in comparison to that of Tompkins, Lentricchia, and Sedgwick, nevertheless resonates with modes of writing that have emerged within feminism, anti-racism studies, and queer studies, where a researcher's situated knowledge or standpoint assumes significance as a source of authority and insight.[45] If the relationship between cinephilia and feminist analysis in Mulvey's "Visual Pleasure" looks like "the tension between love and hate"—"one in which her former 'good object' becomes a 'bad object'"—it is also true that similar tensions characterize contemporary critical work, where writers wrestle with their position and privilege and where "good" cultural objects can also be "bad" ones.[46]

Shumway castigates the academic star system not only for its reliance on the name of the author and its gossipy autobiographies but also for its commitment to individualism: "Marxism, feminism, queer theory, and the various ethnic-studies projects have all attempted to build knowledge collectively. The star system has been and will continue to be an obstacle to such collectivity."[47] Ironically, the star system, which feeds on and contributes to an academic culture of single authorship, may enable the identification of situated knowledges (through autobiographical modes) even as it poses obstacles to the creation and recognition of collective knowledges.

Feminism versus Authorship

In "Visual Pleasure," perhaps paradoxically, Mulvey alludes to collective knowledge—that of feminist spectators within patriarchal culture—and demands collective action as well. Citing the essay's "manifesto form," Lynn Spigel writes that it "began with the language of battle: 'Psychoanalytic theory is thus appropriated here as a political weapon.'"[48] And it concludes with a call to arms, arguing that the "monolithic accumulation of traditional film conventions" must be challenged and undermined to destroy the "satisfaction, pleasure and privilege" offered to "the invisible guest"—the male ego.[49]

Mulvey's proposed solution, to democratize the gaze by "freeing" the camera into its "dialectical" relationship with the audience, explicitly wrests the power of the gaze from any single author. Yet rather than explore the plural possibilities of gazes, Mulvey's "Afterthoughts on 'Visual Pleasure and Narrative Cinema' Inspired by King Vidor's *A Duel in the Sun (1946)*" (1981) pursues instead the "curious spectator, who was, by and large, the product of feminism" and "controls the unfolding of the cinematic image."[50] The practice of curious spectatorship might be thought of as generating a version of multiple authorship, whether through film criticism (formal and informal) or through fan engagement in the prosumer mode.[51] But Mulvey fails to pursue this line of thought, and a version of gaze theory that neglects some of its most radical implications, became feminist film theory's "radiant center."[52] The potential of "freeing" dialectical gazing to animate new ideas about the way meaning is authored collectively remains an unfulfilled promise.

Feminism, Collaboration, and Multiple Authorship

It might seem that I am holding Laura Mulvey personally accountable for the uses and abuses of her essay, which is not my intent. Instead, this academic historiography seeks to reveal the ways "Visual Pleasure" itself was authored not by Mulvey alone but by multiple generations of scholars eager to embrace methodological tools and create better ones. Maggie Humm echoes this sentiment, writing in the autobiographical-critical mode that her recollections of Mulvey's essay "are very much at odds with the later circumscriptions of film theorists." She continues, "Mulvey's essay is to me a more original and creative engagement with the protean zeitgeist moment of emerging visual studies than feminist scripts currently allow."[53]

These "feminist scripts," in my view, championed the singular feminist author along with the powerful concept of the singular male gaze, overlooking the promise of multiply authored and authoring gazes that I associate with Mulvey's intervention. This holds true for both our theorizing about media objects and our academic practice. Academic books and articles are media texts, with their own authorship models and production cultures. Views on and approaches to authorship inform the ways we engage with media texts in our research and also shape our understanding of labor, status, hierarchy, and power within our institutions and our field. Although the concept of knowledge cocreation has emerged within empirical social science research, in film and media studies, "most research questions continue to be defined by the single researcher, and publications to appear in a single authorial voice."[54] Increasingly, media and tech industries and the academy alike romanticize authorship through the figure of the "creative," encouraging the mistaken belief that only certain individuals possess creativity. These ideas about authorship represent a "commercial strategy for organizing audience reception," that holds true in academia as well as in commercial media industries.[55]

The insistence on siting creativity and authority in the single author in academic media studies, evidenced by the continued valorization of single-authored articles and books as the only legitimate currency for tenure and promotion, enables us to maintain the fiction that we work heroically as lone researchers, making discoveries and developing new knowledge. In a rigidly hierarchical professional setting where the diminishing opportunities for tenure and promotion are predicated on a research profile defined by original contributions, it makes perfect sense that we choose not to see our research as a form of collaborative labor. In reality, however, a functioning peer review process (this is an assumption, not an assertion) would ensure that no publication is ever the work of a single individual. Every publication represents a collaboration among scholars through citation and peer review, and between researchers and editors, publishers, designers, copyeditors, and proofreaders.

Given that these very obvious and even mundane ways in which collaboration is necessary to academic research remain opaque or unacknowledged, how could multiply authored or collaborative approaches gain traction within the humanities? In a research landscape dominated by grant funding, digital humanities projects have led the way.[56] Digital humanities projects tend to bring together humanities scholars, computer scientists, and librarians and showcase the power of digital tools over the collaborative interdisciplinary work required to operationalize humanities research questions.[57]

In film and media studies research, the single-authored "gold standard" continues to prevail, although an unexpected and provocative twist has arisen from the emerging methodology of audiovisual criticism. On the face of it, this new research area seems destined to reiterate the least appealing aspects of auteurism, in part because researchers often view themselves as filmmaker-auteurs. However, theorist-practitioner Alan O'Leary argues in "Another Cyborg Manifesto" that a parametric approach to audiovisual criticism, governed by algorithmic constraints rather than the structure of argumentation, produces a posthuman collaboration between scholar, platform, and the original media maker.[58] This approach calls up associations not only with Vertov's *Kino-Eye*, which credits the film camera with contributing an independent way of seeing that supplements human vision, but also with Mulvey's invocation of the "personality" of the "film itself" in her discussion of *Citizen Kane*.

James Morrison rightly points out that one reason for the "roiling passions" attending decades of debates around auteurism is the "dearth of available ideas about the nature of authorship in cinema."[59] Morrison's perceived lack of available ideas can be extended to characterize the nature of authorship in scholarship as well, with O'Leary and Hunter serving as important exceptions. Peter Wollen's polyphonic understanding of auteurism could (and should) be applied to our research, where "networked statements," even in an ostensibly single-authored work, represent the voices of others in the field, from mentors and supervisors to peers, peer reviewers, and students. I have argued the most radical implications of "Visual Pleasure"—the idea of an unconscious yet shared gaze, not attached to or owned by any individual, but accessible to many—might help us to rethink our own work, which I would argue is, and should be, subject to the processes that Hunter characterizes as multiple authorship.

Conclusion

This chapter interrogates "Visual Pleasure" in relation to authorship, arguing that the methodological achievement represented by the concept of the gaze (initially understood as the male gaze, but creating the possibility of multiple authorizing and de-authorizing gazes) was embraced within academic film studies through an auteurist paradigm that dovetailed with the rise of the academic star system. Thus, the truly radical implications of Mulvey's work for the exploration of gendered gazes—including plural and collaborative ways of seeing and knowing, and posthuman partnerships—have yet to be realized in relation to our understanding of visual media as well as academic scholarship.

Notes

Epigraph: André Bazin, "Redécouvrons le cinéma." *L'Information universitaire*, No. 1145 (26 June 1943): EC I, 2. Translated by Blandine Joret, *Studying Film with André Bazin* (Amsterdam: Amsterdam University Press, 2019), 20.

1 Philip Rosen, "*Screen* and 1970s Film Theory," in *Inventing Film Studies*, ed. Lee Grieveson and Haidee Wasson (Durham, NC: Duke University Press, 2010), 264–297.

2 David A. Cook, "Auteur Theory and the 'Film Generation' in 1970s Hollywood," in *The New American Cinema*, ed. Jon Lewis (Durham, NC: Duke University Press, 1998), 11.

3 Peter Decherney, "Inventing Film Study and Its Object at Columbia University, 1915–1938," *Film History* 12, no. 4 (2000): 443–460; Michael Zyrd, "Experimental Film and the Development of Film Study in America," in *Inventing Film Studies*, ed. Lee Grieveson and Haidee Wasson (Durham, NC: Duke University Press, 2008): 182–216.

4 E. Ann Kaplan, "Review of *Inventing Film Studies* (Duke University Press, 2008)," *Screen* 51, no. 4 (2010): 426–430.

5 Shyon Baumann, "Intellectualization and Art World Development: Film in the United States," *American Sociological Review* 66, no. 3 (2001): 404–426.

6 Zyrd, "Experimental Film."

7 Claire Jenkins, "'Counter Cinema' in the Mainstream," *Feminist Media Studies* 22, no. 5 (2021): 1179–1194.

8 Zyrd, "Experimental Film."

9 Baumann, "Intellectualization and Art World Development."

10 André Bazin, "On the *politiques des auteurs*," in *Cahiers du Cinéma: The 1950s: Neo-Realism, Hollywood, New Wave*, ed. Jim Hillier (Cambridge, MA: Harvard University Press, 1985), 248–259.

11 Corinn Columpar, "The Gaze as Theoretical Touchstone: The Intersection of Film Studies, Feminist Theory, and Postcolonial Theory," *Women Studies Quarterly* 30, no. 1/2 (2002): 27.

12 Laura Mulvey, Anna Backman Rogers, and Annie van den Oever, "Feminist Film Studies 40 Years after 'Visual Pleasure and Narrative Cinema,' a Triologue," *NECSUS: European Journal of Media Studies* 4, no. 1 (2015): 74.

13 Maggie Humm, "Feminist Theory, Aesthetics and Film Theory: Mulvey, Kuhn, Kaplan and hooks," in *Feminism and Film* (Edinburgh: University of Edinburgh Press, 1997), 14; Sue Thornham, "On 'Visual Pleasure and Narrative Cinema,'" *Feminist Media Studies* 15, no. 5 (2015): 881–884.

14 Columpar, "The Gaze as Theoretical Touchstone."

15 James Morrison, *Auteur Theory and My Son John* (New York: Bloomsbury, 2018), 6–7.

16 Peter Wollen, quoted in Morrison, *Auteur Theory and My Son John*, 6.

17 Aaron Hunter, *Authoring Hal Ashby: the Myth of the New Hollywood Auteur* (New York: Bloomsbury, 2016), 10.

18 Hunter, *Authoring Hal Ashby*, 7.

19 Columpar, "The Gaze as Theoretical Touchstone," 28.

20 Ziyu Long, Jasmine R. Linabary, Patrice M. Buzzanell, Ashton Mouton, and Ranjani L. Rao, "Enacting Everyday Feminist Collaborations: Reflexive Becoming, Proactive Improvisation and Co-learning Partnerships," *Gender, Work and Organization* 27, no. 4 (2020): 487–506; Trevor Thomas Stewart and Greg McClure, "Freire, Bakhtin, and Collaborative Pedagogy: A Dialogue with Students and Mentors," *International Journal for Dialogical Science* 7, no. 1 (2013): 91–108.

21 Shohini Chaudhuri, *Feminist Film Theorists: Laura Mulvey, Kaja Silverman, Teresa De Lauretis, Barbara Creed* (New York: Routledge, 2006), 2.

22 Michel Foucault and Paul Rabinow, *The Foucault Reader: An Introduction to Foucault's Thought* (London: Penguin, 1991), 114.

23 Foucault and Rabinow, *The Foucault Reader*, 114, 116.

24 Judith Mayne, *Cinema and Spectatorship* (New York: Routledge, 1993), 35–36; Matthew Croombs, "Pasts and Futures of 1970s Film Theory," *Scope: An Online Journal of Film and Television Studies* 20 (2011): 4.

25 J. Feher-Gurewich, "Lacan and American Feminism," in *Beyond French Feminisms*, ed. R Célestin, E. DalMolin, and I. de Courtivron (New York: Palgrave Macmillan, 2003), 239–240.

26 Chaudhuri, *Feminist Film Theorists*, 1.

27 Foucault and Rabinow, *The Foucault Reader*, 119.

28 See Rosen, "Screen and 1970s Film Theory," for a discussion of *Screen*'s impact on film theory.

29 Rachel Fabian, "Reconsidering the Work of Claire Johnston," *Feminist Media Histories* 4, no. 3 (2018): 244–273.

30 Jenkins, "'Counter Cinema' in the Mainstream."

31 Laura Mulvey, *Visual and Other Pleasures. Language, Discourse, Society* (London: Palgrave Macmillan, 1989), 19, 22; David Sorfa, "Laura Mulvey," in *Film Theory and Philosophy: The Key Thinkers*, ed. Felicity Colman (Oxon: Routledge, 2009), 290.

32 Mulvey, Rogers, and van den Oever, "Feminist Film Studies," 70; Mulvey, *Visual and Other Pleasures*, 29.

33 Fatimah Tobing Rony, *The Third Eye: Race, Cinema, and Ethnographic Spectacle* (Durham, NC: Duke University Press, 1996); Caroline Evans and Lorraine Gamman, "The Gaze Revisited, or Reviewing Queer Viewing," in *A Queer Romance: Lesbians, Gay Men and Popular Culture*, ed. Paul Burston, Paul Burston Nfa, and Colin Richardson (London: Routledge, 1995), 12–61; J. Halberstam, "The Transgender Gaze in *Boys Don't Cry*," *Screen* 42, no. 3 (October 2001): 294–298; Kurt Lindemann, "'I Can't Be Standing Up Out There': Communicative Performances of (Dis)Ability in Wheelchair Rugby," *Text and Performance Quarterly* 28, no. 1–2 (2008): 98–115.

34 Sorfa, "Laura Mulvey," 287.

35 Laura Mulvey, *Citizen Kane* (London: BFI, 2012), 17.

36 Mulvey, *Citizen Kane*, 25.

37 Thomas Elsaesser, "The 'New' Film History," *Sight and Sound* 55, no. 4 (1986): 246–251.

38 Chaudhuri, *Feminist Film Theorists*, 10.

39 Linda Nochlin, "Why Have There Been No Great Women Artists?," *Art News*, May 30, 2015 [originally published in *Art News*, January 1971], https://www.artnews.com/art-news/retrospective/why-have-there-been-no-great-women-artists-4201/.

40 Jane Gaines, *Pink-Slipped: What Happened to Women in the Silent Film Industries* (Champaign-Urbana: University of Illinois Press, 2018), 89–90.

41 David R. Shumway, "The Star System in Literary Studies," *PMLA* 112, no. 1 (1997): 86, 94.

42 Shumway, , "The Star System in Literary Studies," 95.

43 Shumway, 96.

44 Mulvey, Rogers, and van den Oever, "Feminist Film Studies," 70.

45 See Sandra G. Harding, ed., *The Feminist Standpoint Theory Reader: Intellectual and Political Controversies* (Hove: Psychology Press, 2004).

46 Sorfa, "Laura Mulvey," 288. For a complex account of Black women's investment in interracial screen relationships, for example, see Kristen J. Warner, "If Loving Olitz Is Wrong, I Don't Wanna Be Right," *Black Scholar* 45, no. 1 (2015): 16–20.

47 Shumway, "The Star System," 98.

48 Lynn Spigel, "Theorizing the Bachelorette: 'Waves' of Feminist Media Studies," *Signs: Journal of Women in Culture and Society* 30, no. 1 (2004): 1215.

49 Mulvey, *Visual and Other Pleasures*, 26.

50 Laura Mulvey, "Looking at the Past from the Present: Rethinking Feminist Film Theory of the 1970s," *Signs: Journal of Women in Culture and Society* 30, no. 1 (2004): 1289. Afterthoughts on "Visual Pleasure and Narrative Cinema" inspired by King Vidor's *Duel in the Sun* (1946), in *Visual and Other Pleasures: Language, Discourse, Society* (London: Palgrave Macmillan, 1989): 29–38.

51 Henry Jenkins, *Fans, Bloggers, and Gamers: Exploring Participatory Culture* (New York: NYU Press, 2006).

52 Humm, "Feminist Theory, Aesthetics and Film Theory," 15.

53 Humm, 4.

54 A. Home, L. A. Chubb, and C. B. Fouché, "Facilitating Co-creation of Knowledge in Two Community-University Research Partnerships," *Collaborations: A Journal of Community-Based Research and Practice* 4, no. 1 (2021): 2; Janice Monk, Patricia Manning, and Catalina Denman, "Working Together: Feminist Perspectives on Collaborative Research and Action," *ACME: An International Journal for Critical Geographies* 2, no. 1 (2003): 91–106.

55 Timothy Corrigan, "The Commerce of Auteurism: A Voice without Authority," *New German Critique* 49 (1990): 46.

56 Marilyn Deegan and Willard McCarty, *Collaborative Research in the Digital Humanities* (London: Routledge, 2012); Twyla Gibson, "Digital Humanities, Libraries, and Collaborative Research: New Technologies for Digital Textual Studies," *College and Undergraduate Libraries* 26, no. 2 (2019): 176–204.

57 Trevor Muñoz, "Digital Humanities in the Library Isn't a Service," 2012, https://trevormunoz.com/archive/posts/2012-08-19-doing-dh-in-the-library/; Alix Keener, "The Arrival Fallacy: Collaborative Research Relationships in the Digital Humanities," *Digital Humanities Quarterly* 9, no. 2 (2015), http://www.digitalhumanities.org/dhq/vol/9/2/000213/000213.html.

58 Alan O'Leary, "Another Cyborg Manifesto," 2021, https://www.youtube.com/watch?v=4QSIOu5JyB8.

59 Morrison, *Auteur Theory*, 3.

Acknowledgments

Our first thanks go to Nicole Solano and her team at Rutgers University Press. Nicole's early enthusiasm for this project and her patience throughout the pandemic helped us usher the collection into being despite what has been for everybody a very trying two years. The collection arose out of a conference we organized at Maynooth University, Ireland, in 2018. Many of the contributors to this volume presented at the conference, and we thank them and all the scholars who contributed to the conference and to the book. We also thank the Department of Media Studies at Maynooth University and the Irish Research Council for hosting and funding the conference. Thanks to colleagues at University College Dublin, especially Sarah Comyn. And thanks to our contributors, for putting together extraordinary work in very difficult circumstances. Finally, we also thank the many feminist conferences and networks—particularly the Women's Film and Television History Network—that have provided platforms for the research contained in these pages to develop.

Notes on Contributors

VIRGINIA BONNER is a professor of film studies at Clayton State University. Her teaching and research focus on independent, documentary, avant-garde, and feminist cinemas; she has published on these topics in *There She Goes: Feminist Filmmaking and Beyond* (2009), *Senses of Cinema*, *Scope*, *In Media Res*, *Ciné-Files*, and *Documenting the Documentary* (2nd ed., 2013).

ABIGAIL CHEEVER is an associate professor of English and film studies at the University of Richmond. She is the author of *Real Phonies: Cultures of Authenticity in Post–World War II America* (2010). Her current research examines the concepts of professionalism and professionalization in New Hollywood cinema.

NICHOLAS FORSTER is a lecturer in African American studies and film and media studies at Yale University. His research focuses on the relationship between race, creative social networks, and media. He has published essays in *liquidblackness*, *The LARB*, and *Black Camera* and is currently writing a biography of the Black actor-director-writer Bill Gunn.

ADRIAN GARVEY teaches at Birkbeck University of London. He has written on James Mason, John Travolta in *Grease*, and silent film stardom in Britain. He is currently researching British film noir and coediting a collection on acting and performance in the films of Alfred Hitchcock.

NICHOLAS GODFREY is a senior lecturer in screen at Flinders University in South Australia. He is the author of *The Limits of Auteurism: Case Studies in the Critically Constructed New Hollywood* (2018).

OLIVER GRUNER is a senior lecturer in visual culture at the University of Portsmouth. His research explores visual histories and Hollywood screenwriters of the 1960s and 1970s. He is the author of *Screening the Sixties* (2016) and coeditor (with Peter Krämer) of *Grease Is the Word: Exploring a Cultural Phenomenon* (2019).

AMELIE HASTIE is the author of *Cupboards of Curiosity: Women, Recollection and Film History* (2007), *The Bigamist* (a BFI "Film Classic," 2009), a forthcoming volume on *Columbo*, and essays on film/television theory and historiography, feminism, and material cultures, including "The Vulnerable Spectator" column in *Film Quarterly*. She teaches at Amherst College.

AARON HUNTER lectures in the Department of Film at Trinity College Dublin. His publications include *Authoring Hal Ashby: The Myth of the New Hollywood Auteur* (2016), *"Being There" and the Evolution of a Screenplay* (2021), and *Polly Platt: Hollywood Production Design and Creative Authorship* (2022).

ALICIA KOZMA is the director of the Indiana University Cinema. She is the coauthor of *Refocus: The Films of Doris Wishman* (2021) and author of *The Cinema of Stephanie Rothman: Radical Acts in Filmmaking* (2022). She holds a PhD from the Institute of Communication Research at the University of Illinois, Urbana-Champaign.

JAMES MORRISON is a professor of literature and film at Claremont McKenna College. He is the author, coauthor, or editor of several books, including most recently *Auteur Theory and "My Son John"* (2018).

KAREN PEARLMAN, senior lecturer in screen at Macquarie University, Sydney, researches creative practice, cognition, and feminist film histories. Her films about Soviet women editors have screened at over fifty festivals and have won twenty-seven awards, including three for best editing, three for best directing, and five for best documentary.

MARIA PRAMAGGIORE is a professor of film and media studies at Maynooth University. She is currently at work on *The Equine Imaginary: Horses in/*

as Cinema and a coauthored book on queer Irish media and cultural history.

ANNA BACKMAN ROGERS is a professor of aesthetics, culture, and feminist theory at the University of Gothenburg, Sweden, and the cofounder and editor in chief of the open-access journal *MAI: Feminism and Visual Culture.*

MARTHA SHEARER is an assistant professor and ad astra fellow in film studies at University College Dublin. She is the author of *New York City and the Hollywood Musical: Dancing in the Streets* (2016) and coeditor of *Musicals at the Margins: Genre, Boundaries, Canons* (2021).

MAYA MONTAÑEZ SMUKLER heads the UCLA Film and Television Archive Research and Study Center. She is the author of *Liberating Hollywood: Women Directors and the Feminist Reform of 1970s American Cinema* (2018).

Index